DANIEL AND REVELATION

Third Edition

DANIEL AND REVELATION

An Independent-Study Textbook by George W. Westlake, Jr. with David D. Duncan

Third Edition

Developed in Cooperation With the Global University Staff

Instructional Development Specialists:
David D. Duncan
George W. Flattery

Illustrators:
Faith McCollough
Jerry McCollough

1211 South Glenstone Avenue
Springfield, Missouri 65804 USA

Global University
Springfield, Missouri, USA

TO BE USED WITH:

Student Packet, Third Edition

Grading Packet, Third Edition

(For Grader's Use Only)

PN 03.10

ISBN 978– 0-7617–1073-8

Previously published as BL1212 *Daniel and Revelation*

Printed in the United States of America

Table of Contents

The Degree Program

This Independent-Study Textbook is one of the courses that comprise the Degree Program. Majors are offered in Bible and Theology, Religious Education, and Intercultural Studies. For additional information regarding the various programs available for study, write to your enrollment office.

Study materials in the Degree Program are designed in a self-teaching format for ministers and Christian workers who want to engage in systematic Bible study at the postsecondary level. These courses will provide many of the necessary tools for practical ministry and Christian witness.

Students may enroll in either individual courses or in a program of study leading to academic certification. However, you should be aware of the possibility that some courses may not fit into a specific study program. When satisfactorily completed courses are applied toward a study program, only those that meet the requirements of the selected program will receive credit toward certification. Therefore, it is important for you to select courses that contribute to your program requirements.

The Degree Program curriculum is under constant evaluation. Revisions and additions will be made in keeping with the goal of providing students with the best possible independent-study learning experiences.

Attention

We have prepared this Independent-Study Textbook to help you successfully complete the course. Please read the course introduction very carefully. By following the instructions, you should be able to achieve your goals for the course, and you should not have difficulty preparing for your final examination.

Address all your correspondence concerning the course to your local enrollment office at the address stamped below. If no address is stamped there, and you do not have the address of the office in your area, then please write to the following address:

Global University

1211 South Glenstone Avenue

Springfield, Missouri 65804

USA

The address of your local office is:

Course Introduction

Daniel and Revelation

What is happening in our world? Where are we headed? What is next in human history? What is God's plan for this world, the human race, our adversary the devil, the saints and the ungodly? How is it all going to end? One of the major subjects of God's Word, *prophecy,* answers these questions. Prophecy has been defined as "history written in advance." Of course, only God can write accurate history ahead of time. Daniel and Revelation are the two outstanding prophetical books in the Bible. Through a series of visions, the book of Daniel presents the unfolding of God's plan —God's timetable —for the nations of the world, particularly for Israel. Revelation portrays the culmination of God's program for all of His creation. Without biblical prophecy, in particular the prophetic *Revelation of Jesus Christ,* we would not know how things are going to end. The Bible would be a story without an end, a mystery that would leave us guessing! Moreover, it would rob us of a part of our blessed hope, for we would be unable to know what awaits the faithful. As it is, we can with Paul anticipate the end:

> No eye has seen,
> no ear has heard,
> no mind has conceived
> what God has prepared for those who love him
> —1 Corinthians 2:9

It is our prayer that as you study Daniel and Revelation, you will receive a fresh revelation of God's glory, power, kingdom, and especially His Son. We pray that the study of these books will give you a greater awareness than ever before that God is in full control. May you also be aware that His plan will be accomplished in all of Creation according to His timing. We hope you will, through prayerful study, receive a fresh vision of Jesus Christ as King of Kings and Lord of Lords. May you have the assurance that: "In honor of the name of Jesus all things in heaven, on earth, and in the world below will fall on their knees, and all will openly proclaim that Jesus Christ is Lord, to the glory of God the Father" (Philippians 2:10–11, TEV).

Course Description

Daniel and Revelation (BIB4072—Credit: 2 hours)

Daniel and Revelation is a study of biblical prophecy that concerns events of the end time. Passages of other Old and New Testament books, in addition to Daniel and Revelation, are studied when such passages help promote a better understanding of biblical prophecy. The unit titles point out the progression of events during the end time. In the final unit of the course, biblical prophecy moves beyond time into eternity. The second coming of Jesus Christ is the central theme of the course. This course also has an ethical emphasis: it is designed to help the student to be ready for Jesus' coming and to encourage others to prepare for His coming (1 John 3:3).

Course Learning Outcomes

Upon the successful completion of this course, you should be able to:

1. Identify major events, terms, time sequences, and personalities referred to in the books of Revelation and Daniel.
2. Describe Jesus' messages to the seven churches and explain how they relate to local churches, individuals, and to the entire church age.
3. Describe the picture of the Antichrist prefigured in Daniel and compare and contrast this with the more specific portrayal of the Antichrist in Revelation.
4. Explain how Gentile world domination is predicted in Daniel and how this will culminate in the Great Tribulation period and the Battle of Armageddon.
5. Describe the punishment that God brings upon the ungodly in Revelation as the trumpets are sounded and the seven last plagues from the bowls of God's wrath are outpoured.
6. Describe the Millennium and list details of life on earth during this period.
7. Compare and contrast what will happen to the wicked and to the righteous before and after the Millennium and the basis upon which the respective destiny of each one is decided.
8. Describe the new earth and life within the New Jerusalem.
9. Appreciate the significance of the blessed hope in the life of each believer and thus purpose to prepare yourself and help others to prepare for the Lord's return.

Resources

You will use *Daniel and Revelation,* an Independent-Study Textbook by George W. Westlake, Jr. as both the textbook and study guide for the course. *The Holy Bible* is also required. Bible quotations in the Independent-Study Textbook are from the New International Version (NIV) unless otherwise noted. Some assignments require you to access the Global University Online Research Center (ORC). Instructions for accessing the ORC are provided in the Undergraduate Writing Assignment Guidelines (UWAG) in the Student Packet.

Content Specialists for the Course

Dr. George W. Westlake, Jr., has been the senior pastor of Sheffield Family Life Center (Assemblies of God) in Kansas City, Missouri, for over 29 years. He has also been active in radio and television ministry for more than 35 years. A speaker at camp meetings, conventions, and seminars, his teaching and preaching ministry is not confined to the United States. He has ministered in Europe, Latin America, Africa, and East Asia. Dr. Westlake has taught at the East Africa School of Theology and is an adjunct faculty member of the Asian Theological Center for Evangelism, the Asia Pacific Theological Seminary, North Central University (Minneapolis, Minnesota), and the Assemblies of God Theological Seminary (Springfield, Missouri).

A published author, Dr. Westlake earned B.A. and M.A. degrees from Central Bible College, Springfield, Missouri, and a D.Min. from Fuller Theological Seminary, Pasadena, California.

David Duncan has worked in the field of education for thirty years. He served as principal of Calvary Bible Institute, Majuro, Marshall Islands for eight years. He holds both a B.A. and a M.A. from California State University – Fullerton. He is a candidate for the D.Min degree at the California Graduate School of Theology and also for the Ph.D. degree at the University of North Texas. Mr. Duncan currently writes and teaches internationally, and serves as an educational consultant.

Study Time

We recommend that you have a regular time for study. Of course, you may take advantage of spare moments to study when you have them, but there is no substitute for a regular study time. Try to complete at least one lesson each week. In a classroom, two or three class sessions would ordinarily be given to each lesson. Studying independently, you may expect to spend from three to six hours on a lesson.

How much time *you* actually need to study each lesson depends in part on your knowledge of the subject and the strength of your study skills before you begin the course. It also depends on the extent to which you follow directions and develop skills necessary for independent study. Plan your study schedule so that you spend enough time to attain the objectives stated by the author of the course as well as your personal objectives.

Study Methods

The Student Packet includes two helpful tools. The “Checklist of Study Methods” and the “Student’s Record Planner” will help you know how to study a lesson, review for a unit progress evaluation on a group of lessons, and prepare for the final examination that covers all of the lessons. If you do not usually study as recommended, you will need to adapt your study methods to achieve the highest success in the course.

Ways to Study This Course

(1) All of your course work except your final examination should be submitted by e-mail. If e-mail is not available, submit by mail or fax.

(2) Although this course has been designed for individual study, there are limited opportunities to join in a study group or class. In that case, the adviser may give you additional instructions. If so, be sure to follow the adviser’s directions.

Lesson Organization, Learning Tools, and Study Strategy

A recommended step-by-step numbered *procedure* for approaching each lesson is presented as part of the introduction to each unit of this course. *The procedure* is a formula for getting the most out of the lesson. Each lesson includes specific components to help you learn the material: (1) the introduction, (2) the highlights or learning activities, (3) the objectives, (4) the outline, (5) the content, (6) the defined words, (7) the learn-by-doing activities or the study questions, (8) the self-test, and (9) the appraisal.

Introduction

Each lesson includes an introduction which serves as a bridge between the previous lesson and new material about to be presented. Read each introduction to review what you have learned thus far in preparation for being introduced to new concepts which build on that foundation.

Highlights or Learning Activities

Global University undergraduate courses have one of two instructional design patterns. These may be identified by the elements listed on the first page of the lessons. One instructional design pattern lists *highlights* before the objectives and includes learning-by-doing activities at the end of the content. The second lists *learning activities* before the objectives and includes study questions in the lesson development.

Highlights

The highlights are a brief summary of the lesson. They give you the key points—or specific views or perspectives related to the key concepts—and let you know what to expect in the lesson. Think about the key points as you study the lesson. Lessons that list *highlights* include "Learn-by-Doing" activities in the lesson development.

Learning Activities

The learning activities are a brief summary of steps to successful study of the lesson. They let you know what to expect in the lesson and guide you in such as way as to help you achieve the objectives of the lesson. Lessons that list learning activities include study questions in the lesson development.

Objectives

The key (important) concepts presented in the lesson are derived from the objectives. Study each objective carefully as you begin each lesson. First, *identify the key concepts presented in the objective* and second, *identify what each objective is asking you to do with the key concepts.* For example, in the objective, *assess the positive and negative ways that colonialism affected the spread of Christianity,* the key concept is *colonialism affected Christianity*. In this objective you are asked to *assess positive and negative ways*—or show the good and bad effects colonialism had on the spread of Christianity.

Outline

The outline gives a succinct picture of the lesson in a few words. It shows each main topic in relation to the development in subtopics. These offer helpful memory cues for acquiring and retaining the lesson content.

Content

The content presents the subject matter. To ensure that the subject matter is learned effectively, *the content* incorporates several learning tools: *objectives, headings, subheads,* and *guiding questions.*

As you study *the content*, (a) refer to the *objective* that relates to the section, (b) identify the key concepts presented in the *objective,* (c) identify what each *objective* is asking you to do with those key concepts, and (d) use the *objective* and *guiding questions* to direct your learning of the important concepts and perspectives. Use *headings* and *subheads* to give you an idea of what will be discussed in each section. Having an idea of what to expect will improve your learning process. *The content* is the substance of the lesson. It should be underlined, highlighted, or otherwise marked to help you remember the key points and significant statements of the author.

Guiding questions (a) directly relate to the key concepts and their relevant perspectives, (b) provide direction for learning in question form, and (c) help you identify the important (key) concepts and their relevant perspectives in each section. The key concepts and relevant perspectives are what the unit progress evaluations (UPEs) and final exam are based on. As you study, try to answer the *guiding questions* and see their relevance to each section.

Study Questions

Some courses include study questions in the lesson development. Most can be answered in the space provided in this book, while others require a notebook in which responses may be written. As you write the answers in your notebook, be sure to record the number and title of the lesson and to write them in correct numerical order. This will help in your review for the unit progress evaluations. You are not required to turn in your answers to the questions.

Do not look ahead at the answers to study questions until you have written your response. If you give your own answers first, you will retain what you study much better. After you complete each study question, check your answer with the one given at the end of the lesson. Then correct any mistakes you made.

These questions are very important. They will help you develop and improve your knowledge and Christian service. The suggested activities, too, will help you use your knowledge in practical ways.

Defined Words

The *defined words* help you understand unfamiliar and unique words used in the lessons. These words are identified in the text with an asterisk (*) superscript. You will find a definition in the left margin and again in the alphabetized glossary at the back of this book. If you are in doubt about the meaning of any other word, you may look it up immediately or when you come across it again in your reading.

Learn by Doing

Some courses include *learn-by-doing* applications at the end of *the content* to suggest ways you can do something practical with the information you have just studied. Some things will be useful to you during the study and others later in your ministry. Explore the possibilities before you move on to another lesson because they will expand your knowledge base and give you more ways to remember the content.

Self-Test

The *self-test* is comprised of an essay related to the lesson and approximately ten multiple-choice questions. Always do these before checking the *answers* located in the Student Packet. The self-test will reinforce your recall of key points.

Appraisal

Some lessons include appraisals. The *appraisal* is your opportunity to analyze the lesson content related to each objective. This is not a test: however, you will elaborate on each objective in essay form. Synthesize the lesson text in your essay. This is an exercise to help you summarize the main points of the lesson. Compare your responses with the key concepts of each objective presented as part of the answers in the Student Packet.

Student Packet

The Student Packet you received with this course contains instructions for taking the unit progress evaluations and the final examination. It also contains the unit progress evaluations and answer keys, project instructions, service learning requirement, CRA instructions and other important forms. Use the checklist on the packet cover to determine which materials you should submit to your enrollment office and when to submit them.

Form and Style Guide

Global University's Undergraduate Form and Style Guide defines the form, style, and documentation system for completing undergraduate writing assignments. The guide can be downloaded free from http://library.globaluniversity.edu/citation.cfm. The guide is also available as a stand-alone document.

Project

The required project asks you to demonstrate an ability to apply the principles taught in the course. This work will give you valuable practical experience in using the knowledge you have gained. The project is in your Student Packet. It is worth 25 percent of your final grade and must be submitted to your enrollment office before you take the final examination. Submit the project by e-mail attachment. If e-mail is not available, submit by mail or fax.

Service Learning Requirement

The service learning requirement (SLR) instructs you to apply principles from the course content to ministry in the church and the community. This practical experience allows you to develop ministry skills while meeting real-world needs. You can find the SLR in your Student Packet. The SLR Report must be submitted to your enrollment office along with your project and CRA (if required) before you take the final examination. Course credit will be granted only after the SLR report is submitted and assessed as satisfactorily completed.

Unit Progress Evaluations and Final Examination

Unit progress evaluation (UPE) scores are *not* counted as part of your final course grade. However, UPE scores indicate how well you learned the material and how well you may do on the final examination. After completing each UPE, check your answers with the answers provided in the Student Packet. You can then review the information in your course materials and Bible concerning points that were difficult for you. Reviewing the lesson objective appraisals, self-tests, and UPEs will help you to prepare for the final examination. Instructions for taking the final examination are in the Student Packet.

Collateral Reading or Collateral Writing Assignment

If you are enrolled in this course for three credits, you may be required to complete a collateral reading assignment (CRA) or a collateral writing assignment (CWA). Check your Student Packet to see if a CRA or CWA assignment is included with your course. The CRA or CWA is worth 35 percent of your course grade for the three-credit course and must be completed within the time limit for the course. Read the instructions carefully before you begin. Submit the assignment by e-mail attachment. If e-mail is not available, submit by mail or fax.

Credit for This Course

To obtain credit for this course, you must complete the assigned project and the service learning requirement (SLR). You must also pass the final examination. The examination must be written in the presence of an approved examining supervisor. Since we have examining supervisors in many countries, it probably will not be difficult for you to meet with the one in your area. Your enrollment office will work out the details with you.

Also, this course may be taken for its practical value only, and not for credit. In this case, you will not need to send in any assignments or take the final examination. The study of this course will enrich your life whether or not you take it for credit.

Course Grade

Your grade for a two-credit course is based on the final examination (75 percent) and the course project (25 percent). If a course is being upgraded to three credits by a collateral reading assignment (CRA), the final examination will be 40 percent of your grade, the CRA will be 35 percent, and the course project will be 25 percent. Although the service learning requirement (SLR) is not graded, you will not receive credit for this course until the SLR assignment is completed and the SLR report is submitted and evaluated as satisfactory.

Your course grade will be listed as 90–100 percent, exceptional; 80–89 percent, above average; 70–79 percent, average; 60–69 percent, below average; or 0–59 percent, fail.

Your Enrollment Office

Your enrollment office will be happy to help you in any way possible. Ask your adviser any questions you may have about arrangements for your final examination. Be sure to allow sufficient time so plans can be made accordingly. If several people want to study the course together, ask your adviser about special arrangements for group study. May God bless you as you begin your study.

THE CORE OF END-TIME EVENTS

Lessons...

1. An Overview of the Book of Daniel
2. Perspectives of the Coming World Ruler
3. Perspectives of the Coming Times of Distress

Procedures...

1. Observe the objectives for key points.
2. Reflect on the headings and subheadings.
3. Study the content identifying key points (highlight, underline, etc.) as you read.
4. Answer the self-study questions.
5. Do the self-test to reinforce key concepts.
6. Review the lessons in this unit in preparation for the Unit Progress Evaluation.

An Overview of the Book of Daniel

We begin our study of the books of Daniel and Revelation with an overview of the book of Daniel. It has been observed that Daniel is, generally, a prophetical history of Gentile world power from the reign of King Nebuchadnezzar to the coming of Christ. The prophets in general emphasize God's power and sovereign rule in relation to Israel as He guides the destinies of His chosen people through the years until their final restoration. By contrast, Daniel's emphasis is on God's sovereign rule in relation to Gentile world empires. His prophecies reveal God as the One who overrules in their affairs until the time of their destruction at the second coming of Christ.

It is essential for the student of Bible prophecy to study the book of Daniel in its entirety in order to receive the full benefit of its message. This book presents a great prophetic message, but it also contains spiritual, practical messages. While its content inspires readers with a vision of the future, they also bring comfort to the distressed. As we examine its background, structure, and various emphases, we pray that you will be sensitive to the direction of the Holy Spirit as He makes prophetic truth deeply meaningful to you.

the activities...

- Read the introduction to this Independent-Study Textbook (hereafter referred to as the IST). Give particular attention to the sections that explain the lesson organization and study methods. This section contains instructions that are important to your success in this course. Notice the course learning outcomes for your study of the course. They all are important, but some may stand out to you. Underline those you feel would be particularly helpful to you. You may also want to list learning outcomes of your own.
- Study the lesson outline and objectives. These will help you to identify the things you should try to learn as you study this lesson.
- Work through the lesson development in this IST. Be sure to read all Scripture references given, do the required exercises, and check your answers.
- Take the self-test at the end of this lesson and check your answers carefully with those given in the Student Packet. Review any items you answer incorrectly.

the objectives...

1.1 *Identify accurate descriptions of the city and empire of Babylon and the purpose of Daniel's ministry.*

1.2 *Discuss the structure, theme, date, and authorship of the book of Daniel.*

1.3 *Explain the basic issue in Daniel's first test of faith and why it was so significant.*

1.4 *Identify the elements of the image in Nebuchadnezzar's dream and state the significance of the dream and the term times of the Gentiles.*

1.5 *List the main truth of Daniel 4.*

1.6 *Explain the basic nature of Belshazzar's sin.*

1.7 *Identify key elements in the sixth conflict.*

the outline...

1 The Background of the Book of Daniel
- **a** The City of Babylon
- **b** The Geography of Ancient Babylon
- **c** The Historical Setting
- **d** The Religious Setting

2 Essential Facts About the Book of Daniel
- **a** The Structure of Daniel
- **b** The Matter of Authorship
- **c** The Date and Theme

3 The Personal History of Daniel
- **a** The First Conflict: An Initial Test of Faith
- **b** The Second Conflict: Pagan Magic Versus Heavenly Wisdom
- **c** The Third Conflict: Idolatry Versus Loyalty
- **d** The Fourth Conflict: A King's Pride Versus God's Sovereignty
- **e** The Fifth Conflict: Man's Impiety Versus Divine Sovereignty
- **f** The Sixth Conflict: Jealousy Versus God's Providential Care

Identify accurate descriptions of the city and empire of Babylon and the purpose of Daniel's ministry.

The Background of the Book of Daniel

The City of Babylon

The primary setting of the book of Daniel is the city of Babylon, the center of the Babylonian Empire. Babylon was a golden city in a golden age. Excavations have revealed the glory that Babylon once achieved. Within the city's massive walls were broad avenues, canals, temples, and palaces. The Ishtar Gate led through double fortifications, which were embellished with rows of bulls and dragons of enameled brick. A tall ziggurat (pyramid style) built in eight stages overlooked the city. The hanging gardens of the city, according to the Greeks, were one of the seven wonders of the world. Babylon reached the height of her glory under King Nebuchadnezzar (605–562 BC). His goal was to demonstrate his might and to make the city splendid and secure.

The Geography of Ancient Babylon

Ancient Babylon lay between the Tigris and Euphrates Rivers in an area commonly referred to as the *Fertile Crescent.* From the two mighty rivers which began in the mountains of Armenia (modern Turkey), soil was carried downstream for centuries toward the Persian Gulf, building up a rich alluvial plain. This fertile plain became the cradle of ancient civilization. In fact, ancient writers referred to Babylonia as the bread basket of the world.

The city of Babylon was situated relatively near the southern part of this plain. The combination of the fertile soil, extensive irrigation canals, and a climate conducive to farming enabled Babylon to support a large population. These positive natural qualities undoubtedly encouraged the development of culture, education, and civic enterprise.

The Historical Setting

The older Babylonian Empire arose to prominence in the ancient Middle East in the second millennium before Christ. More than a millennium later a new or Neo-Babylonian Empire emerged as a powerful nation-state about 626 BC as Nabopolassar successfully resisted Assyrian opposition to his rule over Babylon. As the recognized king of Babylon, he moved quickly to consolidate his power. He purposed to establish control over the lucrative trade routes and commerce of the eastern Mediterranean. While his son Nebuchadnezzar was involved in military campaigns in this area about 605 BC, Nabopolassar died, leaving his kingdom and growing empire to his son. And under his able leadership Babylon rose to prominence as an empire.

Earlier in 605 BC, Nebuchadnezzar had defeated the Egyptian army at the battle of Carchemish and established Babylon as the dominant political power in the region. As a result, he gained control of Judah which had been under Egyptian rule since 609 BC when King Josiah was defeated at Megiddo (Jeremiah 46:2). Before he returned to claim the kingdom, Nebuchadnezzar visited Jerusalem and took captives (among them Daniel and his friends) and treasures from Jerusalem and returned to Babylon (Daniel 1:1–7).

Nebuchadnezzar returned to Jerusalem in 597 BC to reinforce his control over the Jews because King Jehoikim apparently had neither paid tribute to Babylon nor remained loyal to Babylonian rule. In fact, King Jehoikim had turned to Egypt for support. During this siege, he died and his successor, King Jehoichin, surrendered to Nebuchadnezzar (2 Kings 23:34–24:14). As the preceding Scripture reference indicates, Nebuchadnezzar removed all the treasures from the temple of the Lord and the royal palace. He also took many of the people of Jerusalem captive, including the officers, fighting men, craftsmen and artisans, and the king and royal family. Then in about 586 BC after a long siege, Nebuchadnezzar destroyed the temple and the city of Jerusalem, removed King Zedekiah to Babylon, and left only the poorest people to cultivate the land and vineyards (2 Kings 24:18–25:12).

apostasy
the losing of one's religious faith or moral principles

The Religious Setting

During the last one hundred years before Judah went into exile to Babylon, the religious life of the nation was marked by a cycle of *apostasy and spiritual recovery. The rule of Athaliah, Ahaz, and Manassah brought unrestrained idolatry to God's people. But the religious reform begun under Joash gained momentum under Uzziah and reached its zenith of recovery under Hezekiah. However, following Hezekiah's reign, Manasseh plunged Judah into gross idolatry,

astrology
study of the stars to tell what will happen; study or science which assumes that stars and planets exert a direct influence on people

divination
act of seeing the future or discovering what is obscure by supernatural or magical means

occultism
use of the mysterious or magical; belief in and use of evil spirits and their power

including worship of planets, human sacrifice, and devil worship. He approved of *astrology, *divination, and *occultism—all of which were practiced regularly. Although he underwent a significant change after he was taken captive to Babylon, the reform he initiated did not represent true revival. Judah was committed to idolatry and returned to it as soon as he died.

Josiah, who came to the throne about 640 BC, gave Judah both godly leadership and genuine reform. It appeared that God was giving Judah a stay of execution, prolonging judgment for her years of spiritual adultery and general ungodliness. During Josiah's reign, Judah extended her borders in part because of the declining influence of Assyria. A spirit of optimism prevailed: the Law was being kept as never before and Jeremiah's prophetic ministry (which began in Josiah's thirteenth year-about 627 BC) was a powerful influence for righteousness.

Word in 614 BC that Asshur had fallen and in 612 BC that Nineveh had fallen must have encouraged Josiah to get involved in international affairs. For some reason, he decided to oppose Pharaoh Necho in his efforts to assist the declining Assyrian forces against Babylon. Josiah's intent was ill-advised and led to his death, plunging Judah once again into spiritual apostasy that could only lead to judgment. Thus Daniel and his people were taken captive to Babylon, and the army of Nebuchadnezzar completely destroyed the city of Jerusalem and ravished the countryside (2 Chronicles 36:17–21). According to an earlier prophecy given by Jeremiah, these desolations were to last for seventy years (Jeremiah 25:11). In fact, Daniel 9:1–2 opens with a reference to this very prophecy.

demoralized
having been weakened, or disheartened

With their national freedom gone, their temple destroyed, their people in captivity, the Jewish remnant was *demoralized. These were times of serious trouble and great unhappiness. Under conditions such as these could people still believe in God? Was it possible to live one's religion in a strange land? Was there a future for God's people or was this the end? Such questions were on the hearts and lips of earnest Jewish exiles. (See Psalm 137:1–6 for a brief view of the devastating effect the captivity had on Jewish people.)

Moreover, large numbers of captives, attracted by the glamour and wealth of Babylon, were ready to give up their religion for the sake of material success and prosperity. Some of these captive Jews who were so discouraged felt that since the old faith was finished, they should just conform to the pagan culture and customs of Babylon. At such a time, Daniel was raised up to encourage his discouraged brethren. By his faithful, godly life, he proved that one could live for God in a pagan environment and that it pays to serve God. The visions God gave him assured the exiles that God was in control of history and that their future was secure.

1 Circle the letter preceding each TRUE statement.

a The city of Babylon was located near the northern end of the Fertile Crescent close to the source of the Tigris and Euphrates Rivers.

b The climate, weather, and natural features of Babylonia favored the development of a large population.

c The architect of the Neo-Babylonian Empire was the father of Nebuchadnezzar whose name was Nabopolassar.

d King Josiah led Judah back to God, and he also extended Judah's political influence at the expense of the declining Assyrian Empire.

e In order to maintain a balance of power in the area, the Egyptian army was on its way to support the failing Assyrian Empire against Babylon when King Josiah interfered.

f Life for captives in Babylon was superior to life in Judah; therefore, most Jews quickly gave up their religion for paganism.

2 Based upon our study to this point and a careful reading of 2 Chronicles 36:15–17, Judah went into exile because

Because they mocked and despised the prophets and messages of God.

3 Daniel was raised up as a prophet in exile primarily to

a) remind exiles that their punishment was less than they deserved.
b) encourage his people who were discouraged and disillusioned.
c) assure his people that God is in control of history.
d) all of the above.
e) both b) and c) above.

Discuss the structure, theme, date, and authorship of the book of Daniel.

Essential Facts about the Book of Daniel

The Structure of Daniel

The content of Daniel may be divided into two roughly equal parts. One Bible scholar has given us an outline in which chapters 1–6 are seen primarily as a narrative of personal biography and local history which refer to six moral conflicts that concerned Daniel and his companions. Chapters 7–12, in this scholar's outline, concern visions and prophecies that relate to the controlling hand of God as it arranges the scenes in the ongoing story of history. This suggested outline may at first glance seem to divide the book into strictly *narrative* and *prophetic* portions. However, in chapter 2 we will find one of the most sublime prophecies in all the Word of God. For our purposes in this study, we will consider the content based on the following outline:

I. Personal Biography and Local History of Daniel
- **A.** Chapter 1: The First Conflict—The First Test of Faith
- **B.** Chapter 2: The Second Conflict—Pagan Magic Versus Heavenly Wisdom (The Times of the Gentiles)
- **C.** Chapter 3: The Third Conflict—Idolatry Versus Loyalty to God
- **D.** Chapter 4: The Fourth Conflict—A King's Pride Versus God's Sovereignty
- **E.** Chapter 5: The Fifth Conflict—Impiety Versus Divine Sovereignty
- **F.** Chapter 6: The Sixth Conflict—Jealousy Versus God's Providential Care

II. Gentile Nations, Israel, and the World Ruler in Prophecy
- **A.** Chapter 7: The Four Beasts
- **B.** Chapter 8: The Ram and the Goat
- **C.** Chapter 9: The Seventy Sevens
- **D.** Chapter 10: The Glory of God

E. Chapter 11: The Flow of History From Medo-Persia to the End-time

F. Chapter 12: The Great Tribulation and the Resurrection

The Matter of Authorship

Very little is known about the author of this remarkable book; however, it appears that Daniel was born either of royalty or nobility (1:3). The outstanding thing about Daniel from his youth to old age is his moral courage or simply his unchanging godliness. Daniel is one of the few men about whom God says only good. In fact, Daniel is called "highly esteemed" (9:23, 10:11, 19). We cannot help but connect Daniel's early faith and moral courage with the influence of godly King Josiah and the prophet Jeremiah. It was in the third year of King Jehoikim that Daniel was taken to Babylon as a prisoner (1:1). King Josiah had been dead for about four years. If Daniel was between eighteen and twenty years of age when he was taken to Babylon, he must have been between fourteen and sixteen when Josiah died.

Josiah's reign was long (thirty-one years), and it appears that Daniel was born sometime near the middle of his reign. Being of princely descent, Daniel was undoubtedly close enough to the king and his godly activities to be deeply influenced by the rediscovery of the Law, the repair of the temple, the restoration of worship, and the great national Passover that was observed (2 Chronicles 35:1–19). In the thirteenth year of Josiah, Jeremiah began his powerful, public ministry (Jeremiah 25:3), which was still being exercised at Jerusalem when Daniel was carried into captivity. The influence of these two great men was never lost on the future prime minister. More than sixty years later we see Daniel still pondering the words of Jeremiah concerning the seventy years of captivity (9:2).

While some modern scholars have tried to discredit the prophetic nature of the book and the status of its author, these matters were settled conclusively by our Lord. He referred specifically to "the prophet Daniel" (Matthew 24:15) and to his prophecy about the future "abomination that causes desolation" (Mark 13:14) which is in focus in Daniel 9:27. Our Lord thus confirmed the book as prophecy and the author as a prophet.

The Date and Theme

The time frame included in the book of Daniel covers a period of about seventy-three years. It includes the entire period of Judah's exile in Babylon and extends into the kingdom of Medo-Persia. It appears to have been written during the sixth century before Christ.

Daniel does not direct his prophecies to the people of his times, nor does he rebuke his people for their sins. Neither does he make a stirring appeal for repentance and revival. His message is a revelation of the majesty and sovereignty of God. You will probably note that he frequently uses the phrase "The God of heaven." In this book we shall see that God, in His infinite wisdom and power, rules over the affairs of empires and people, and both are ultimately bent to His will. *The theme, then,* is *the sovereignty of God.* We shall also note that special attention is focused on the *Times of the Gentiles* and the events that bring the church age to its glorious, victorious conclusion.

4 Circle the letter preceding each TRUE statement.
- **a** The book of Daniel falls into two roughly equal parts: chapters 1–6 and 7–12.
- **b** All the prophetic content of Daniel is located in the latter part of the book.
- **c** There is little evidence in Scripture to support the claim that Daniel is a prophetic book.
- **d** By nature the book of Daniel may be termed a "rebuke for sin and a call for repentance."
- **e** The date of composition for the book of Daniel appears to have been about the sixth century before Christ.

5 In your notebook discuss the structure, date, theme, and authorship of the book of Daniel.

The Personal History of Daniel

In order to help you understand both the historical and the prophetical nature of the book of Daniel, we shall use the outline suggested earlier. This will help us with the sequence of events both in Daniel's life and in the historical events predicted by the prophet. Since our focus in this course is prophecy, we will concentrate on the *prophetic* chapters, giving them more attention than the purely historical narrative chapters.

Explain the basic issue in Daniel's first test of faith and why it was so significant.

The First Conflict: An Initial Test of Faith

Daniel 1:1–21

self-indulgence
act of gratifying ones own desires, appetites, and passions with too little regard for the welfare of others

abstinence
the act of keeping oneself from doing or entering into something

At the very outset of the book we are introduced to the first conflict of the youthful exiles. It is a conflict between pagan *self-indulgence and godly *abstinence. At this point Daniel and three of his friends—Hananiah, Mishael, and Azariah—are being trained in the king's college for service to the king. They are required to partake of a diet that contains things forbidden by the Old Testament Law (vv. 3–5). On the surface this one issue might seem to be a small matter; however, it was only part of a total policy to destroy the young men's faith in God. Verses 6 and 7 show that the young men were given new names. Apparently this was an attempt to blot out their past life with its emphasis on God and to identify them with Babylon. Whereas their old names identified them with the God of Israel, their new names identified them with the heathen gods of Babylon. See Figure 1.1 below.

Meaning of the Hebrew Name	**Meaning of the Babylonian Name**
Daniel: God Is Judge	Belteshazzar: Bel's Prince
Hananiah: Jehovah Is Gracious	Shadrach: Inspiration of Rach
Mishael: Who Is What God Is	Meshach: Who Is What Shach Is
Azariah: The Lord Helps	Abednego: Servant of Nebo

Figure 1.1

These four young Jewish princes were exposed to the corrupting influences of pagan court life, the idolatry of their teachers, and the ungodly customs of Babylon. Moreover, their homeland was devastated; their religious center was destroyed; and their freedom was gone. Yet, they were not affected because they resolved in their hearts to be faithful to God (v. 8). Verses 8–20 show that because of their decision to put God first, Daniel and his friends were honored by God. They gave no sign of indecision; they knew what was right and they resolved to do it. Thus, the first test proved to be a stepping stone to more responsible service and a more effective witness for God. Moreover, it indicated a set of mind that indicated the young men's priorities and the value they attached to their faith in God.

6 Which verses in chapter 1 state the issue of the first test and the method the four young men used to overcome it?

....

7 Explain the nature of the first test and why it was so important.

....

....

Identify the elements of the image in Nebuchadnezzar's dream and state the significance of the dream and the term times of the Gentiles.

The Second Conflict: Pagan Magic Versus Heavenly Wisdom

Daniel 2:1–49

The Image (The Times of the Gentiles)

As you observed when you read Daniel 2, the second major conflict involves the challenge of pagan magic to divine wisdom. Let us examine the setting.

As many ambitious kings before and after him, Nebuchadnezzar was concerned about the extensive empire he was building and the course of the future (v. 29). Would it last? Would wise heirs maintain what he had achieved? Or would his achievements be lost because of his descendants' incompetence, unconcern, or foolishness? In his concern God gave this heathen king a dream that revealed an outline of the history of the world from his own time to the second coming of Christ.

sorcerers
those who practice sorcery, wizardry, or magic

King Nebuchadnezzar dreamed a strange and fascinating dream soon after he became king (v. 1). The dream troubled him so much that he could not sleep. Even worse, however, he forgot what he had dreamed. Thus, he called for his esteemed magicians and *sorcerers to use their magical powers to help him recall and interpret the dream, but this was not to be. They were baffled by the incredible request, for no man can possibly know what another has dreamed (vv. 2–7). Their pagan magic failed notably to respond to the king's challenge; therefore, he decreed that *all* the wise men of Babylon, including Daniel and his three friends, were to be killed.

When Daniel learned of the king's decision, he asked the executioner why the king had acted so harshly. When he learned that pagan magic had failed and created a serious crisis, Daniel asked permission to speak to the king. The wise young man assured the king that he would interpret the dream if he were given some time (vv. 14–16). Having spoken in faith and knowing that God is the Revealer of mysteries, Daniel urged his friends to pray that God would reveal the dream and its interpretation. This solution would satisfy the king's demand, and it would show the superiority of divine wisdom over all pagan magic. Moreover, it would free Daniel and his friends from the penalty of death.

8 Review verses 17–28 carefully. What do these verses reveal about the spiritual state of Daniel and his three friends?

....

....

Verses 28–30 contain three key phrases that help us understand the dream better. Daniel speaks of "days to come" (v. 28), "things to come" (v. 29), and "what is going to happen" (v. 29). These expressions stress the fact that the dream is a picture of future things. It is a prophecy and it deals with things that had not yet happened. It concerned the days ahead—even the distant future.

Nebuchadnezzar must have sat spellbound as Daniel told him precisely what he had dreamed. The king had seen an enormous, dazzling image. Its head was made of gold, its chest and arms of silver, its belly and thighs of bronze, its legs of iron, and its feet and toes of iron and clay. Fascinated, the king watched as a rock was cut out of a mountain but not by human hands. This rock struck the image on its feet and crushed it to bits. And the pieces of the battered image were swept away like chaff before a wind, leaving no trace of their existence. Meanwhile, the rock became a huge mountain and filled the earth (vv. 31–35).

Lest God's people miss the point of this dream of the future, God gave a precise reference point: the *head of gold* (vv. 36–38). The image, which symbolizes human government, pictures the rise and succession of empires that have had a primary impact on the people of God from the kingdom of Babylon to the setting up of the kingdom of our Lord Jesus Christ. These empires were not *world* empires, but each of these, as we shall see, has had a profound effect on the destiny of Israel.

The prophet, inspired by the Holy Spirit, gave the interpretation. The king, as the head of the Babylonian kingdom, was the *head of gold* (vv. 36–38). Babylon would be succeeded by another kingdom, which was symbolized by silver (v. 39). Comparing verse 32 with 39, we see that this succeeding kingdom was represented on the image by the two arms and breast. History records that Babylon gave way in the Middle Eastern imperial struggle to the two-part kingdom of Media and Persia. (We will use the term *Medo-Persia* hereafter).

Medo-Persia held imperial control for a little over two hundred years. Then it was succeeded by "a third kingdom" (v. 39), represented by the belly and thighs of bronze on the image. Again secular history records that as the empire of Medo-Persia declined, the powerful new Grecian kingdom under its best known leader, Alexander the Great, rose to prominence. The Grecian or *Hellenistic* influence was spread by Alexander's conquests to a vast area from Greece to Persia and throughout the Middle East, including Egypt, for a period of about three hundred years.

As Hellenistic civilization waned, a powerful, new, and far greater empire arose. It was symbolized on the image by the legs of iron (v. 40). Rome absorbed what the previous kingdoms had controlled and added greatly to these domains. As you may know, the Roman Empire was divided into two parts: the Eastern and Western Empires. Rome, which was the capital of the western division, lasted until AD 476, but the eastern division of the empire with its capital at Constantinople stood until AD 1453. And while the empire as such died, a number of the nations of which it was composed continued to exist as independent nation-states.

The interpretation continued with the explanation of another government that would arise, symbolized on the image by the feet and toes part of iron and part of brittle clay. This future governmental unit, the prophet said, would be partly strong and partly brittle. And it represents man's last attempt to rule on earth. The final rule of man will be characterized by people who lack the desire and commitment to form a unified world government. In this time of inherent disunity in what appears to be a ten-nation confederation (v. 44, "in the time of those kings"), God will break into the affairs of mankind to establish His never-ending kingdom. (We will discuss this ten-nation government later on in greater detail.)

There is progression in this dream as Babylon gives way to Medo-Persia, Greece, and Rome. Then there is the final, loosely knit ruling unit of the end time. Some Bible scholars believe that as the feet and toes are extensions of the legs, so this image symbolism suggests that the final ruling unit will come from the nation-states or peoples from which the old Roman Empire was formed. However, your IST author concludes that since iron represents Rome on this image, and since the feet and toes are part iron *and* clay, this final *entity will be composed partly of old Roman Empire countries, and partly of countries not included in the old Roman Empire (the clay).

entity
something that has real and separate existence

Notice that no natural cause accounted for the fall of the stone, for it was "cut out of a mountain, but not by human hands" (v. 45). The golden age for which natural man has longed will not come about by natural processes but by divine intervention in the affairs of men. A new movement external to the world and its system will change the course of history. The crushing stone, which represents God's intervention, destroys the symbolic image in the days of the feet and toes, grinding them to powder. As man's kingdom ends, nothing is left, but the Stone rolls on until it fills the whole earth. Man's work is *temporal; only the divine is eternal. God's kingdom will endure.

temporal
not religious or sacred; worldly; secular; lasting for a time only

As we conclude this section, we want to place this dream in perspective. Beginning with Nebuchadnezzar's conquest of Judah and the resulting captivity of the Jewish remnant, a period of time began on God's *prophetic time clock* which we call "the times of the Gentiles" (Luke 21:24). This expression in general refers to the period of time when Israel's people and land are under the control of Gentile nations. It will end with the total destruction of human government in its final form: a ten-nation confederation headed by a person we will learn to know as the Antichrist. His defeat will take place at the second coming of Christ.

Thus ended the second conflict. Nebuchadnezzar was filled with gratitude as he thanked the prophet for this marvelous service (v. 46). In addition, even though he was a pagan, the king expressed his sincere feelings: Daniel's God was "God of gods and Lord of kings" (v. 47). Pagan magic was clearly no match for heavenly wisdom! Moreover, Daniel and his three friends were promoted in the administration of public affairs in Babylon.

9 Match the part of the image (right) with the kingdom or government to which it refers (left).

.... **a** The Medo-Persian Empire	1) Head of gold
.... **b** The Roman Empire	2) Breast and arms of silver
.... **c** The Ten-Nation Confederation	3) Belly and thighs of bronze
.... **d** The Babylonian Empire	4) Legs of iron
.... **e** The Grecian Empire	5) Feet of iron and clay

10 The second conflict of Daniel concerns
a) religious externals, ceremonial requirements, and compromise.
b) the superiority of divine wisdom over pagan magic.
c) a contest between radically different cultures for supremacy.
d) personal versus group religious convictions.

11 What is the significance of the image dream and the term *times of the Gentiles*?

....

....

The Third Conflict: Idolatry Versus Loyalty

Daniel 3:1–30

Chapter 3 gives details of Nebuchadnezzar's attempt to impose a uniform system of religion on his subjects. He may have believed that this would unify his empire. Whatever his reason, he set up a huge image and demanded that everyone worship it whenever the appropriate signal was given. There was no room for an alternative loyalty. Simply put, the issue was this: one must either bow to the image or burn in a blazing furnace. This decree meant that the young Jewish civil servants must decide whether to keep their spiritual convictions and loyalty to God or to adopt the standard imposed by Babylon. Fortunately, the decision was not difficult because these young men had already showed their faith in God and commitment to His Word.

Thus, when the time came, their minds were already made up. They showed by their behavior that it takes more than a king's command to make true servants of God sin against their convictions. The result was an immediate sentence of death; however, as multitudes watched, the faith of these three devout youths was rewarded. In the midst of the blazing furnace they were freed, accompanied by *a fourth Person* who looked like a son of the gods (v. 25). They walked out of the furnace of death to the glory of God and the admiration of the assembled Babylonian leaders. Once again, they were promoted in the civic affairs of Babylon.

12 Describe briefly the issue involved in the third conflict.

....

....

List the main truth of Daniel 4.

The Fourth Conflict: A King's Pride Versus God's Sovereignty

Daniel 4:1–37

As you read chapter 4, you may have noticed that King Nebuchadnezzar was given a number of dramatic experiences that involved the "Most High God." Even though God demonstrated His power and wisdom to the king, nothing seemed to change his haughtiness and pride. As we shall see, God warned him through a remarkable vision about this reckless attitude, but more was required before the king was ready to humble himself and give God the rightful place in his thinking and actions. Keep these things in mind as you examine this conflict.

Nebuchadnezzar was enjoying peace in his spacious city following his far-flung conquests. His energy had been turned from the task of consolidating his empire to refining his rule over the affairs of Babylon. His government was running smoothly like a well-oiled machine. As a result, he was able to turn his attention to internal developments. He began massive public works projects, including the building of fortifications, a moat, and a fresh water supply for the city. Streets were paved and abundant food supplies were stored. The city was beautified with palaces, temples, attractive public buildings, and the famous hanging gardens.

The king was apparently well-satisfied with his imperial and domestic achievements; however, at this point God gave Nebuchadnezzar a dream (vv. 4–17) that was intended to bring about a change in his attitude and behavior. Daniel, who interpreted the dream (vv. 19–27), advised the king to repent and change his actions and attitude in order to avert judgment. Whatever his immediate reaction, the king soon forgot the advice. Just one year later he boasted, "Is not this the great Babylon I have built . . . by my mighty power and for the glory of my majesty?" (v. 30). Immediately judgment fell!

The result was that the king lost his sanity, and for an extended period of time he lived apart from people in the open fields (vv. 30–33). During this time his kingdom was maintained for him by his advisors. After this period of extreme abasement, he was restored to his kingdom. As a result of this conflict, the king's proud spirit was broken and his spiritual priorities were reordered as he gladly acknowledged God's control over the affairs of people (vv. 17, 25, 32). The main point of this chapter is to impress upon us that God is sovereign in establishing and maintaining the kingdoms of men.

13 The main lesson or truth taught in Daniel 4 is that

....

Explain the basic nature of Belshazzar's sin.

The Fifth Conflict: Man's Impiety Versus Divine Sovereignty

Daniel 5:1–31

Chapter 5 introduces a final scene in the history of Babylon. The kingdom of Babylon is in obvious decline. A powerful army of Medes and Persians surrounds the city. King Nabonidus is away from the city, and his eldest son, Belshazzar, acts as king-regent in his absence. This is the setting in which the young king-regent chooses to throw a wild party. Made bold by his drinking, the proud young ruler commands that the sacred vessels taken from the temple in Jerusalem be brought to use in toasting the gods of Babylon. This haughty move of *impiety brings an immediate reaction from God: the fingers of a hand appear and write a strange message on the wall (v. 5). The king is terrified; his nobles are baffled. This, then, is the conflict of chapter 5.

impiety
lack of respect or reverence for God

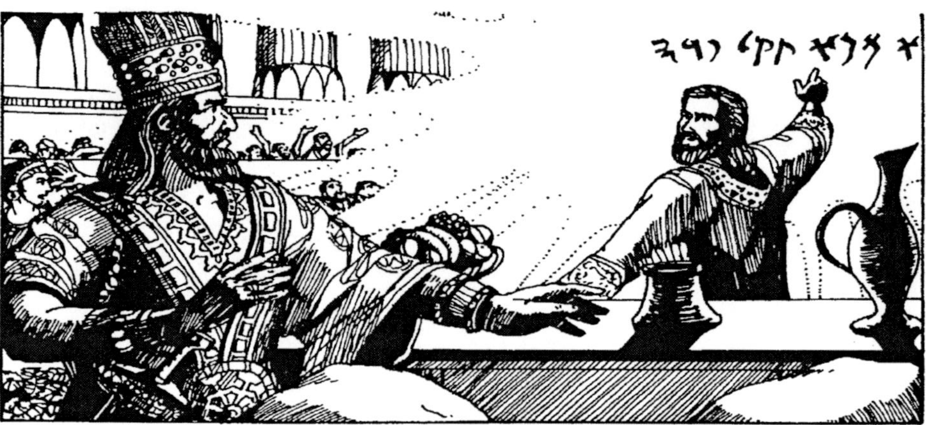

The terrified ruler sent for his enchanters, astrologers, and diviners to interpret the message, but none could help. The queen mother, however, remembered the service Daniel had given during Nebuchadnezzar's reign (vv. 10–12). So Daniel was brought to the king and promised a great reward if he could interpret the writing. He would be made the third ruler in the kingdom. (Belshazzar, as we mentioned, reigned the kingdom jointly with his father, Nabonidus.) Brushing aside the promised rewards, Daniel moved quickly to the meaning of the mysterious message.

This was a crucial hour in Babylon's history. *In spite of the knowledge that his grandfather Nebuchadnezzar had been greatly humbled for his arrogance, Belshazzar had ignored his accountability to God.* Furthermore, he had presumed to insult the God who controlled life itself by drinking out of the sacred vessels that had been dedicated to Him. Beyond this, he had dared to praise the worthless and lifeless idols of Babylon. Therefore, his actions were weighed in the divine scales, and he was found to have fallen short of what God required. The kingdom of Babylon had reached its end; it was to be succeeded by the Medes and Persians (the breast and arms of silver on the image of Daniel 2).

Daniel 5 ends with a terse statement: "That very night Belshazzar . . . was slain" (v. 30). With this solemn comment we see that man is responsible before God. God holds us responsible for the light and knowledge we receive of Him. Verses 18–21 show the extent of Belshazzar's knowledge of God and verses 22 and 23 reveal his willfulness in rejecting this knowledge. Sin against the light of God's Word and will is called *willful* or *presumptuous* sin. Hundreds of years earlier David prayed to be delivered from this type of sin (Psalm 19:13), and each of us, likewise, ought to be aware of the need to live responsibly in the light God has given us. Thus, Babylon fell and was succeeded by the joint kingdom of Media and Persia.

14 The best description of the fifth conflict is man's
- a) genius versus God's mercy.
- b) weakness versus God's faithfulness.
- c) uncertainty versus God's omnipotence.
- d) impiety versus God's sovereignty.

15 Explain briefly the nature of Belshazzar's sin.

....

Identify key elements in the sixth conflict.

The Sixth Conflict: Jealousy Versus God's Providential Care

Daniel 6:1–28

As chapter 5 ended, we saw Babylon fall and Darius the Mede take the kingdom in behalf of the Medo-Persian Empire. Now Daniel and his fellow exiles are under the control of this empire. Nevertheless, we see that Daniel has a place of prominence as one of three chief administrators over the realm (vv. 1–2). In this position Daniel so distinguished himself that the king intended to make him the chief administrator (v. 3). This intent, however, caused an undercurrent of criticism and jealousy among other administrators and satraps.

While Daniel was both a foreigner and an exiled Jew, he was also a distinguished civil servant: trustworthy, diligent, and incorrupt (vv. 4–5). The reason for the reaction of Daniel's enemies was jealousy over his promotion and perhaps prejudice because of his country, people, and religion. Verses 6–9 tell of their conspiracy to *trap* Daniel into breaking a legal statute and incurring the death penalty.

The conspirators knew they could count on Daniel's consistent behavior toward God (v. 10). What a powerful testimony that was! And so, Daniel's prayer to God was used as evidence to support the charge that he was disloyal to the king and subject to the death penalty (vv. 11–14). Since they could not legally reverse a law of the Medes and Persians, the sentence was carried out. Even so, the king knew the power of Daniel's God to deliver and he encouraged Daniel to believe that God would rescue him (v. 16). In fact, God did intervene, bringing protection and deliverance to Daniel and destruction to his enemies (vv. 17–24). Once again, steadfast faith in God in the midst of conflict and confrontation with evil brought glory to God and promotion to His servant. The evidence here is that God's providential care for His people can be depended on in all situations. One who puts his faith and trust in God will not be ashamed.

16 Circle the letter preceding each TRUE statement.

a The focus of the narrative shifts from Babylon to the realm of the Medes and Persians.

b Once Babylon fell, all Jewish exiles returned immediately to their homeland.

c Daniel's service under Nebuchadnezzar and his successors as a counselor led to a place of authority under Medo-Persian rule.

d The sixth conflict suggests that when one builds his life on faith and trust in God, he can expect to see God's providential care revealed.

e Daniel's enemies were not so much concerned about his race, religion, or cultural differences as they were about his qualifications for public office.

Self-Test

After you have reviewed this lesson, take the self-test. Then check you answers with those given in your Student Packet. Review any questions you answer incorrectly.

True-False. Write **T** in the blank space preceding the following statements if the statement is TRUE. Write **F** if it is FALSE.

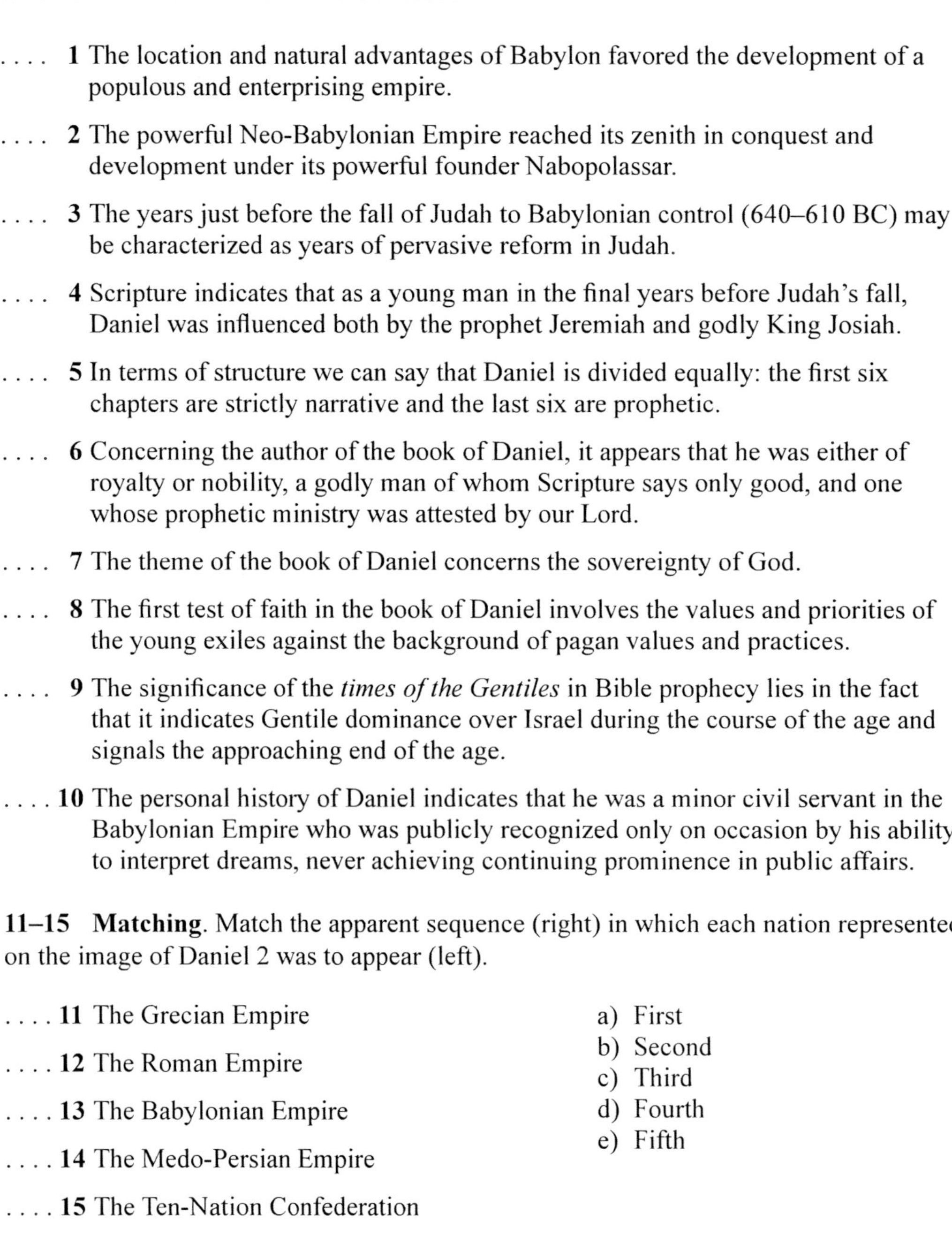

.... **1** The location and natural advantages of Babylon favored the development of a populous and enterprising empire.

.... **2** The powerful Neo-Babylonian Empire reached its zenith in conquest and development under its powerful founder Nabopolassar.

.... **3** The years just before the fall of Judah to Babylonian control (640–610 BC) may be characterized as years of pervasive reform in Judah.

.... **4** Scripture indicates that as a young man in the final years before Judah's fall, Daniel was influenced both by the prophet Jeremiah and godly King Josiah.

.... **5** In terms of structure we can say that Daniel is divided equally: the first six chapters are strictly narrative and the last six are prophetic.

.... **6** Concerning the author of the book of Daniel, it appears that he was either of royalty or nobility, a godly man of whom Scripture says only good, and one whose prophetic ministry was attested by our Lord.

.... **7** The theme of the book of Daniel concerns the sovereignty of God.

.... **8** The first test of faith in the book of Daniel involves the values and priorities of the young exiles against the background of pagan values and practices.

.... **9** The significance of the *times of the Gentiles* in Bible prophecy lies in the fact that it indicates Gentile dominance over Israel during the course of the age and signals the approaching end of the age.

.... **10** The personal history of Daniel indicates that he was a minor civil servant in the Babylonian Empire who was publicly recognized only on occasion by his ability to interpret dreams, never achieving continuing prominence in public affairs.

11–15 Matching. Match the apparent sequence (right) in which each nation represented on the image of Daniel 2 was to appear (left).

.... **11** The Grecian Empire

.... **12** The Roman Empire

.... **13** The Babylonian Empire

.... **14** The Medo-Persian Empire

.... **15** The Ten-Nation Confederation

a) First
b) Second
c) Third
d) Fourth
e) Fifth

Answers to study questions

9 **a** 2) Breast and arms of silver
b 4) Legs of iron
c 5) Feet of iron and clay
d 1) Head of gold
e 3) Belly and thighs of bronze

1 **a** False
b True
c True
d True
e True
f False

10 b) the superiority of divine wisdom over pagan magic.

2 the people despised God's words and failed to walk according to His Law; therefore, after His patience was exhausted, God brought judgment upon the people, their cities, and their land.

11 The image dream gives a view of the general course of history from Nebuchadnezzar until the Second Coming. The times of the Gentiles refer to the time when Israel and her land are under Gentile control.

3 e) both b) and c) above.

12 Your answer. It involved the loyalty of three Hebrew youths to God and their willingness to die, if need be, for their convictions.

4 **a** True
b False
c False
d False
e True

13 God is sovereign in establishing and preserving the kingdoms of men.

5 Your answer should include the fact that a rough outline of Daniel has chapters 1–6 as Personal Biography and Local History; whereas, chapters 7–12 concern Gentile nations, Israel, and the World Ruler in Prophecy. The date of composition is set in the sixth century before Christ. The theme of the book is the sovereignty of God. Daniel wrote the book and was either of the seed royal or of the nobility. His authorship is attested by Jesus in the Gospels.

14 d) impiety versus God's sovereignty.

6 Verses 3–5 state the general conditions and verse 8 gives more specific details.

15 Basically, it was willful sin against the light and knowledge God had given.

7 The issue was whether the Jewish youths would renounce their faith in God and become Babylonians. It indicated clearly their values and priorities at the outset of their public life.

16 a True
b False
c True
d True
e False

8 Your answer. They had true spiritual character, a deep trust in God, faith in His ability and desire to meet their personal needs, and appreciation for what He is. Also, they lived their faith in honor and humility.

Perspectives of the Coming World Ruler

In Lesson 1 we were introduced to the book of Daniel and to the personal history of the prophet in chapters 1–6. In addition to many background facts, we considered important aspects of Bible prophecy. Among other things, we focused attention on the phrase *times of the Gentiles* and what it implies in God's plan for human history. Now we turn to the second half of Daniel, chapters 7–12, to add to the knowledge we have already gained. Since this material is so extensive, we will divide the content into two fairly equal lessons. Lesson 2 will cover chapters 7–9, and Lesson 3 will deal with chapters 10–12.

You may recall from the outline given in Lesson 1 that the content for the second half of Daniel, as this lesson title shows, concerns the future. Certain Gentile nations, Israel, and the coming world ruler are introduced and examined at length in chapters 7–12.

Our prayer is that you will seek to learn what the Bible has to say about these important subjects. Also, we trust you will not be led aside either by sensationalism or foolish speculation as you examine these matters and adjust your life accordingly. May the Holy Spirit especially quicken your mind now as you begin this lesson and may He also give you a desire to grow in your knowledge of the truth and to apply it to your daily life.

the activities...

◊ Before you begin to study the lesson, scan Daniel 7–9 to get an overview of the content. Then read each chapter more carefully as you come to it in the lesson development.

◊ Work through the lesson development according to the procedures given in Lesson 1.

the objectives...

2.1 *Describe Daniel's beast vision and identify points of similarity between it and the vision of Nebuchadnezzar's image.*

2.2 *Recognize examples of the interpretation of this vision that flow logically out of the text.*

2.3 *Explain what key figures in Daniel 8 symbolize and their biblical prophecy significance.*

2.4 *Identify key elements in the explanation of the phrase seventy sevens in Daniel 9:24–27.*

2.5 *Describe the progression of revelation in Daniel 2, 7, 8, and 9, and its significance.*

the outline...

1 The Four Beasts
The Interpretation

2 The Ram and the Goat
3 The Seventy Sevens
4 Review and Application

Describe Daniel's beast vision and identify points of similarity between it and the vision of Nebuchadnezzar's image.

The Four Beasts

Daniel 7:1–28

The vision of Nebuchadnezzar in chapter 2 is often called the *image vision*. In that vision, God revealed a particular course that Gentile rule would take from Nebuchadnezzar's day to the end of the *times of the Gentiles*. In chapter 7 the content is frequently called the *beast vision*. The subject matter, as you have probably noticed, is similar in both visions. In one vision, however, the point of view is that of a pagan ruler who sees man's rule as splendid, progressive, and refined. In the other, though, man's rule is seen from God's point of view as beastly, degrading, and corrupt.

In both visions we see four kingdoms or political entities which appear to have an important role in God's program. In chapter 2 God gave the key to interpret the symbolism represented by the image. And so the meaning was fairly simple for us to grasp through various stages until the final period of man's rule. As we examine chapter 7, let us see if there is a similar key in the text that will give some clue to the identity of the various elements.

Daniel saw four beasts come out of the sea. According to Revelation 17:15, the sea represents "peoples, multitudes, nations and languages." From the sea of humanity, then, the first beast arose. It was like a lion and had the wings of an eagle. The prophet saw that its wings were torn off, and it was lifted up from the ground and was given a man's heart (v. 4). The second beast was like a bear. It was raised up on one side and it had three ribs in its mouth, and it was commanded to arise and eat its fill of flesh (v. 5). Daniel next saw a beast like a leopard that had four wings on its back. Moreover, it had four heads and it was given authority to rule (v. 6). Finally, the prophet saw a nondescript beast. It was large and powerful and it had great iron teeth. This beast crushed and ate its victims and trampled what it did not eat. It also had ten horns; however, as Daniel watched, another *little horn* arose among the ten and it uprooted three of the ten. This *little horn* had eyes like the eyes of a man and a boastful mouth (vv. 7–8). However, the arrogance of the *little horn* and the beast was cut short and destroyed by divine appointment (vv. 9–12). Then one like a son of man came to take charge of an eternal kingdom (vv. 13–14).

In verses 9–14, we have a magnificent preview of the conclusion of this age. The Ancient of Days in all His glory and heaven's angelic hosts take their places to witness the end of rebellion and sin. Not only is there majestic glory before which all opposition is destroyed, but also the appearance of the Son of Man to set up His eternal kingdom. This vision gives us a foretaste of the glory that awaits us at Christ's coming when our bodies will be liberated from the effects of the curse and we shall be like our Lord (1 Corinthians 15:35–55; Philippians 3:20–21; 1 Thessalonians 4:13–18; 1 John 3:2).

Before we move on to consider the interpretation, let us consider some points of similarity between the visions of chapters 2 and 7. Both involve a progression of kingdoms or political entities. And a ten-nation order (ten toes and ten horns) rises out of the fourth kingdom of each. (The legs of iron are the fourth kingdom of 2:40, and the nondescript beast is the fourth kingdom of chapter 7.) In both visions God intervenes in the time of the ten-nation entity to end man's rule and establish His eternal rule. In chapter 2 we seem to have a *general* outline, but in chapter 7 we have helpful details that give us a more complete picture.

1 Circle the letter preceding each TRUE statement.

a The symbolism suggested by the sea, according to Scripture, is the violence of nature.

b We can say most accurately that Daniel's vision of chapter 7 is a less detailed prospect of the future than that of Nebuchadnezzar.

c The visions of the king and the prophet suggest both a terminal point for earthly kingdoms and the certain rule of God in the future.

d The activity of the *crushing rock* of chapter 2 seems to have its parallel in the activity of the *Son of Man* in chapter 7, in which he receives universal dominion.

e The final scenes of human government and the accession of the Son of Man presented help us to understand the course of the future.

2 In your notebook describe the beast vision of chapter 7.

Recognize examples of the interpretation of this vision that flow logically out of the text.

The Interpretation

Daniel 7:15–28

Daniel was troubled by the vision and wanted very much to know what it meant. Thus, he asked one who appeared in the vision what it meant (vv. 15–16). This one told Daniel the four beasts represented four earthly kingdoms; however, this informer quickly added "But the saints of the Most High will receive the kingdom and will possess it forever" (v. 18). Unfortunately, this brief explanation does not tell us specifically what kingdoms the beasts represent.

As we shall see in chapter 8, there is a continuation of reference to kingdoms that had an impact on God's people in Daniel's day and following. This has led some Bible scholars to believe that Daniel 7 simply reinforces the progression of kingdoms set forth in chapter 2. Your writer suggests that these first three beasts may symbolize modern nations that will support the final world ruler. Verse 17, he believes, indicates that these beasts are four kingdoms that will arise in the future, and Daniel is writing during the Neo-Babylonian period, which had existed for some time. You will also notice when we discuss Revelation 13, that these three beasts are mentioned in connection with the final world ruler in verse 2. Daniel 7 and Revelation 13 are the only places where these three beast symbols appear together in Scripture.

Somehow the fortunes of God's people are tied to those of the nations symbolized in the visions given in Daniel. We saw in chapter 2 that the *times of the Gentiles* began with the Babylonian conquest of Judah. Moreover, the rule of the Medes and Persians helped preserve the nation of Israel after her captivity and brought about the resettlement of the Jewish exiles. Grecian or Hellenistic rule gave Israel, among other things, a preview of the end-time rule of a shrewd and treacherous ruler. Roman rule brought Israel both great benefits and some sobering limitations for an extended period of time. Let us keep these facts of Israel's history before us as we continue with the interpretation.

In verses 19–22 the prophet appears to interrupt his informer in order to get to the heart of the vision: the fourth beast and the activity related with it. The informer takes up the interpretation in verse 23 and answers the prophet's questions, adding greatly to our knowledge of the details of end-time events.

coalition
alliance of political parties or groups for some special purpose

The fourth beast, says the informer, is a kingdom or political entity that will have a mighty impact on the earth. Its rule will be extended efficiently and irresistibly (v. 23). Ten kings or governmental leaders joined together in some sort of alignment will come from this kingdom (v. 24). Then after the rise of this ten-king *coalition, another *king* different from the ten will arise and subdue three of the ten (v. 24). Taking control of their domains, this ruler, described earlier as the *little horn,* will make himself supreme ruler. He will speak against God and he will oppress God's people. Moreover, this powerful leader will attempt to change set times and laws that are apparently sacred and very meaningful. He will succeed in his purposes for "a time, times and half a time" (v. 25). However, he will be deprived of his power and destroyed by the coming kingdom of God (v. 26). Then the people of God will rule the earth under Him (v. 27). These facts give us insights into the concluding events of this age in addition to those we examined in chapter 2. Now let us focus our attention on several facts from the prophet's questions and the interpretation and place them in perspective.

From this fourth kingdom a ten-nation coalition will arise in the end time (v. 24). Out of this entity another *king* or leader will arise (compare v. 7 with v. 8). In due course this one called the *little horn* will emerge and displace three of the ten kings (vv. 8, 20–21, 24–25). In practical terms, he will assume control of the coalition or *empire* and eliminate three of the ten leaders by force, establishing himself as absolute ruler. This person is arrogant, boastful, impressive, and seemingly inspired by an infernal purpose. He is actively hostile toward God, speaking blasphemous words against Him and oppressing His people. In fact, he strikes at God through his people and succeeds in defeating them for 3 1/2 years, 42 months, 1260 days, or "a time, times and half a time" (vv. 22, 25). Then he is judged and destroyed, but the people of the Most High will rule and reign under God forever. See Figure 2.1 below.

RECURRENT TIME SEGMENT IN DANIEL AND REVELATION	
TIME	**LOCATION**
Time, times, and half a time	Daniel 7:25; 12:7; Revelation 12:14
42 months	Revelation 11:2; 13:5
1260 days	Revelation 11:3; 12:6

Figure 2.1

As we review this marvelous preview of the future, we have some more specific information to add to what we gained in chapter 2. While we have not dealt with the identity of the first three beasts which is not clearly given, we can be sure of this: the final ten-nation coalition will arise out of the fourth empire (possibly in a revised form). Moreover, we see that a strong leader will take control of this *empire.* Thus, for the first time in the biblical record we get a glimpse of one who, along with other names, is called the Antichrist. And we learn something about his nature, method of operation, and final destiny.

Above all, we have gained important details about the events of the end time. These can help us to understand more about the times in which we live and our responsibilities in the light of these facts.

3 Circle the letter preceding each TRUE statement.

a The informer told Daniel that the four beasts represented four aspects of human government.

b The nations symbolized by the image and beast visions appear to be important because of their effect on the destiny of the people of God.

c It may be said that Daniel was much more concerned about the fourth beast and what proceeded from it than he was with the first three beasts.

d The ten-nation coalition or empire is an entity from the past which we can readily identify.

e The *little horn* and *another king* are the terms used to describe one who will gain control over the ten-nation entity.

f The method by which one known as the *little horn* gets control of the coalition is by peaceful diplomacy.

4 The leader of the ten-nation entity will exercise power

a) for a period of three and one-half years.
b) over God's people, defeating them during his rule.
c) only in the area of governmental control.
d) all the above.
e) both a) and b) above.

5 Circle the letter preceding each statement that represents an accurate example of interpretation that flows out of the text.

a The four beasts represent Babylon, Medo-Persia, Greece, and Rome.

b The ten-nation entity is the final end-time example of man's rule.

c The leader of the ten-nation entity will exert force in order to demonstrate his control over the *empire.*

d Just before the coming of the Son of Man, the people of God will be mightily oppressed by a godless ruler who will speak against God and prosper as he oppresses God's people.

e The beasts represent the major powers of the world today under the corporate leadership of the United Nations Organization.

6 In your notebook tell what Christian believers can know about end-time events based on the text we have considered.

Objective 2.3

Explain what key figures in Daniel 8 symbolize and their biblical prophecy significance.

The Ram and the Goat

Daniel 8:1–27

In the final year of Belshazzar's reign, Daniel had a vision which outlined the course of two empires of the relatively near future. As you read verses 1–14, you probably noticed that two central figures occupied the scene of action: a ram and a goat. The focus at first was on the ram as he moved south, north, and west at will. Nothing could resist his advances as he grew and became great. Then, however, the prophet saw a goat with one prominent horn between his eyes move rapidly out of the west and attack the ram, overpowering him completely. The goat in turn became great, but at the height of his power his notable horn was broken. In its place four prominent horns grew up, but from one of these another horn emerged. It started small and grew gradually toward the south, the east, and the *Beautiful Land.* As it became great, it overthrew some, established itself as prince, and prospered for a time, elevating evil and trampling truth to the ground. The prophet was told that this time of chaos would last for some 2300 days or a bit less than seven years. Then truth would be reestablished and right would prevail.

This is the substance of the vision which Daniel saw. Naturally, he was puzzled by it and sought to understand its meaning. At this point an angelic messenger came to his assistance (vv. 15–18). As in chapter 2, God gives us the key we need to unlock the identity of the two countries symbolized by the ram and the goat. The ram stands for the joint kingdom of Media and Persia (v. 20). The two horns represent the kings of this kingdom. A careful comparison of verse 3 with secular history reveals a remarkable thing: Media was the stronger part of this joint kingdom at the beginning, but gradually Persia came to dominate it. Scripture says that "One of the horns was longer than the other but grew up later" (v. 3). Secular history records that the conquests of Medo-Persia were to the south, north, and especially to the west. For slightly over two hundred years this powerful empire held sway in the Middle East, but then it faced an irresistible force from the west.

Verse 21 gives us the identity of the goat and amplifies the information given in verses 5–7. The goat symbolizes the kingdom of Greece and the prominent horn, its first king. From secular history we learn of the rise of Alexander the Great and his lightning-like conquests as he swept eastward to take over the empire of Medo-Persia. Because his conquest was so complete, we often refer to the empire he forged as *Hellenistic Civilization.* (The Greeks were also known as *Hellenes.*) However, Alexander's career ended after a dozen years and his empire was ultimately divided among four of his generals. Two of these who are significant to our studies in Daniel are Ptolemy and Seleucus. Ptolemy developed a powerful kingdom in Egypt and Seleucus did the same in greater Syria, which after the beginning of the second century included the biblical land of Palestine. Thus, Alexander's kingdom was broken up, and the four divisions did not have the same power that he had wielded (v. 22).

We now move to the content of verses 9–14, which is interpreted in verses 23–25. The prophet was told that a powerful leader would emerge from one of the four divisions of the Grecian Empire. He would start small but grow in power through *intrigue, diplomacy, and political maneuvering. When he gained power, he would rule ruthlessly, imposing his will and evil values on others. Moreover, he would attack the *holy people,* debase spiritual values, and succeed for a time. Nevertheless, Daniel is told that as this leader exalts himself against the Prince of princes, he will be destroyed. Let us consider what message this vision had for God's people of that day and what message, if any, it has for the people of God in the end time.

intrigue
underhanded planning to accomplish some purpose

Historical and religious literature of this period gives us valuable information about the fortunes of Alexander's vast empire. For example, the Jewish historian Josephus leaves us a wealth of material on the division of Alexander's empire and the fortunes of his successors in his *Antiquities of the Jews.* And the *Apocrypha,* a series of noninspired writings of this period, give us additional historical information about the kingdoms of Ptolemy and Seleucus and their successors.

Early in the second century before Christ (around 175 BC), the throne of the Seleucid Empire became vacant. A member of the Seleucid family, Antiochus IV, who was in Greece at the time, determined to get control of the throne even though he was not the crown prince. With the help of a king who was sympathetic to his purposes, to whom he pledged future friendship and assistance, Antiochus gained control of the Seleucid kingdom. Once in power, he consolidated his position by giving lavish gifts and bribes. The record shows that Antiochus came to power by flattery, bribery, and deceit. He began in a small way but soon became great. In fact, for a brief period of time he exercised a degree of control over the Ptolemaic kingdom. However, his ambition to formally unite the Seleucid and Ptolemaic Empires was forbidden by the Roman Senate. At this point, the frustrated king turned his energies elsewhere.

Having reigned for some eight years, the deceitful, arrogant king turned to the *Beautiful Land* (v. 9) and the *holy people* (v. 24), a fairly obvious reference to Palestine and the Jews as these terms are used elsewhere in Daniel (see Daniel 9:24). In an effort to destroy the root of Jewish nationalism and impose a uniform system of religious loyalty on his many subject peoples, Antiochus forbade Jewish worship. This included the reading of the Law, celebration of ceremonial feasts, and the rite of circumcision. Moreover, he decreed that his Jewish subjects must transfer their religious loyalties to him, adopt pagan values, and honor pagan feasts. Knowing the intensity of their faith, Antiochus attempted to use military power to force them to comply. From 168 BC onward for the next three and one-half years, devout Jews endured cruel *atrocities as the ruthless king stopped at nothing that would break Jewish spirit and thus enable him to achieve his purpose.

atrocities
monstrous wickedness or cruelty; very cruel or brutal acts

Antiochus replaced the incumbent high priest with one who would carry out his godless policies. He killed in cold blood those who circumcised their boy babies and those who kept the Jewish feasts. However, his ultimate offense was to defile the sacred Torah scrolls with the grease of a pig before he destroyed them. Then he sacrificed a pig upon the altar in the temple to show his contempt for the Law. Naturally, this led God-fearing Jews to forsake temple worship. However, the king's enforcers pursued the people to their villages in order to get them to accept the new policies. The faithful were required either to defile themselves with the meat of swine or be killed, but this was too much. A godly priest, Mattathias, raised the flag of revolt, and one of his sons, Judas Maccabaeus, became the leader of a fearless guerrilla band that eventually drove the Seleucid armies out of the land. The king, however, was not present to witness the failure of his system. Instead, he was in the eastern part of his kingdom where he died a strange and mysterious death.

We see that the careful unfolding of prophecy concerns Medo-Persia, Greece, and elements of the divided Grecian Empire. Carefully and logically the scene unfolds to reveal a *diabolical leader who came to power by intrigue, cruelty, and force. This Seleucid ruler is clearly identified in history, and it appears that he fulfilled the prophecy accurately and completely. Since all elements of this prophecy were fulfilled so fully, one is led to ask: "Why did God focus so much attention on such a brief period of Israel's history?" The question, we feel, leads us to examine other end-time prophecies to see if another such person may be anticipated. Chapter 2 revealed an end-time entity, but it gave no hint of leadership. However, chapter 7 spoke clearly of the ten-nation coalition and an arrogant leader who will wage war on God's people for three and one-half years until he is destroyed by Christ's coming. Thus we see that another person *like* Antiochus will come into power in the end time. This fact has led many Bible scholars to conclude that in Antiochus IV we have a preview of the coming Antichrist. Keep these facts in mind as you move on in your study of Daniel and Revelation.

diabolical
very cruel, wicked, or fiendish

7 Based on our studies thus far, which of the following summarizes best the content and purpose of Daniel 8?

a) The focus is primarily on the rise, development, and destiny of Medo-Persia and Greece in history.
b) It emphasizes the background, rise, and fall of Medo-Persia and Greece in order to locate and identify a king who is especially important in his relationship with God's people.
c) It looks beyond Medo-Persia, Greece, and kingdoms that grew out of them in order to focus on and identify precisely a coming world ruler.
d) It interpreted the 'writing on the wall for Belshazzar.

8 Circle the letter preceding each TRUE statement.

a As in chapter 2, there is a key that identifies the two main symbolical figures in chapter 8.
b Details from secular history add greatly to our understanding of the outline given in this chapter's prophetic message.
c While the breakup of Alexander's empire produced four parts, the focus in Daniel concerns just two of these elements.
d The biblical record indicates clearly that the stern-faced master of intrigue would come to power by force alone.
e According to the biblical record, the cruel leader was to be entirely unsuccessful in his efforts to promote deceitfulness, overthrow God's people, and set himself against God.
f Looking to the future, in which Daniel 2 and 7 also give some details about events at the end of the age, the future *little horn* will not be destroyed by any human foe; he will meet his end at the hands of God.

Identify key elements in the explanation of the phrase seventy sevens in Daniel 9:24–27.

The Seventy Sevens: Daniel 9:24–27

Daniel 9:1–27

A careful reading of Daniel 9 reveals some very important facts. Among other things, we see that Daniel is concerned about the ruin of his homeland. It had lain in a state of desolation for many years. In fact, the Lord had spoken through Jeremiah the prophet, saying that this ruin would last for seventy years (Jeremiah 25:11; 29:10). "Why the desolation? Why seventy years?" you may ask. The immediate cause of desolation, of course, was the sin of God's people who rejected His Word, messengers, and initial judgment (2 Chronicles 36:15–21). The longer-term cause, however, seems to have been the people's rejections of God's system of honoring the sabbatical year. (Compare Leviticus 25:14 with 2 Chronicles 36:21.) Since Israel had apparently failed to give the land its Sabbath years for a period of 490 years, the people owed the land seventy years of rest.

9 From your reading of the Scriptures in this section, God commanded the people of Israel to rest their land one year out of

a) 7 years.
b) 70 years.
c) 490 years.
d) 50 years.

Your writer believes that Daniel was thinking about this initial 490-year period as he prayed in Daniel 9:1–19. The period of judgment had nearly run its course. Restoration was now in view as the prophet pleaded for his people. At this point, Gabriel came to tell him about another 490-year period which concerned Israel's future. The verses you have read in Daniel 9:24–27 are known as "the prophecy of the seventy weeks." (The word translated *sevens* in the NIV is translated "weeks" in the KJV.) Conservative scholarship overwhelmingly regards this time as "weeks of years," that is, a seven or "week of years" equals seven years.

Beginning with verse 24, we observe six things that Gabriel says will happen to Daniel's people (Israel) and to his holy city (Jerusalem). Remember: this prophecy is directed to Israel, not the church. These six elements appear to include God's entire redemptive purpose for Israel. Then in verses 25 and 26, Gabriel explains this time period with its special order of *sevens* in more detail. First, note how many *sevens* stand between the decree to restore and rebuild Jerusalem and the coming of the Anointed One. There are a total of sixty-nine *sevens* (weeks of years). Amid all the facts that seem to be crowded into these verses, we see that:

1. Jerusalem (from Daniel's perspective) was to be rebuilt in times of trouble (following the exile).
2. After sixty-nine *sevens*, the Anointed One would be cut off and have nothing.
3. The people of a coming ruler would destroy the city and the sanctuary, ushering in ruin, war, and desolation.

Now let us examine these facts a bit more in detail. The Anointed One, the ruler, is Jesus Christ. The Hebrew word *Messiah* means "anointed one," as does the Greek word *Christ.* The phrase "will be cut off" clearly refers to Jesus' first coming. Between the decree to rebuild Jerusalem and the cutting off of Christ two segments of time would go by. They may be described graphically as in Figure 2.2.

7 sevens	(7x7 years)	=	49 years
+62 sevens	(62x7 years)	=	434 years
69 sevens	(69x7 years)	=	483 years

Original time period	70 sevens	(70x7 years)	=	490 years
Decree to rebuild Jerusalem until Messiah	– 69 sevens	(69x7 years)	=	483 years
Balance of time remaining	1 seven	(1x7 years)	=	7 years

Figure 2.2

On the preceding chart, we see that one *seven* remains to accomplish the six things mentioned in verse 24 for Daniel's people, Israel, and his holy city, Jerusalem. Now as we examine verse 26, we learn what was to happen to the Anointed One, the city, and the sanctuary. The Anointed One was to be "cut off." Some scholars have calculated that 483 years after the decree to rebuild Jerusalem, Jesus rode into Jerusalem on Palm Sunday proclaiming Himself, by this act, as Messiah (Zechariah 9:9 and Matthew 21:4–11). Shortly thereafter, He was cut off when He gave His life as a ransom for sinners. Jesus' death occurred sometime between AD 29 and AD 33.

Secondly, Daniel's city, the city of Jerusalem, was to be destroyed, as was the sanctuary (v. 26). This historic event, however, did not take place until AD

70. After a long and bitter siege, the Roman general Titus destroyed the city. His troops were so angered by the fierce resistance of the Jews that they burned the magnificent temple Herod had built. In the intense heat, the gold of the temple melted and ran into the cracks of the marble. To get the gold, Roman soldiers pried apart the very stones of the temple, fulfilling the words of Jesus in Matthew 24:2: "... not one stone here will be left on another; every one will be thrown down." But this was some forty years after Jesus was cut off. How do we account for this gap between Jesus' death and the destruction of Jerusalem? In prophecy, the prophets recorded future events as the revelation came to them; however, they did not always understand the time elements in their fulfillment. Peter refers to these gaps in fulfillment, noting the concern of the seers who predicted both the sufferings of Christ and the glory afterwards (1 Peter 1:11). Your writer believes that there is here a prophetic time gap of about forty years of which Daniel was apparently unaware.

Daniel 9:27 now refers to one simply noted as "he." This is the "ruler who will come" of verse 26. This ruler is distinctly different from the ruler mentioned in verse 25. He is spoken of in the future tense in verse 26. Now, in verse 27 we come to another piece of the time element mentioned by Gabriel. Sixty-nine sevens have already passed; only one seven, the *seventieth seven*, remains. Your writer believes that an unknown gap of time passes between the events noted above in the first sixty-nine sevens and what is yet to occur in the final seven decreed in verse 24. Nearly 2000 years have passed since the events of the first sixty-nine sevens passed into history, but the events prophesied for the final seven, we believe, lie just ahead.

Let us consider verse 27 closely. The "he" referred to is the one who is called "Antichrist." We have discussed him in our commentary for chapters 7 and 8 in some detail, and we shall focus on him especially in Revelation chapters 13 and 17. Daniel here notes that this one will make a contract with Israel for a period of "one seven," that is, seven years. Halfway through this seven, however, he will break the contract, end religious freedom, and set up a false system of worship. His rule will continue until its decreed end at Armageddon. We have included a simple chart of the 490 years decreed in the seventy sevens of Daniel 9:24–27 in Figure 2.3.

PASSAGE OF TIME IN THE SEVENTY SEVENS OF DANIEL 9:24–27				
Decree to Restore Jerusalem	First Coming of Christ		Rapture of the Church	Revelation 16:16 Armageddon
7 Sevens (7x7 years) |--------49 years-------|	62 sevens (62x7 years) |-------434 years ------|	Time Gap	Time, times and ½ time (The Antichrist Covenant) |-----------3 ½ years---------|	Time, times and ½ time (Abomination to the End) |--------3 ½ years------|
|--------------------483 years--------------------|			|-------------------------7 years------------------------|	

Figure 2.3

10 Daniel 9:24–27 concerns Daniel's people and the holy city. Name these people and this holy city.

....

11 Circle the letter preceding each TRUE statement.

a In Daniel 9, it appears that two (2) 490-year periods are in view: one concerns the past and one concerns Israel's future.

b The word translated *seven* or *sevens* in Daniel 9:24–27 represents seven-year time segments and has been called "weeks of years."

c The total time period in view in Daniel 9:24–27 is seventy sevens, and in this single 490-year period God's redemptive program for Israel is completed.

d The destruction of the city and sanctuary of which Gabriel spoke occurred in AD 70 under the Roman general Titus.

e A coming ruler will make a seven-year contract with Israel, but he will break the contract and prohibit religious freedom after three and one-half years.

f Between the first sixty-nine sevens and the final seven, there is a large gap in which the Anointed One will usher in everlasting righteousness.

12 Daniel 9:25 indicates that between the decree to rebuild Jerusalem and the first coming of Christ

a) 490 years will go by.
b) 483 years will go by.
c) 434 years will go by.
d) 49 years will go by.

It is important to understand that the final seven years have to do with God's completion of the things stated in the prophecy of the seventy sevens to restore the nation of Israel. A careful reading of Jeremiah 31:31–40 and Romans, chapters 9–11, points out that: 1) God selected the people of Israel, 2) they are temporarily blinded, and 3) they will be restored. This restoration, we believe, will take place in the final seven-year period. Again we remind you that *these seven years are for Israel—not the church!*

We may thus summarize the events of this last period as it concerns Israel. First, the Antichrist, an apparently strong man, will make a seven-year contract with Israel. This might possibly be a guarantee of security for Israel in the midst of the surrounding nations who are hostile to her very existence. Such a contract would guarantee peace for the Middle East. However, Israel's people, who are largely self-sufficient, will apparently need something to force them to recognize their need of a Savior. When the contract is broken, the Jewish people will lose their religious freedom and suffer unparalleled persecution as we shall see.

13 Circle the letter preceding each TRUE completion. In the seventieth seven, the people of Israel will apparently

a negotiate a security contract with a strong leader.

b continue to be self-sufficient until the Lord brings in everlasting righteousness.

c suffer when their contract is broken and their spiritual liberty is denied.

d recognize their extreme need of a Savior when their religious liberties are gone.

e face a future of extreme persecution as God completes His redemptive program for them.

Describe the progression of revelation in Daniel 2, 7, 8, and 9, and its significance.

Review and Application

In Lesson 2 we have added more specific facts to our knowledge of future events. Each vision has added important facts, helping us to see progress in divine revelation and a more complete picture of the concluding events of this age. Now let us go back briefly to what we have studied here and in Lesson 1.

Daniel 2 gave a broad outline of the course of human government from Nebuchadnezzar to the coming of the Crushing Stone. We saw that only four nations whose affairs were intertwined with those of God's people were in focus. Then out of the fourth kingdom we learned that the final form of man's rule will be a ten-nation entity or coalition that will arise to exercise control. However, it will not have the essential elements needed to produce true and lasting unity. It is said to be composed of *iron* and *baked clay* which symbolize both strength and brittleness, a combination that produces neither unity nor longevity. This coalition's end, however, is not brought about by inherent weakness but by God's breaking into the affairs of man. God's kingdom, we observed, grew until it filled the whole earth, crushing man's rule and bringing in a new, eternal order.

Chapter 7 added details to the broad outline given in chapter 2 and increased our knowledge of future events, bringing into focus those involved in the concluding scenes of human history. We learned that the ten-nation coalition of chapter 2 will be headed by one described as the *little horn* in contrast with the other horns of the fourth beast (kingdom). This ruler will get rid of three leaders of the coalition as he assumes total control and consolidates his position. Moreover, he will actively assert himself against the Most High in bold and defiant words and actions, oppressing God's people and changing set times and laws. He will prosper in his wicked, arrogant policies, we saw, for three and one-half years, but in the end he will be destroyed by the power and majesty of God at the coming of our Lord. After the judgment of the wicked, our Lord will initiate His eternal kingdom. Now we have examined specific facts about judgment, the destiny of the wicked, the second coming of Christ, and our Lord's coming kingdom.

Chapter 8 gave us what appears to be a preview of the coming ruler, including insights into his rise to power, deceitful nature, tactics, and end. In the historic figure of Antiochus IV we see many of the evil qualities that will characterize the end-time ruler; however, the future ruler will display them on a much larger scale. For example, Antiochus IV was a wicked, deceitful master of intrigue. He was also a persecutor of God's people, the Jews, and he succeeded for a while; nevertheless, he was destroyed but not by human power. These things suggest that the future coalition ruler will come to power by a combination of *manipulation and diplomacy. He may initially "have a hand of iron in a velvet glove," as he moves to gain control of the coalition, but he will soon show his true intent as he destroys three leaders and makes himself absolute ruler. Then he will initiate his policy against God's people, against truth and righteousness, and against God Himself, but in the end he will be destroyed by divine judgment.

manipulation
clever use or influence; change made for one's own purpose or advantage

Finally in chapter 9 we saw that God revealed a significant time table for His people composed of seventy sevens. In this time schedule, God intended to put an end to sin, atone for wickedness, and bring in everlasting righteousness.

We learned that between the decree to restore Jerusalem and the coming of the Messiah sixty-nine sevens or 483 years passed. The final or seventieth seven remains to be fulfilled, and it surely will be! We learned that in this final seven-year period a ruler, the Antichrist, will come forward to make a seven-year pact or treaty with the Jews (9:27). This event promises to be hailed as the most brilliant stroke of diplomacy ever, for it will bring about a guaranteed peace in the war-torn Middle East. However, halfway through the contract period, this deceitful ruler will change his policy, ending religious freedom and initiating abominable policies that will desolate the temple and drive faithful Jewish worshipers away. This policy will continue until the end predicted for this ungodly one known as the *Antichrist.*

With the foregoing glimpses of the future and the people involved in its concluding events, we are equipped to live and serve more effectively. In a practical sense, this knowledge should help us to understand the significance of events that take place in our world as we move rapidly toward the conclusion of this age. It should also lend a sense of urgency to our efforts to complete the unfinished task of reaching lost people with the gospel of Jesus Christ.

14 Based on our study to this point, match the order of events (right) with the actions or events listed (left).

.... **a** The treaty between the deceitful ruler and the Jews is broken.	1) First
.... **b** The ten-nation coalition is destroyed and replaced by the coming kingdom of the *Crushing Stone.*	2) Second
.... **c** The *Master of Deceit* makes a seven-year treaty with God's people, the Jews.	3) Third
.... **d** Religious freedom is taken from God's people, many of them are destroyed, and some kind of sacrilege causes the temple to be destroyed.	4) Fourth
.... **e** Through intrigue and diplomacy, the *Master of Deceit* takes control of the ten-nation coalition.	5) Fifth

15 What is meant by the progression of revelation in Daniel 2, 7, 8, and 9?

....

....

16 What is the significance of progressive revelation?

....

....

Self-Test

Multiple choice: Select the best answer.

1 In Daniel 7 the beasts are said to symbolize
- a) the character of mankind.
- b) the nature of people without God.
- c) kingdoms that arise from the earth.
- d) qualities of kingdoms that existed in the past.

2 The *little horn* of chapter 7 and the *small horn* which grew out of one of the four prominent horns that came from the goat in chapter 8 apparently represent
- a) the same person.
- b) a powerful end-time ruler.
- c) the head of a ten-nation entity.
- d) all of the above.
- e) both a) and b) above.

3 A comparison of chapter 8 and secular history from about 330 BC to 160 BC indicates that the prophecy concerning the *small horn* received primary fulfillment in the person of
- a) Alexander the Great.
- b) Antiochus IV.
- c) Ptolemy Philadelphus.
- d) Xerxes.

4 Apparently the details given concerning the *small horn* of Daniel 8 were intended to
- a) serve as a preview of the coming Antichrist.
- b) warn Israel of future difficult days under Seleucid rule.
- c) provide further details for secular historians.
- d) all of the above.
- e) both a) and b) above.

5 Two animals in chapter 8, a ram and a goat, symbolized the historical kingdoms of
- a) Rome and Babylon.
- b) Media and Persia.
- c) Medo-Persia and Greece.
- d) Greece and Rome.

6 Based on our study to this point, it appears that the ten-nation coalition may perhaps arise out of
- a) some form of the old Roman Empire.
- b) an entity composed of totally different elements from any previous empire.
- c) a current creation of select well-to-do nations.
- d) an ecclesiastical entity that is both historical and current.

7 It appears that the person who will be known as *Antichrist* will gain control of the ten-nation coalition by means of
- a) force alone by which he will crush his opposition.
- b) a combination of intrigue, deceit, and ultimately force.
- c) the common consensus of leaders of the ten-nation entity.
- d) the vast support he will have among people.

8 The *Master of Deceit* will succeed in his evil designs against God and His people until he meets his end
a) by defeat in battle as he defends the coalition.
b) at the hands of leaders of the coalition who resent him.
c) by natural death at the end of a long and successful reign.
d) by being destroyed through some supernatural means.

9 The first sixty-nine of the seventy sevens of Daniel's vision concerned the
a) decree to restore Jerusalem, the Anointed One, and His being cut off.
b) destruction of Jerusalem and the coming of the Antichrist .
c) rise and fall of Babylon and extended to the fall of Rome.
d) rise of Rome, its treatment of the Anointed One, and the rise of the Antichrist.

10 The seventieth seven of Daniel 9 concerns the
a) future, including the revelation of the Antichrist.
b) making and breaking of the pact between the Antichrist and the Jews.
c) second coming of Christ to destroy the ten-nation coalition and all resistance to His rule.
d) all of the above.
e) both b) and c) above.

Answers to study questions

9 a) 7 years.

1 a False
b False
c True
d True
e True

10 The people are the Jews; the city is Jerusalem.

2 You should be able to indicate the successive rise of the four beasts, but especially the fourth one and how he is described. You should note the rise of the little horn and his uprooting three of the original ten horns. Finally, you should have noted that he meets his end at the hands of the Ancient of Days, which is followed by the rule of the Son of Man.

11 a True
b True
c False
d True
e True
f False

3 a False
b True
c True
d False
e True
f False

12 b) 483 years will go by.

4 e) both a) and b) above.

13 Items **a**, **c**, **d**, and **e** are true.

5 Items **b**, **c**, and **d** are true.

14 a 3) Third
b 5) Fifth
c 2) Second
d 4) Fourth
e 1) First

6 Your answer. Just before our Lord returns, a powerful leader will take over a ten-nation entity, displacing three of ten leaders of that entity in the process. He will be strongly anti-God, a persecutor of God's people, and very successful in his efforts for three and one-half years. Then he will be overthrown and destroyed by the judgment of God, and his rule will be replaced by the eternal reign of our Lord Jesus Christ.

15 This term refers to the move from a general outline of the future in chapter 2 to more specific details in each additional chapter.

7 b) Chapter 8 emphasizes the background, rise, and fall of Medo-Persia and Greece in order to locate and identify a king who is especially important in his relationship with God's people.

16 We get a more complete picture of God's truth as we study it in its entirety. One chapter does not necessarily provide all the facts on the subject.

8 **a** True
b True
c True
d False
e False
f True

Perspectives of the Coming Times of Distress

We have now examined in-depth 9 of the 12 chapters of Daniel. In Lesson 2 we traced the progress of revelation from the general outline given in chapter 2 through many additional details given in chapters 7, 8, and 9. We now continue with the second half of the material on Gentile nations, Israel, and the coming world ruler in chapters 10–12.

Most of us seldom consider who or what is involved in the spiritual realm and the serious nature of spiritual warfare. For example, do you ever wonder why we do not receive more prompt answers to some of our prayers? Chapter 10 gives us insights into the cause of at least some delays. Then chapter 11 provides details from history some of which anticipate events of the future. Finally, chapter 12 gives us a sharper focus on the seventieth seven, including facts about a source of help God will provide for His people during this difficult time.

As we conclude Unit 1, we trust the content will give you a renewed sense of mission and lend a sense of urgency to your service for Christ. We also pray that this first unit of study will create a desire in your heart to know more about prophetic truth and its application to your Christian life and service.

the activities...

◇ Study the lesson according to the procedure given in Lesson 1 and take the self-test when you have completed the lesson development.

◇ Be sure to look in the glossary for the meanings of any key words you do not know.

◇ Review the lessons in this unit in preparation for your unit progress evaluation (UPE). Read the instruction page in your Student Packet, then turn to Unit Progress Evaluation 1. When you have completed the UPE, check your answers with the answer key provided in your Student Packet. Review any items you may have answered incorrectly. (Although UPE scores do not count as part of your final course grade, they indicate how well you learned the material and how well you may perform on the final examination.)

the objectives...

3.1 *Identify elements of the revelation and vision received in Daniel chapter 10.*

3.2 *On the basis of Daniel 10, describe what is involved in spiritual warfare.*

3.3 *Identify key factors in the prophecies concerning Persia and Greece.*

3.4 *Explain the importance of the Ptolemys and Seleucids in biblical history and the value of this information in validating Bible prophecy.*

3.5 *Relate key elements in prophecy about Antiochus IV that were fulfilled in history.*

3.6 *Give evidence that distinguishes the king in verses 36–45 from Antiochus IV who is described in verses 21–35.*

3.7 *State evidence which locates the events of Daniel 12 in the last half of the seventieth seven.*

the outline...

1 The Glory of God
- **a** Traumatic Revelation
- **b** Spiritual Warfare

2 The Flow of History: From Medo-Persia to the End Time
- **a** Persia and Greece
- **b** The Ptolemaic and Seleucid Empires to Antiochus IV
- **c** Antiochus IV Epiphanes: Prototype of the Antichrist
- **d** The Coming Antichrist

3 The Time of Distress

Identify elements of the revelation and vision received in Daniel chapter 10.

The Glory of God

At this point in the study, we meet the world of spiritual forces in the heavenly realms (Ephesians 6:12). Through the experience of the prophet Daniel, we are able to understand more fully the part that spiritual warfare plays in the affairs of men and nations. Chapter 10, which gives us the setting and background for another of Daniel's visions, reveals the emotional and spiritual pain that attended this experience. The primary purpose of the vision is to give a detailed explanation of the fortunes of the Jewish people in the future under the rule of Medo-Persia, Greece, and Syria (the Seleucids). Then, overleaping the rule of one Seleucid king, Antiochus IV, we are given a preview of the coming world ruler, the Antichrist, of whom Antiochus IV was simply a type. The vision of chapters 10–12 thus expands the content of chapter 8 and shows that these prophecies develop in a progressive way. What began as a general summary of the future of human government in chapter 2 is expanded in 7, 8, 9, and 11–12 to include minute details that concern particular crises through which Daniel's people will go.

Traumatic Revelation

Daniel 10:1–12

As we begin our study of the last chapters in the book of Daniel, we examine first the majesty and glory of God that the prophet received as recorded in chapter 10. According to verse 1, the revelation caused Daniel great concern. His concern was probably for his people as we shall see. This concern led him to fast before the Lord and left him very weak (compare verses 2 and 3 with verse 8).

We should remember that Daniel had not returned to his native land two years earlier when the decree had been issued for this purpose (2 Chronicles 36:23). Perhaps it was because of the plight of his fellow-Jews and the desolation of his homeland that made him grieve and fast for this three-week period.

Some Bible scholars believe that the hardships of the returned exiles caused Daniel grave concern (Ezra 4:1–5). Moreover, the building stoppages caused by Samaritan opposition were no doubt a major burden for him also (Ezra 4:24).

At the end of the three-week period, however, Daniel was visited by a supernatural being apparently in answer to his prayer. Your writer believes that God gave Daniel this glorious vision to take away his fear and worry about dramatic future events, undoubtedly the turbulent conditions of war included in the seventieth seven. Also, it was to give him understanding when these events would occur and to strengthen him.

preincarnate
describes activities of our Lord before He was embodied in flesh and became *God with us*

awesomeness
having the power to inspire emotion in which dread, wonder, and veneration are variously mingled

Your writer believes that the supernatural being Daniel saw was the *preincarnate Son of God. Many times when men have fully dedicated themselves to God in prayer and fasting, He has appeared to them in some glorious manifestation of His grace and sovereign power. The extreme brightness and glory of this heavenly visitor caused the prophet to fall down before Him. And even as the *awesomeness of the moment struck the prophet with a sense of his own unworthiness, consciousness faded and he fell into a deep sleep. Notice in the following chart (Figure 3.1) the similarity between the supernatural being in Daniel's vision and John's vision of Jesus Christ in Revelation 1.

Item	*Daniel*	*Revelation*	*Meaning*
Clothing	"dressed in linen"(v.5)	"robe reaching to his feet" (v. 13)	Dignity
Belt	"gold" (v. 5)	"golden" (v.13)	Very Valuable
Eyes	"like flaming torches" (v. 6)	"like blazing fire" (v.14)	All-seeing
Lower Body	"legs like . . . burnished bronze" (v. 6)	"feet. . . like bronze glowing" (v.15)	Steadfast
Voice	"like the sound of a multitude" (v. 6)	"like the sound of rushing waters" (v. 15)	Strength and Authority

Figure 3.1

We see that in addition to the glory of the vision, there is abundant symbolism. The clothing of the priests in the Old Testament was made from linen (Exodus 28:39–43). Linen indicates purity and righteous acts, as we shall see in our study in the book of Revelation. The belt of gold speaks of royalty, and crysolite is the substance from which the seventh foundation in the New Jerusalem is composed (Revelation 21:19–20).

Daniel 10:7 says that none of the men who were with Daniel saw the vision. What happened to them seems to imply that they were not men of God, for God chooses to reveal spiritual truths to His servants—not to others. A comparison of Daniel 10:8–10 with Revelation 1:17 shows that Daniel was affected by this glorious vision in much the same way that John was affected by his vision of Christ.

trauma
an emotional shock which has a lasting effect on the mind

From Daniel 10:10 it appears to your writer that someone different from the being described in verses 5–6 now sets the prophet on his hands and knees. Daniel needed help because of the *trauma of the vision and his own weakness from three weeks of fasting. Daniel's intercessory prayer in chapter 9 and his fasting in this chapter indicate the kind of man Daniel was. It is not surprising, therefore, that he is referred to in verse 19 as a man highly esteemed, for he lived close to God. God loves all of His people, but there are those who draw closer to Him, to whom He can reveal greater truths. (See Exodus 33:11 and James 2:23 for examples of this.) *Is it your desire to be that close to Jesus?* It is His desire for you to be that close! James 4:8 says: "Come near to God and He will come near to you." You can be just as close and intimate with God as you determine to be, but you must follow that determination with those practices in your life that bring you close to Him.

1 Circle the letter preceding each TRUE statement.

- **a** The revelation that Daniel received concerned the judgment that was about to be visited on his people, the Jews.
- **b** The war that was revealed to Daniel seems to refer to the future seventieth seven.
- **c** The vision brought Daniel both understanding of the revelation he had received and a glimpse of God's glory.
- **d** Visions, it seems, are given to encourage and uplift as well as to inform God's people about the course of the future.
- **e** The vision gave Daniel some understanding of when the prophesied events, in relation to others, would occur.
- **f** We can safely assume that special revelations and visions are not given to all God's people but are reserved for those who draw especially close to Him.

On the basis of Daniel 10, describe what is involved in spiritual warfare.

Spiritual Warfare

Daniel 10:13–21

As we come to the last section of chapter 10, God gives us a marvelous insight into the nature of spiritual warfare. Verse 13 tells us *why* Daniel had to wait so long for an answer to a prayer he had prayed and that God had heard three weeks earlier. Notice in verse 13 who hindered the angelic messenger from coming to Daniel and for how long he hindered this messenger. Observe also who came to help this messenger. (We have chosen to call this one simply a *messenger* to distinguish him from what we believe was the preincarnate Son of God. Obviously, the Son of God does not need any assistance from Michael or anyone else!)

From the discussion in these verses and in verses 20 and 21, it appears that there are angels who represent various kingdoms. In this case, the angel who stands for Persia is seen as the adversary of God's messenger. In order to break the spiritual barrier, Michael, the archangel, came to the messenger's assistance and overcame the hindrance of the evil angel.

Here we see a spiritual principle: there is within the ether waves or heavenlies around us a multitude of *spiritual forces.* (The apostle Paul describes these spiritual forces of evil in Ephesians 6:12.) More specifically, there are specific evil angels commissioned to withstand or hinder God's purpose concerning a nation. Here, perhaps, the evil prince was trying to prevent the kingdom of Persia from helping the Jews return to and restore their native land. After three weeks of delay, Michael, the protector of the Jews (Daniel 12:1), was sent to join the conflict, helping this angelic messenger so that the answer might come to Daniel. And while for the moment the conflict between this angel of God and evil angels was interrupted, it would continue (vv. 20–21).

The purpose of the vision, given in verse 14, was "to explain to you [Daniel] what will happen to your people in the future, for the vision concerns a time yet to come." And surely the details which follow in chapters 11 and 12 are remarkably precise and comprehensive concerning the future of the Jewish people under Antiochus IV, as the historical record shows.

The practical value of this example lies in the insights it gives concerning spiritual warfare. While this particular example concerns a nation, the principle of spiritual opposition is the same for individuals. Satan is the accuser of the believers, a task he pursues day and night (Revelation 12:10). We know that delays in answer to our prayers are not denials. God hears us just as He did Daniel, but there are hindrances and obstacles that can make us wonder if the heavens are brass above us. Apparently within His sovereignty, God allows these days to strengthen our faith, but, as in this case, the answer ultimately comes.

2 In terms of the spiritual warfare described in chapter 10, we can say most accurately

a) this particular case was not a good example of normal spiritual warfare.
b) here we have an example of the usual opposition to God and His servants that goes on continually.
c) while there are angels that stand for nations, spiritual opposition does not extend to individuals.
d) there is not enough evidence here or elsewhere in Scripture to indicate anything about the true nature of spiritual warfare.

3 Circle the letter preceding each TRUE statement.

a Answers to prayer may on occasion be delayed because of spiritual opposition.
b Scripture seems to indicate that there is, in addition to messengers from God and angels that stand for nations, a more powerful rank of angels which is represented by Michael.
c Spiritual opposition comes only when matters of the future are concerned.

4 Describe briefly what is involved in spiritual warfare.

....

....

....

The Flow of History: From Medo Persia to the End Time

In this final vision, God gave Daniel a predictive preview of the course of the empire under Persian, Grecian, Ptolemaic, and Seleucid rulers. This was essential because the welfare of the Jewish people was bound up in these kingdoms. They controlled Jewish land and dictated policies that had an important effect on Jewish religious, cultural, and political values.

skeptics
those who question the truth of theories or apparent facts

While not all of this prophetic preview of history was given in great detail, many of the events foretold were fulfilled with amazing accuracy. This prompted early *skeptics to insist that Daniel's account must be a historical narrative compiled after the events occurred rather than valid prophecy. For the person who denies the supernatural element in the Word of God and in God's relationship with man, this is a logical conclusion. However, those who accept the miraculous element in God's dealings with man recognize that the supernatural simply involves God's intervention in suspending His own natural laws. They understand that the infinite God has frequently broken through the finite realm of man, ministering to his immediate needs and revealing future events with remarkable clarity. The multitude of fulfilled prophecies is evidence of this fact.

One student of biblical prophecy has indicated that in the first 35 verses of Daniel 11, there are some 135 prophetic statements—all of which are now fulfilled. This writer's thesis is that the accuracy of the prophetic word in this case gives us confidence to believe that those which are still unfulfilled will be fulfilled with the same degree of accuracy.

We do not have space to refer to all of these prophetic statements in Daniel 11:1–35, but we will list some of them and their fulfillment to strengthen your faith in the accuracy of God's prophetic Word.

Identify key factors in the prophecies concerning Persia and Greece.

Persia and Greece

Daniel 11:1–4

Daniel's word may have reassured the Persian king that his dynasty would continue for some time. It was in no immediate danger of being replaced. According to the prophetic word, three more Persian kings—each one not notably different from the one he succeeded—would rule before a truly notable fourth king would come to the Persian throne. He would be rich and aggressive toward neighboring countries. In fact, Daniel predicted that he would generate support for his objective, the invasion of Greece, by stirring up his people to an emotional peak for this purpose.

Concerning the fourth king, we identify him as Xerxes I (486–468 BC). Cyrus was then in power over the Medo-Persian realm (539–529 B.C). The three who were to precede the notable fourth king were Cambyses (529–522 BC), Smerdis (522–521 B.C), and Darius Hystaspes (521–486 BC). Let us note what the historic record has to say about Xerxes I.

avenge
inflict, execute, or carry out deserved or just punishment (upon someone)

The kings that preceded Xerxes I accumulated vast wealth through their victories over Lydia, Babylon, and Egypt, as well as their own severe taxation program. Xerxes I added to this wealth, for he had one grand objective: to invade Greece and *avenge an earlier defeat. He thus raised a mighty army for this end, but his invasion attempt was defeated in 480 BC at the Battle of Salamis. And with his defeat Persia's power and glory began to fade, although the empire lasted for nearly another 150 years.

One of the significant results of the *Greek Campaign* of Xerxes I was that it angered the Greeks. Thus, when Alexander the Great came to power, his consuming passion was to crush Persian military power completely and to destroy every trace of the Persian empire.

Verses 3 and 4 predict the rise of a mighty king who would rule with great dominion and do according to his will. After reaching his zenith, however, he would depart, leaving his realm to be divided four ways—but not to his descendants.

History reveals that Greece was united under Philip of Macedon (338 B.C); however, before he could launch into empire-building, he was assassinated (336 BC). His son, Alexander, assumed control of the kingdom and in very short order confronted and defeated all Persian resistance. Then, in less than a dozen years, Alexander built an empire that reached from Greece in the west to India in the east. However, in 323 BC at the height of his conquests, he died, leaving no suitable heir. One of his generals tried in vain to administer the empire, but within a short time it was divided among four of Alexander's generals. Thus, the overall unity was destroyed and with it Alexander's dream of establishing Hellenistic Civilization. Above all, the prophecy that stated "It will not go to his descendants" was fulfilled to the letter.

Alexander's empire was carved up by four of his generals: Cassander, Lysamachus, Ptolemy, and Seleucus. Of these four only the latter two concern the balance of this prophecy. *Ptolemy* seized control of Egypt and Israel, and *Seleucus* occupied Persia, Syria, and Asia Minor. It is the conflict of these two kingdoms and their effect on the Jewish people that concern us in the following verses.

We notice that the vision moves quickly over the Persian period and the exploits of Alexander the Great, a time span of slightly over two hundred years (539–323 BC). It then focuses on a time when Alexander's far-flung empire was divided into four political entities.

5 Circle the letter preceding each TRUE statement.

a The message concerning the future of the Persian Empire was one that would have tended to encourage the Persian king.

b Persia's wars against Greece aroused intense hatred in Greeks and led to the final downfall of Persia's empire.

c The mighty leader who would do as he pleased, rule with great power, and not leave his kingdom to his heirs is identified as Cyrus of Persia.

d The empire which would be divided into four parts after the death of the mighty king would then become much stronger.

Explain the importance of the Ptolemys and Seleucids in biblical history and the value of this information in validating Bible prophecy.

The Ptolemaic and Seleucid Empires to Antiochus IV

Daniel 11:5–20

Having predicted that Alexander's empire would be broken up and divided to the four winds of heaven, the angel spoke of two branches of this empire. The first, the Seleucid or Syrian branch, was located to the north of Israel and would be under the rule of Seleucus and his descendants. The second branch, the Egyptian, was located to the south of Israel and would be under the control of Ptolemy and his descendants.

The significance of the angel's continued message, which concerns just these two branches, lies in the fact that Israel lay between them and was continually involved in their history. Throughout most of the time between about 300 BC and 198 BC there was intermittent war between the two empires. Both empires used the *Holy Land* for a battleground, wasting the land and killing its people. Since the two empires were located north and south of Israel, their leaders are referred to here significantly as the "king of the North" and "the king of the South."

The Ptolemys controlled the land of Israel from the breakup of Alexander's empire (323 BC) until 198 BC when control passed to the Seleucid armies of Antiochus III, the Great. With these background facts before us, we will consider briefly the prophecies of verses 5–20, which cover about 140 years, and how they were so remarkably fulfilled. Indeed, one great benefit of these facts is that by comparing prophecy with history we see prophecy beautifully *validated.

validated
made valid; given legal force; confirmed

Verse 5 refers to Ptolemy I Soter, the king of Egypt. The commander spoken of is Seleucus I, who for a time served as a general in Ptolemy's army. Later, however, Seleucus I won some major victories and established himself as king over Syria. He became much stronger after he defeated Media and firmly established the Seleucid dynasty.

Verse 6 refers to Ptolemy II Philadelphus, the king of Egypt, and Antiochus II Theos, king of the Seleucid or Syrian Empire. Because of the strength of the king of Egypt, Antiochus divorced his wife, Laodice, and married Bernice, the daughter of the king of Egypt. Observe how accurately the prophecy in this Scripture was fulfilled. These two kings did make an alliance that was sealed by the marriage of Antiochus and Bernice; however, as soon as Ptolemy died (within two years), Antiochus divorced Bernice and remarried Laodice. Laodice first poisoned Bernice and then her husband, Antiochus II, because she feared him. Then she put her son Seleucus Callinicus on the throne.

Verses 7–9 relate to Ptolemy III Euergetes, who attacked the *king of the North,* Seleucus Callinicus, to avenge the murder of his sister Bernice. He not only avenged the death of his sister, but also carried off a wealth of plunder, precisely as the Scripture predicted. He could have conquered Syria at this time, but he neglected to do so. Instead, he turned his attention to internal problems in his kingdom. In time Seleucus invaded Egypt, but he was soundly defeated and crept home with a very small part of his army.

Verses 10–12 concern the sons of Seleucus Callinicus. Seleucus III Ceraunus and Antiochus III come into focus as they struggle for supremacy in the area and successfully extend their power. After just two years, however, Seleucus III Ceraunus was murdered, and his brother, Antiochus III, took the kingdom and challenged Ptolemy IV Philopater, the king of Egypt. Initially, Antiochus III was defeated with a tremendous loss of men and equipment (vv. 11–12). For some twelve years there was a period of relative peace between the king of the South and the king of the North. During this time, Antiochus extended his control over Persia, Bactria, and into India as he raised the kingdom to its greatest glory.

Verse 13 indicates the care he would take to ensure that this time he would not fail to defeat the king of the South. Assisted by Philip, the king of Macedonia, and some *renegade Jews (14), Antiochus III totally crushed the forces of Ptolemy V Epiphanes (v. 15). As a result of this victory, Ptolemaic rule over Israel was ended permanently, and Antiochus III was firmly in control of the "Beautiful Land"(v. 16). However, Antiochus also intended to overthrow Ptolemy V; therefore, he began making plans to invade Egypt. Instead, he decided to ally himself with his opponent and secure the bargain by giving his daughter, Cleopatra, in marriage to Ptolemy. (This is not the Cleopatra of Roman history.) He felt that after the marriage his daughter would work for him against her husband, but as Scripture indicates, his plans did not succeed (v. 17).

renegade
deserter from a religious faith; traitor

Verses 18 and 19 predict the end of this ambitious king. Antiochus III, as these verses suggest, turned his attention to further conquest, and by 196 BC he had conquered most of Asia Minor. His empire stretched from western Asia Minor to India, but his appetite for yet further land was not satisfied. Thus, in 192 BC he turned to the west and invaded Greece, intending to add that kingdom to his dominions. However, in a series of encounters with the Roman commander Scipio, Antiochus was defeated totally and completely just as Daniel predicted (v. 18). As a result, he lost not only his claims to Greece, but also western Asia Minor. Moreover, he was required to pay huge sums of money to Rome and send twenty hostages to Rome, among them his son Antiochus IV, to guarantee peace. However, in the attempt to raise the huge *indemnity required by Rome, the king began to loot temples. And while doing this, he was slain, fulfilling Daniel's prophecy that "he will stumble and fall, to be seen no more" (v. 19).

indemnity
payment for damage, loss, or hardship; money demanded by a victorious nation at the end of a war as a condition for peace

The son of Antiochus III, Seleucus IV Philopater, fell into the same trap as his father. In trying to raise the huge sums of money required by the kingdom and the Roman indemnity, he sent out his tax collector to raise the revenue wherever he could. Heliodorus, his agent, tried to rob the temple in Jerusalem, but seemed to be miraculously restrained. Soon thereafter, Heliodorus poisoned his master, once again confirming Daniel's prophecy that he would "be destroyed, yet not in anger or in battle"(v. 20). The stage was now set for the succession to the Seleucid throne.

6 According to our discussion, the Ptolemys and Seleucids were important in biblical history because
- a) both were great world empires in their respective days.
- b) they were direct family heirs of Alexander the Great.
- c) Israel lay between them and was involved in their history.
- d) they gave birth to the Roman Empire.

7 From 323 BC until 198 BC we can say most accurately that control of Israel was in the hands of the
- a) Ptolemys, the king of the South.
- b) Seleucids, the king of the North.
- c) kings of the South and then in those of the North from time to time as the two kingdoms vied for control of the region.
- d) leaders of each kingdom, Ptolemaic and Seleucid evenly.

8 Explain the value of the prophetic facts given in verses 5–20 to the student of Bible prophecy.

....

....

....

Relate key elements in prophecy about Antiochus IV that were fulfilled in history.

Antiochus IV Epiphanes: Prototype of the Antichrist

Daniel 11:21–35

At this point Scripture focuses on Antiochus IV Epiphanes, the stern-faced king and master of intrigue we discussed in Lesson 2. In that setting we noted that he is a symbol or picture of the coming Antichrist. In the following paragraphs we want to consider both the prophecy and fulfillment and the possible relationship between the facts of history and the coming one whom they seem to portray.

contemptible
deserving contempt or scorn; mean; low; worthless

Verses 21–24 portray a vivid picture of Antiochus IV's accession, the methods he employed, and his beginning as a *contemptible person. (Among other things Antiochus did in the course of seizing power was to assume the title *Epiphanes,* which means "illustrious" and shows us something about his conceit.) When he learned in Athens of his brother Seleucus IV Philopater's death, Antiochus IV made immediate plans to gain control of the Seleucid kingdom. First, he secured the assistance of Eumenes II, king of Pergamum, to help him seize control of the kingdom. Eumenes II was happy to do so because he was concerned about the growing threat of the Romans and felt he needed a future ally. The new king first consolidated his position and then set up effective financial and administrative control over the kingdom. (You may recall that because of Antiochus III's defeat at the hands of Rome huge indemnity payments had to be made.) In fact, Antiochus IV was able to raise revenue to make the payments to Rome and to finance his own lavish lifestyle as well.

usurper
one who seizes and holds (power, position, authority) by force

All resistance that came against the new regime was destroyed. Heliodorus, the treasurer of his late brother's kingdom and the would-be *usurper of the throne, tried unsuccessfully to regain the throne, but to no avail (v. 22). Moreover, Antiochus IV removed Onias III, the high priest at Jerusalem, from office and replaced him with an evil, self-seeking substitute. In so doing, the king destroyed a prince of the covenant. His long-term goal was to destroy the Jewish faith and make all his subjects loyal to the same pagan gods (and later transfer both their loyalty and worship to him).

The prophecy speaks in verses 23 and 24 about the methods of Antiochus IV. They indicate that he would use diplomacy at first to gain political ends, but then he would act deceitfully, ignoring the provisions of his agreements. And since his foes were unprepared to resist his military advances, he would win amazing victories such as his forefathers had never seen. In addition, he would spread the loot from his conquests among his followers. History records with amazing precision that this is just what took place in Antiochus IV's rise to power.

The prophecy continues in verses 25–28 with predictions about Antiochus IV's victorious war with Egypt. Scripture indicates that the king of the South would be hindered by plots devised against him and deceptive agreements made with the *master of intrigue* from the North. Also predicted were the fruit of Antiochus IV's victories and his policy against the *holy covenant.* Let us see what history records about this subject matter.

Antiochus IV was successful in his first invasion of Egypt. His objectives were to assert his own claim to the Seleucid Empire and to establish the claim of his nephew, Ptolemy VI Philometer, to the throne of the Ptolemaic throne. Part of the policy of Antiochus IV, which gave him temporary power in the purely internal matters of the Ptolemys, was his use of *deception. He and his nephew practiced deceit as they sat at the same negotiating table; neither one was willing to keep his promises (v. 27).

deception
a deceiving; a being deceived; a thing that deceives; trick meant to deceive; fraud; sham; hoax

On his way back from Egypt to Antioch, Antiochus IV stopped in Israel to begin his program of forced *Hellenization.* He had already set up a *puppet* high priest when he destroyed the "prince of the covenant" (v. 22) and removed the honor attached to the office. All of this fit his purpose to unify all the diverse people of his realm by imposing a common culture, religion, and language. All of his subjects except orthodox Jews conformed to his policy—even apostate Jews—even though it meant doing things that were totally alien to their faith and spiritual heritage. Moreover, wherever the evil king turned, he prospered, and he used the plunder he won to buy friends and win favor among his far-flung subjects.

The next verses in this prophecy (29–35) look to the attempts of the wicked king to extend his empire to include that of Egypt and his rebuff by the ships of the western coastlands. These verses also deal with his attempt to abolish the *holy covenant,* destroy those who were faithful to it, as well as their brave resistance, and his ultimate failure. Once again, let us see what history records about this aspect of the evil *master of intrigue.*

In 168 BC Antiochus IV invaded Egypt in an attempt to gain control of that kingdom. He was preparing to attack Alexandria when a Roman general ordered him to quit and return home. Frustrated by this humiliating turn of events and news that there was an *insurrection in Jerusalem, Antiochus IV returned to Antioch by way of Jerusalem and vented his anger on the people of the city. In addition, he began to force his state religion on the Jewish people.

insurrection
a rising against established authority; revolt; rebellion

In order to hasten the process of breaking down Jewish resistance to his policies, Antiochus IV *desecrated the temple and abolished the daily sacrifice. He defiled the Torah scrolls in the temple, also, and ordered all other sacred scrolls to be destroyed. He forced priests and people alike to eat swine's flesh, forbade the observance of holy days, and the circumcision of baby boys. Furthermore, he insisted that Jews observe pagan holidays. Worst of all, however, he set up an image of Zeus Olympius in the temple (who was supposedly personified in Antiochus IV himself). This was "the abomination that causes desolation" (v. 31). Thus, the satanically inspired king did in fact "vent his fury against the holy covenant" (v. 30).

desecrated
having been used or treated without respect

Faithful Jews were appalled by this *sacrilege and steadfastly resisted his efforts. Many Jews, however, recanted. Those he was able to entice from their faith he corrupted with flattery and bribery (v. 32). As this madman continued enforcing his policies with vigor and cruelty, resistance mounted. The faithful, as we learned in Lesson 2, raised a standard of revolt. Both militarily and religiously they moved to throw off the oppressive yoke and to return the worship of Jehovah to its rightful place.

sacrilege
an intentional injury to anything sacred

This time of terrible suffering served several purposes: (1) the wicked were confirmed in their folly, and (2) the wise were purified and tested, their faith was strengthened as they made the ultimate commitment to God (vv. 33–35).

The faithful fell for a time, but as we saw in Lesson 2, they united behind Mattathias and his son Judas Maccabaeus. First, the gains of the Seleucid king were canceled in the countryside through an effective guerrilla warfare campaign. Then, in four major battles the forces of the Maccabees defeated the best armies of the Seleucid Empire and pacified the conquered territory. Then they cleansed the temple and reestablished the covenant rituals and appropriate worship.

This dramatic account anticipates the coming *holocaust under the Antichrist and gives us a preview of the future so that we can know that survival for the faithful is possible. After our review questions, we will turn from the preview to that which it anticipates.

holocaust
great or wholesale destruction; complete destruction by fire, especially of animals or human beings

9 Circle the letter preceding each statement that relates accurately elements of prophecy about Antiochus IV that were fulfilled in history.

- **a** Antiochus IV came to the throne of Syria as the rightful and natural heir.
- **b** Early in his rule Antiochus IV suffered numerous military defeats, but as time went on he became successful.
- **c** The method by which Antiochus IV conducted his diplomacy may be described best as deceitful.
- **d** Antiochus IV's attempt to expand his control to include the kingdom of Ptolemy was stopped forever by Rome.
- **e** Antiochus IV's efforts to wipe out the religion of the Jews was based on his desire to bring overall unity to his realm.
- **f** The forced Hellenization policy met with failure because of the united efforts of faithful Jewish people who were willing to die for their faith in God.

Give evidence that distinguishes the king in verses 36–45 from Antiochus IV who is described in verses 21–35.

The Coming Antichrist

Daniel 11:36–45

At the beginning of verse 36, please notice the subtle break in the story thread. As we noted earlier, prophecy does not concern itself with history as such; history is important or significant as it effects the Jews and their land. Antiochus IV, as a person, was important in the stream of history primarily, we believe, to give us a preview of the coming Antichrist. And for this reason we suddenly realize that the prophecy no longer refers to Antiochus IV. Rather, it bypasses all the intervening years and moves to the time of the end, when Antichrist will do many of the things which Antiochus did in his *forced Hellenization program.* The final *little horn* (Daniel 7:8, 24–26) will rule in Daniel's seventieth seven. His reign will signal the beginning of the final, dreadful judgment, which is of special concern to Israel.

In verses 5–20 we examined the struggles of two dynasties: the Seleucid and Ptolemaic. The kings of each were referred to as the kings of the North (Seleucids) and the kings of the South (Ptolemys) on the basis of their location in relation to Israel. Then in verses 21–35 the focus narrowed to include the reign of one contemptible person who for a brief period controlled the Seleucid Empire: Antiochus IV. Now, however, we have in verse 36 one who is called simply "the king." A careful examination of "the king's" characteristics reveals that obvious differences exist between him and Antiochus IV, the subject of the preceding verses. We shall note some of these differences in a brief comparison.

Verses 36–39 give a description of *the king's* characteristics, which suggests that he is just being introduced. Since verses 21–35 have already given a fairly complete review of Antiochus IV's qualities and rule, we would be surprised to see them repeated at this point. Then in verses 40–45, we see facts stated that are not consistent with what we know of Antiochus IV. He did not attack the Libyans and Ethiopians, and he was not concerned about tidings out of the north and east. It was the power of Rome from the west that kept him from conducting his second Egyptian campaign. Moreover, in verse 40 he is distinguished from the king of the North; whereas, Antiochus IV was a *king of the North.*

The king's conquests, according to prophecy, would cause many countries to fall. Antiochus IV's warlike tendencies, by contrast, did not result in the fall of many countries. In effect, during his rule the wars in which he engaged were local affairs. And while he devastated the holy land, he did not set up his campaign tent there as his provisional headquarters. These facts appear to support the notion that verses 36–45 have in view the coming Antichrist and not the historical subject of verses 21–35.

Verses 40–45 deal with major Middle Eastern clashes that will emerge as the coming ruthless leader exerts his will in the affairs of this region. From our previous views of this powerful leader, we see that he will head a powerful coalition, and few other world leaders will be able to challenge him. If he is not himself a Middle Easterner, he could well anger those in the area by insensitivity to their cultural and religious heritage. One who will resist his control will be the king of the South. In the past, as we have seen, this term referred to the king of Egypt. But since modern Egypt is a relatively minor power, it may indicate an Arab coalition under the leadership of an Egyptian. In the 1950s Egypt headed such a coalition which was known as the United Arab Republic (UAR). The UAR did not last partly because Arab nationalism and Islamic fundamentalism were only beginning. However, a new and more powerful coalition of Arab states may well arise to fulfill the requirements of this prophecy. This is an interesting possibility to consider as we evaluate the future *king of the South.*

This fierce leader will arouse the fury of a future king of the North. As we have seen, this reference in history applied to kings of the Seleucid or Syrian Empire. However, Syria today is neither a major military power nor able to challenge a super power in battle, and she does not have a fleet of ships with which to support her attack as verse 40 suggests. But to the north of Syria lies the Commonwealth of Independent States made up of republics of the former Soviet Union, and these republics control one of the most powerful fleets in the world. A northern leader with this power base could obviously challenge "the king." It is quite interesting that the former Soviet Union is deeply involved in the Middle East militarily and economically. So it is fair to say that the Commonwealth of Independent States will continue to be interested in the strategic importance of this region and to be involved diplomatically, militarily, and economically in its destiny.

Again we cannot identify these end-time leaders, but it is interesting to watch how the focus of the world is drawn increasingly to the Middle East. Its political tensions, energy resources, strategic location, and maturing nationalism demand that it occupy the attention of the nations. We suggest that you read Ezekiel chapters 38 and 39 to consider future events that will involve Israel now that she has been regathered from the four comers of the earth. One thing is sure: there will be a massive invasion from the north and the time sequence suggested by Ezekiel seems to fit in well with the latter part of the seventieth seven.

Daniel indicates that Israel will be crushed after this would-be peace advocate turns against her in the middle of the seventieth seven (vv. 41, 44–45). Many countries, Egypt included, will fail, but Edom, Moab, and the leader of Ammon will be delivered from his hand. It appears that this strong ruler will concentrate his efforts on Northeast Africa, especially in Egypt, Libya, and Ethiopia. But whereas Antiochus IV faced opposition from the west (Rome), this ruler will face opponents from the north and east. He will react to this opposition with fury, and many people will die (v. 44). He will establish his headquarters in Israel, but his rule will come to an abrupt end as he meets an irresistible force from above: the Crushing Stone of Daniel (2:34–35, 44).

10 State at least two bits of evidence from verses 36–45 that distinguish *the king* from Antiochus IV who is described in verses 21–35.

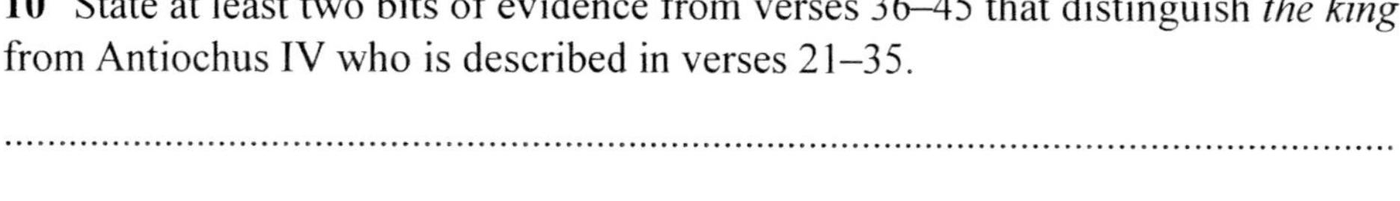

11 Circle the letter preceding each TRUE statement.

- **a** Evidence suggests that Antiochus IV appears in history to give God's people a preview of the coming Antichrist.
- **b** The Middle East will figure prominently in the seventieth seven and it will be the scene of intense fighting.
- **c** By comparing the king of the South and the king of the North in history with what is spoken of these same ones in the future, we gather that Egypt and Syria are not intended.
- **d** Scripture here suggests that *the king,* whom we have identified as the coming Antichrist, will concentrate on the Middle East apart from Northern Africa.
- **e** The future Antichrist will be challenged primarily by forces from the west.

State evidence which locates the events of Daniel 12 in the last half of the seventieth seven.

The Time of Distress

Daniel 12:1–13

In chapter 12, we see the theme of the end-time rule of the Antichrist continued and expanded. We also find here the *purpose* of the time of distress, God's plan to preserve the faithful, and the incredible future of those who overcome.

In the midst of the seventieth seven, as we learned in our study of chapter 9, God's people will face the greatest distress they have ever known and they will need help. God will not desert them; He will involve Michael, the mighty angel He has designated to protect Israel, to deliver them. Revelation 12:7–9 indicates something of this mighty spiritual struggle which will finally result in the deliverance of God's people (v. 1). Matthew 24:21–29 and Luke 21:20–26 speak of the degree of distress this period will bring about. Zechariah 13:8–9 and 14:2 also refer to the devastation that will result as these days come to a close. The remnant that survives will be made up of those whose names are written in God's book.

Verse 2 refers to the multitudes that will be resurrected. The first group mentioned, the righteous, will be raised to enter millennial blessedness after this time of distress. The second group, the wicked, will be resurrected after the millennial reign of Christ to shame and eternal contempt (compare Revelation 20:4–6 with 20:11–15). The reward for righteousness and faithful service will be eternal blessedness (v. 3). These things, Daniel is told, are for the time of the end, so he is told to seal the words of the scroll (v. 4).

At this point two other angelic beings appear and join the one clothed in linen. One of them asks: "How long will it be before these astounding things are fulfilled?" (vv. 5–6). Raising both hands to heaven to indicate the solemnity of the message, this mighty one says: "It will be for a time, times and a half a time. When the power of the holy people has been finally broken, all these things will be completed" (v. 7). Three and a half years will thus be involved in this time of distress. However, observe what is to be done: the power of God's people is to be broken. In this time of distress God's people will be crushed so completely that they will have to *look up.* Thus, as this time of distress at the end of the seventieth seven comes to a dramatic conclusion, Jews will look to God for redemption. And He will pour upon them the spirit of grace and supplication, and Israel's remnant will be saved (Zechariah 12:10–14; 13:1–6).

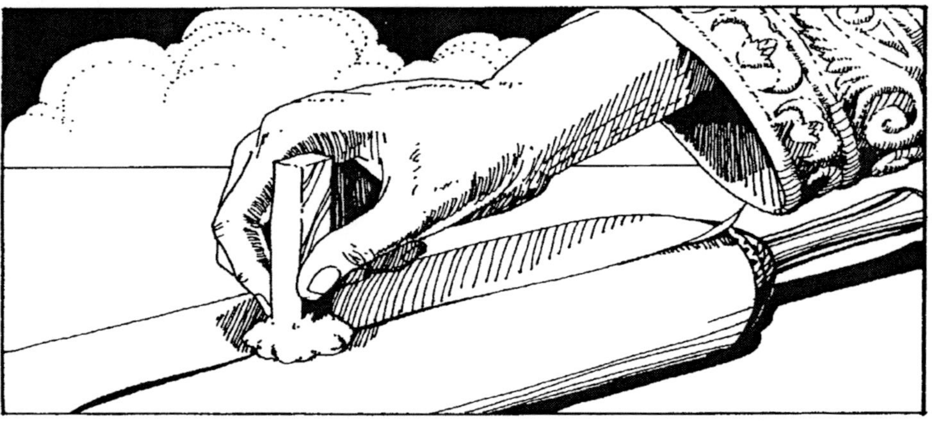

paradox
statement that may be true but seems to say two opposite things; for example: "More haste, less speed"

The last days, as verse 10 notes, will present a *paradox. Wickedness will be apparent everywhere and will be growing like an irresistible tide, and the wicked will not understand. These are the terrible times Paul speaks of in 2 Timothy 3:1–5. To people of the world, there will be only gloom and hopelessness ahead. The words of one poet reflect this prospect when he states that "the world won't end with a bang but with a whimper." However, in this time of distress the great Refiner of gold will purify, refine, and perfect His people.

Verses 11 and 12 speak of days that extend beyond the 1260 days or 3 1/2 years. We do not know exactly why these extra days are included; however, they may be required for the cleansing of the land and the temple. Some Bible scholars also suggest that during these days the judgment of nations will occur (Matthew 25:31–46). It may be that these extra days are required to set in motion the new government and to prepare people for a period of normalcy following the rule of the Antichrist. Whatever this may involve, Daniel is urged to carry on his work and he is assured that in the future he will be raised to receive his eternal inheritance.

Thus we conclude our study of Daniel. We trust that you have received a good foundation for your prophetic studies. We trust it will help you as you move on to consider other prophecies in the book of Revelation.

12 In your notebook write a brief description of the events of the seventieth seven based on what we have studied to this point.

13 In your notebook state evidence which indicates when the events of Daniel 12 will occur.

Self-Test

True-False. Write **T** in the space preceding each statement that is TRUE. Write **F** if it is FALSE.

.... **1** Visions are given to God's servants to encourage them, strengthen them in their labor, and inform them.

.... **2** Since God is no respector of persons, we can safely say that God gives visions to any of His children regardless of their relationship to Him.

.... **3** Daniel's vision of chapter 10 greatly increases our knowledge of the nature of spiritual warfare.

.... **4** The chief value of fulfilled prophecy is its ability to validate history.

.... **5** The amazing fulfillment of prophecy gives us confidence to believe that those yet unfulfilled will be fulfilled with the same degree of accuracy.

.... **6** Fulfillment of the prophecy that Xerxes I would be far richer than any Persian kings before him and that he would incite everyone against Greece points to the accuracy of prophecy.

.... **7** One of the most amazing prophecies is that of the mighty one who would appear, rule with great power, and depart, leaving his empire not to his heirs but to four others. We have seen that this referred to Alexander the Great.

.... **8** Antiochus IV's rise to power is amply verified by history, but it was not predicted by the prophets.

.... **9** The coming time of distress for the Jews will occur during the second half of the seventieth seven which is in the future.

.... **10** Daniel 12 indicates that there will be one general resurrection in which all the dead, good and evil, will face a bright new future.

Unit Progress Evaluation 1

Now that you have finished Unit 1, review the lessons in preparation for Unit Progress Evaluation 1. You will find it in your Student Packet. Answer all of the questions without referring to your course materials, Bible, or notes. When you have completed the UPE, check your answers with the answer key provided in your Student Packet, and review any items you may have answered incorrectly. Then you may proceed with your study of Unit 2. (Although UPE scores do not count as part of your final course grade, they indicate how well you learned the material and how well you may perform on the final examination.)

Answers to study questions

7 a) Ptolemys, the kings of the South.

1 **a** False
b True
c True
d True
e True
f True

8 The value of these prophetic facts is in their ability to verify the accuracy of the Word of God. The evidence shows that each prophecy received an amazing fulfillment.

2 b) here we have an example of the usual opposition to God and His servants that goes on continually.

9 You should have circled **c**, **d**, **e**, and **f**.

3 **a** True
b True
c False

10 Verse 40 distinguishes *the king* from the king of the North. Also, this verse says that *the king* will invade many countries, including Ethiopia and Libya, which was not true of Antiochus IV in history.

4 Based on what we read in chapter 10, we see that answers to the prayers of God's people can be hindered by evil angels. The important thing, however, is that there is no power that can hinder the prayers getting through to God. And if we are patient, the answers to our prayers will come.

11 **a** True
b True
c True
d False
e False

5 **a** True
b True
c False. This leader is identified as Alexander the Great. It would not have the power the mighty king had exercised.
d False

12 Your answer should include the major points we have listed. The seventieth seven will begin with the coming to power of a crafty leader of a ten-nation coalition. He will make a peace pact with the Jews for seven years, but he will break it after three and one-half years. Then he will turn in fury on the Jews and seek to destroy them; however, they will be helped by Michael and the godly will be delivered. Before He sets up His eternal kingdom, God will break in on the ungodliness of the end time and end the rule of the Antichrist. Then the wicked will be resurrected to shame and the righteous to eternal blessedness.

6 c) Israel lay between them and was involved in their history.

13 The evidence in chapter 12 suggests that the time of great distress will occur in the second half of the seventieth seven. It says plainly that it will last for three and one-half years. By comparing this evidence with what is given in Daniel 9 about the seventy sevens, we conclude that the time of great distress will commence when the coming ruler breaks his pact with the Jews.

THE COMMENCEMENT OF END-TIME EVENTS

Lessons...

4 Understanding the Book of Revelation

5 What John Saw

6 Letters to Ephesus, Smyrna, and Pergamum

7 Letters to Thyatira, Sardis, Philadelphia, and Laodicea

Procedures...

1. Observe the objectives for key points.
2. Reflect on the headings and subheadings.
3. Study the content identifying key points (highlight, underline, etc.) as you read.
4. Answer the self-study questions.
5. Do the self-test to reinforce key concepts.
6. Review the lessons in this unit in preparation for the Unit Progress Evaluation.

Understanding the Book of Revelation

Daniel and *Revelation* are two of the outstanding books of prophecy in the Bible. They have an important message for Christians today. They show us that the Creator, who began the world and created all that is in it, will also bring everything to the conclusion He has designed. They show us that He is the God of history. He is in full control of the future. In this lesson, we will consider the book of Revelation as a whole. In later lessons we will study its specific messages in more detail.

As we begin our study of *Revelation*, we will examine its theme and content, and we will consider the special form in which it is written. We should also learn how to interpret the book of Revelation. To do this we will learn certain principles of interpretation to help us understand its message.

Most important of all, we will discover that the book of Revelation reveals Jesus Christ. He is its great Subject and Object. Jesus is the One in whom all God's plans will be completed. It is our prayer that each student will—in every lesson of this course—receive a fresh vision of God's glory, power, kingdom, and especially His Son. We pray that this vision will inspire each one to live for Jesus with more dedication than ever before.

the activities...

- ◊ Study the lesson according to the procedure established in Lesson 1.
- ◊ Remember to write your *own* answers to the study questions before looking up the answers at the back of this lesson. This procedure will help you to learn the material more quickly.
- ◊ Take the self-test at the end of this lesson, and check your answers carefully with those given in the Student Packet. Review any items you answer incorrectly.

the objectives...

4.1 *State the meaning of the term* revelation *and the theme of the book of Revelation.*

4.2 *Identify the subject of the book of Revelation.*

4.3 *List the evidence regarding the authorship of the book of Revelation and the date it was written.*

4.4 *Arrange in order an outline of the book of Revelation giving topics, headings, and references within the main outline divisions.*

4.5 *Identify the parenthetical enlargement portions of the book of Revelation.*

4.6 *Identify four basic systems of interpretation of the book of Revelation.*

4.7 *Describe the principles for interpreting the prophetic message of the book of Revelation.*

4.8 *Identify principles that assist one to interpret the prophetic message properly.*

the outline...

1 An Overview of the Book
- **a** Name and Theme
- **b** Subject
- **c** Author and Date of Writing

2 A Description of Its Contents
- **a** Main Divisions
- **b** Parenthetical Enlargements

3 Guidelines for Understanding Its Message
- **a** Four Basic Views of Its Meaning
- **b** Special Features of Its Form
- **c** Principles for Interpreting Its Meaning

State the meaning of the term revelation *and the theme of the book of Revelation.*

An Overview of the Book

We will begin our study of the book of Revelation with an overview of its *name*, *theme*, *subject*, and *author*.

Name and Theme

Names of the books of the Bible are important. For example, the first book of the Bible is called *Genesis*, a word that comes from the Greek language and means "generations." The phrase "these are the generations of" occurs over and over in the book and actually marks divisions in its outline. In Hebrew, the language in which the book was originally written, the name of the book is *Bereshith*, an expression that means "in the beginning." This phrase is used in the first sentence of the book. The name of the final book of the Bible is also found in its first sentence.

1 Turn to Revelation 1:1 in your Bible and write in your notebook the phrase which contains the name of the book.

The word *revelation* is a translation of the Greek noun *apokalupsis*, which means "that which is unveiled." The verb form *apokalupto*, "to unveil," is also found in the Greek New Testament. These words are used in various Scripture passages to express two main ideas. First, they refer to God's action of revealing things to our understanding. Second, they refer to the visible appearing of Jesus Christ. However, a third idea can also be seen in the New Testament. The phrase found in 1 Peter 1:13, for example, does not necessarily refer only to the future appearing of Jesus Christ. It can also be translated as "the grace that is being brought to you at the revelation of Jesus Christ" (a continuous present-tense rendering of the phrase). The truth expressed is that we can be strong now because there is a constant unveiling of Jesus Christ to us as we walk with Him.

2 Match the appropriate main idea (right) with the Scripture passage (left).

. . . . **a** Matthew 11:25	1) The revelation of things to our understanding
. . . . **b** Matthew 16:17	2) The visible appearing of Jesus Christ
. . . . **c** 1 Peter 1:7	
. . . . **d** 1 Peter 1:12	

The second main idea, the visible appearing of Jesus Christ, is the theme of the book of Revelation. This theme is sounded like a trumpet in chapter 1, verse 7:

> Look, he is coming with the clouds, and every eye will see him, even those who pierced him; and all the peoples of the earth will mourn because of him. So shall it be! Amen.

3 In your notebook state the meaning of the term *revelation* and give the theme of the book of Revelation.

Identify the subject of the book of Revelation.

Subject

As you may have noticed, the title of the book of Revelation is not simply *The Revelation*; rather, it is *The Revelation of Jesus Christ*. So it is an unveiling, a making manifest, a revealing of a *person*, Jesus Christ.

4 Read Luke 24:13–27 and answer the following questions:

a About whom did Jesus talk to the disciples (v. 27)?

....

b From what Scriptures did He teach (v. 27)?

....

Do you understand that the Bible is a book about Jesus Christ? From the "In the beginning" of Genesis until the final "Amen" of Revelation, there is one majestic figure who walks on every page of God's book: it is God's Son. He is the subject and the object of it all. Moreover, in its final chapters, He is seen in the fullness of His person, position, and accomplishments—past, present, and (most of all) future.

5 The book of Revelation contains many pictures of its great Subject. Copy the following list of the pictures in your notebook, leaving space after each one. As you read through Revelation in this course, some study questions will require you to write after each picture or figure of Christ the chapter and verse or verses where it appears.

—The Judge of His Church

—The Alpha and Omega

—The First and the Last

—The Amen

—The Beginning and the End

—The Firstborn from the Dead

—The Owner of the Keys of Hades and Death
—The Faithful and True Witness
—The Lion of the Tribe of Judah
—The Root of David
—The Lamb
—The High Priest
—The Possessor of the Seal of God
—The Ruler of the Kings of the Earth
—The Son of Man
—The Living One
—The Owner of the Earth and Sea
—The Wielder of the Harvest Sickle
—The Son, a Male of Israel
—The Trampler of the Winepress of the Wrath of God
—The Rider of the White Horse
—The King of Kings
—The Lord of Lords
—The Morning Star
—The Light of Eternity
—The *Go'el* (Kinsman Redeemer)

In the book of Revelation, Jesus Christ is active. He *speaks*, *moves*, *conquers*, *judges*, *and rules*. He *commands* John to copy His dictation and to send it to the seven churches. He *calls* John to "Come up here" (Revelation 4:1). He *takes* the seven-sealed book out of his Father's hand. He *opens* the book. He *stands* on Mt. Zion with converted Israel. He *reaps* the harvest of the earth, *rides* on a white horse, *tramples* the winepress of the wrath of God, and *rules* throughout eternity.

The book of Revelation is not only a revelation of Jesus Christ, but also the revelation from Him to His servants of the series of events that will take place to complete the plan of God.

6 The subject of the book of Revelation is
a) the life of Jesus on earth and His relationship to the church.
b) Jesus Himself, what he has done, is doing, and will do.
c) the explanation of the teachings Jesus gave about God.

List the evidence regarding the authorship of the book of Revelation and the date it was written.

Author and Date of Writing

Within the book of Revelation there are several references to the identity of its author.

7 Read Revelation 1:1, 4, 9; 22:8 and answer the following questions in your notebook, giving the chapter and verse reference or references from these parts of Revelation for each answer.

a Who states that he is the author of the book?
b What relationship did he have to Jesus Christ?
c What relationship did he have to those to whom he directed his message?

In addition to references you have just studied, several other facts about the book of Revelation indicate that it was written by John.

In their writings, a number of leaders of the early church attribute the authorship of the Revelation to the apostle John. Among these are Justin Martyr (AD 163–217), Tertullian (AD 145–220), and Origen (AD 185–254). These early church fathers are known to have been men of integrity and strong personal commitment to Jesus Christ. Their testimony therefore carries much weight in matters of early church history. As we shall see, however, other men of that time have different convictions about the identity of John. Moreover the precise date when the Revelation was written can not be known with certainty. Some scholars place the date between AD 64 and 68, during the reign of the Roman emperor Nero. However, the early church writers who refer to the date of writing, place the writing date between AD 91 and 96, during the reign of Domitian. This appears to be the most logical choice based on internal evidence, secular history, and the testimony of early church leaders.

As noted above, some scholars are not convinced that Revelation was written by the apostle John, and they deny his authorship. Their basic argument is that the style of writing in Revelation is too different from that of John's Gospel and his Epistles. It is true that the styles are different, but they are different because the subject matter is different. There are very few references to the Old Testament in the Gospel and the Epistles of John, for their subject matter is different. In them the focus is God reaching out to man in His Son, Jesus Christ, and the life man has in Him as a result. In Revelation, by contrast, it is estimated that there are between three and four hundred references to the Old Testament. This is true because its subject is great judgment, and John is expressing the prophecies of the Hebrew Old Testament in the Greek language.

Though the basic subject matter of Revelation differs from that of John's other writings, Revelation is very similar to them. For example, John is the only New Testament writer to use the Greek word *logos*, "word," in a personal way. He calls Jesus the *Logos* in the following Scriptures: John 1:l-3, l4; 1 John 1:1; Revelation 19:13. He also uses the Greek word *nikao*, "overcome," in John 16:33; 1 John 2:13–14; 4:4; 5:4–5; and 17 times in Revelation. Outside of John's writings, this word is used only three times (Luke 11:22; Romans 3:4; 12:21). The prophecy of Zechariah 12:10 is quoted in John 19:37 and referred to in Revelation 1:7. In both of these places the Greek verb *ekkenteo*, "pierced," is used, a word that is not found anywhere else in the New Testament or in the *Septuagint. These similarities are significant. Along with the other evidence that John wrote Revelation, they present strong evidence that the writer of this book is the same person as the one who wrote the Gospel and Epistles of John. The evidence presented indicates that the writer of Revelation is John the apostle and beloved disciple of Jesus.

Septuagint
the Greek translation of the Old Testament that was made, according to ancient tradition, in about the third century before Christ

8 In your notebook list four facts which support the conclusion that the book of Revelation was written by the apostle John during the reign of Domitian (AD 91–96).

Arrange in order an outline of the book of Revelation giving topics, headings, and references within the main outline divisions.

A Description of Its Contents

Main Divisions

In Revelation 1:19 Jesus Himself states the three main subjects of His message.

9 According to Revelation 1:19, what three things was John supposed to write?

....

....

Study the following outline, which is divided according to these three subjects and is based on the wording of the Greek text.

The Book of Revelation

I. The Prologue, 1:1–8

II. What You Have Seen, 1:9–20 (The Vision of Christ)

III. What Is Now, 2:1–3:22 (The Messages to the Churches)

IV. What Will Take Place Later, 4:1–22:6 (After These Things)

- **A.** The Church in Glory, 4:1–5:14
- **B.** The Great Tribulation, 6:1–19:21
- **C.** The Millennium, 20:1–6
- **D.** Gog and Magog, 20:7–10
- **E.** The Great White Throne, 20:11–15
- **F.** All Things New, 21:1–22:6

V. The Postscript, 22:7–21 (Be Ready)

Of course, many other outlines of Revelation have been made. One of the most famous ones is the outline which is based on the series of sevens that are found in the book. (This outline is included in the Global University course, *New Testament Survey*.)

10 Write the number of the outline division of the book of Revelation (right) in front of each topic, heading, or reference which belongs to that division (left).

. . . . **a** All Things New
. . . . **b** The Vision of Christ
. . . . **c** What You have Seen
. . . . **d** Be Ready
. . . . **e** The Messages to the Churches
. . . . **f** Revelation 1:1–8
. . . . **g** Revelation 2:1–3:22

1) The Prologue I
2) Main Division II
3) Main Division III
4) Main Division IV
5) The Postscript V

Identify the parenthetical enlargement portions of the book of Revelation.

Parenthetical Enlargements

parenthetical enlargement a close-up view, a fuller description, of one part of a subject that has already been mentioned

In writing, a **parenthetical enlargement* is a close-up view, a fuller description, of one part of a subject that has already been mentioned. For example, one may view an entire town from a distance and receive an overall view. Then he may walk up close to one individual house and notice its details. The close-up view of the house is like a parenthetical enlargement.

Parenthetical Enlargement is a close-up view, a fuller description, of one part of a subject that has already been mentioned.

There is a good example of a parenthetical enlargement in the account of Creation in Genesis 1 and 2. In chapter 1, all six days of Creation are presented, including the creation of man and woman, given in verses 26–30. Then in chapter 2:4–25, there is a longer, more detailed description of one event of day six: the creation of man and woman.

The book of Revelation is presented in the same way. John gives a narrative in proper order. Then he enlarges on important subjects that he has already mentioned. To interpret the book of Revelation accurately, it is important to place these parenthetical enlargements properly. With one exception, chapter 14, the parenthetical enlargements give details of events already stated. Chapter 14, however, looks forward or anticipates events that are to follow. See Figure 4.1 for the parenthetical enlargements of the book of Revelation.

Chapter	Subject of Parenthetical Enlargement
7	The 144,000 of Israel and the white-robed multitude
10	The mighty angel with the scroll
11:1–14	The two witnesses
12	The woman, the son, and the dragon
13	The two wild beasts
14	The 144,000 of Israel (again), the final preaching of the gospel, the announcement that Babylon has fallen, the final harvest, and the winepress
17	The two wild beasts and the great prostitute
18	Babylon

Figure 4.1

11 Circle the letter preceding each example of a parenthetical enlargement.

a The account of Creation in Genesis 1
b A fuller description of a subject which is briefly mentioned in another part of a narrative
c An orderly account of a series of events in their correct sequence
d The picture of Babylon in Revelation 18
e The description of man and woman in Genesis 2:4–25

Guidelines for Understanding Its Message

You have studied some basic facts about the theme and content of the book of Revelation. In this section of the lesson you will consider some important principles to follow as you seek to understand the message of the book.

Identify four basic systems of interpretation of the book of Revelation.

Four Basic Views of Its Meaning

There are four basic views or systems of interpretation of the book of Revelation. These are the *preterist*, the *historicist*, the *idealist or spiritual*, and the *futurist*. We will evaluate each one briefly, and we will assess the strengths and weaknesses of each.

Preterist. Those who hold this view teach that the prophecies of Revelation were fulfilled in the struggles of the early Christians against Rome. The beasts mentioned in the book represent the Roman Empire under the Caesars, who demanded that they be worshipped as God. The events foretold in the book came to a climax at either the destruction of Jerusalem in AD 70 or the fall of Rome in AD 476. Thus, its message has little or no meaning for the present time.

Historicist. In this view the book presents a description of the course of history leading up to our time. Individuals who hold this view identify various prophecies of the book with the rise of the Huns, Napoleon, Islam, and so forth. It is difficult to find two persons holding this view who agree on what is represented by any particular symbol.

allegory
a long and complicated story with an underlying meaning different from the surface meaning of the story itself

Idealist or Spiritual. According to this view the book is a spiritual *allegory which shows the triumph of God over Satan, of good over evil. The book makes no references to any specific events. Its pages reveal principles which depict the constant warfare between the forces of Satan and the forces of God.

Futurist. Futurists believe that the book is literal. By literal they do not mean that the Antichrist is going to have seven heads and ten horns. Rather they believe that the events and personages referred to in the book are literal events and people. According to this view the majority of the prophecies have not yet been fulfilled. They are to have a future fulfillment. The events described in chapters 1–3, according to this view, have taken place; however, still in the future are the judgments, resurrections, raptures, Antichrist, false prophet, Great Tribulation, Battle of Armageddon, *Millennium, and the new heavens and earth. Futurists point out that the book calls itself a prophecy.

Millennium
the period of a thousand years during which Christ is expected to reign on earth

A number of Bible scholars who have studied the book of Revelation hold views which cannot be strictly classified into just one of the preceding categories. For instance, many hold the spiritual view, but they also agree that there is a prophetical element in the book and that the final events are going to take place.

Unlike the futurists, however, they do not believe that the prophecies of the book refer to specific events that can be clearly defined.

There can be little doubt that the early church saw in the book of Revelation a picture of the Roman Empire in its opposition to and persecution of the Christians. As a part of its purpose, the book certainly served as an encouragement to the struggling church of the first three centuries. It is also apparent that the book of Revelation does show the ultimate victory of God over the forces of Satan. Beyond its message of comfort to the early church and the simple assurance that good will triumph over evil, there was little else to commend this prophecy to early Christians.

Thus, while admitting some of the merits of other views, the viewpoint presented in this course is basically that of the futurist. We believe that this viewpoint conforms best to the content of the book, for *the book does describe events that must take place to complete the plan of God—events that will take place in the future.*

12 Write the number of the system of interpretation of the book of Revelation (right) in front of each sentence which expresses that view (left).

. . . . **a** The prophecies refer to actual events which will take place in the future to complete God's plan.	1) Preterist 2) Historicist 3) Idealist/ Spiritual 4) Futurist
. . . . **b** The prophecies were fulfilled during the time when the early Christians suffered persecution by Rome.	
. . . . **c** Some who hold this view believe that the prophecies were fulfilled when Jerusalem was destroyed in AD 70.	
. . . . **d** The events described represent a spiritual allegory of the continuing struggle between God and Satan.	
. . . . **e** Prophecies are identified with specific persons and events of the past, such as Napoleon and the rise of Islam.	

Describe the principles for interpreting the prophetic message of the book of Revelation.

Special Features of Its Form

apocalyptic
like a revelation; portending a violent upheaval; Apocalyptic also describes a class of Jewish and Christian visionary literature written between 200 BC and A.D 200.

As you know, the Bible contains writings on many different subjects and in many different forms. For example, it contains the psalms of David, the proverbs of Solomon, the prophecies of Isaiah, and the letters of Paul. Some of the prophetic writings in the Bible are given in a form called **apocalyptic*, a style that has several distinctive features. Four books of the Bible that are considered to be especially apocalyptic in form are the prophecies of Daniel, Ezekiel, Zechariah, and Revelation.

As you continue your study, you will learn more about the apocalyptic features of both Daniel and Revelation and what they mean. The following paragraph presents the three main features of the apocalyptic style found in the biblical books, along with examples from the book of Revelation:

1. *In the apocalyptic writings, signs and symbols are used to convey spiritual truth.* For example, notice the expression "made it known," which occurs in

Revelation 1:1. This is a translation of a Greek word which literally means "to signify," "to show with signs." Signs and symbols are used throughout the book. John states "I saw" over sixty times (see 1:12 and 14:6 for examples). He states twenty-eight times "I heard" (see 5:11 and 12:10 for examples). In addition, he specifically indicates that he was "shown" something (see 4:1; 17:1; 21:9–10; and 22:1 for examples).

2. *The apocalyptic writings show future victory for the forces of God against the forces of Satan.* See, for example, the victory over Satan which is presented in Revelation 12:7–12 and 20:7–10.
3. *In apocalyptic writings, angelic beings intervene to explain events.* This is illustrated by the appearance of the angel in Revelation 10:9–11 and 17:15–18.

The apocalyptic style was also used by nonbiblical writers. Though their writings resemble those of the biblical books in some ways, there are some important differences. For example, nonbiblical apocalyptic books contain an extremely pessimistic view of the life of the godly. By contrast, the biblical writers are optimistic. They show that although the godly suffer persecution, God blesses His people with peace and joy in the midst of tests and trials of faith. They have a relationship with Him that nothing can destroy.

13 Circle the letter preceding each description of a distinctive feature of apocalyptic literature which is found in the book of Revelation.

a) Use of signs and symbols to convey spiritual truth
b) Identification of John the apostle as the author
c) Use of the word *apokalupsis*
d) Intervention of angels who appear to explain events
e) Pessimistic view of the life of the godly
f) Portrayal of the ultimate victory of God over Satan

Identify principles that assist one to interpret the prophetic message properly.

Principles for Interpreting Its Meaning

There are four important principles to follow when one interprets the prophetic message of the book of Revelation. We have listed them below. The first three need to be applied because Revelation is a prophetic book. The fourth needs to be applied because the prophecy of Revelation is given in an apocalyptic form.

Principle Number 1: Let the Scriptures interpret themselves. In Revelation John recorded the pictures and scenes which he saw, and it is our task to interpret these signs based on the teachings of the rest of the Word of God. Two things to remember when we interpret these signs are: 1) the Bible is its own best interpreter, and 2) when the obvious makes the best sense, any other sense is nonsense. The context of the book of Revelation is the whole Bible.

Principle Number 2: Apply the rule of prophetic perspective. As the apostle Peter pointed out in 1 Peter 1:11, the prophets had glimpses of future events, but they did not always understand them or see the time elements involved in their fulfillment. Often, reading prophecy is like looking at the sky and seeing a multitude of stars. We are not aware of the vast distances between them nor of the fact that some are much closer to us than others.

14 Read Isaiah 61:1–2 and Luke 4:16–21. In your notebook write a short paragraph to explain why you think Jesus stopped reading where He did.

Even though Isaiah saw "the year of the Lord's favor" and "the day of vengeance of our God" in the same vision, he did not see the time gap between the two events. Here is where proper prophetic perspective, or viewpoint, is needed. The first event was fulfilled when Jesus ministered on earth; the second will not be fulfilled until the Great Tribulation. Since the second has not yet been fulfilled, the gap between the two events is already about 2000 years long.

Principle Number 3: Recognize the possibility of double fulfillment of prophecy. The prophets whose messages are recorded in the Old Testament were primarily preachers to their own generation, not foretellers of the future. They warned the people of their day about an impending Day of the Lord which would shortly come as a judgment for sin and idolatry. Yet their messages point beyond what happened in their own time and forward to the great Day of the Lord which is described in the book of Revelation. For example, the prophet Joel mentions the Day of the Lord (Joel 1:15; 2:1–2, 11, 31). In Joel's day, judgments certainly were coming upon Judah in the near future; however, there is a final Day of the Lord yet to come, the one pictured in Revelation 19. Thus, Joel's prophecy will have a double fulfillment.

Principle Number 4: Understand the use of signs and symbols. Many signs and symbols such as animals, colors, numbers, and objects appear throughout the book of Revelation. They are used to express certain meanings. According to one writer, J. B. Smith, there are forty-six symbols the book itself interprets. Other symbols are not interpreted. However, there is general agreement on the meanings of many of those that are used. The following chart (Figure 4.2) gives several of the most important symbols used in Revelation along with the meanings that are usually assigned to them.

Type of Symbol	***Symbol***	***Meaning***
Numbers	One two three four six seven ten twelve	God confirmation trinity earth man, evil divine fullness, (occurs 54 times) political completion final completion
Animals	lamb horses wild beasts frogs lion	Jesus military might Antichrist and False Prophet demons Jesus
Colors	white pale red purple emerald green black	purity, ancientness death bloodshed, war imperial luxury rest, refreshment calamity, distress

Figure 4.2

After careful study of Revelation, it is your writer's belief that the meanings of the symbols on the above chart remain constant throughout the book.

You have already been introduced to some of the pictures of Christ that are found in Revelation, and you have undoubtedly become more aware that God is in control of the future. Our prayer is that this study will challenge you to live a consistent Christian life as we come nearer to the return of Jesus Christ.

15 Match each statement (left) with the principle of prophetic interpretation (right) that the statement relates most closely to (left).

. . . . **a** Joel's prophecies about the Day of the Lord had a fulfillment in his time and will also be fulfilled at the end of the age.

. . . . **b** The symbol of the lamb is interpreted to mean Jesus.

. . . . **c** The fulfillment of two events described in the same verse can be separated by many hundreds of years in time.

. . . . **d** Other prophecies in the Bible are compared with those given in Revelation in order to understand the ones given in *Revelation*.

. . . . **e** While Jesus was in the synagogue at Nazareth, he referred to His own ministry there by reading only part of the messianic prophecy on Isaiah 61:2.

1) Principle that Scriptures interpret themselves
2) Principle of prophetic perspective
3) Principle of double fulfillment
4) Principle of the use of signs

Self-Test

Multiple choice: Select the best answer.

1 As used in the title of the book of Revelation, the word, *revelation* means the
a) unveiling of the meaning of spiritual experience.
b) visible appearing of Jesus Christ.
c) giving of spiritual knowledge to believers.
d) unveiling of things to the understanding of believers.

2 The main subject of Revelation is the description of
a) events in the earthly life of Jesus.
b) spiritual forces which are arrayed against the godly.
c) Jesus Himself in the past, present, and future.
d) symbols related to the destiny of the nation of Israel.

3 An indication that the apostle John wrote the book of Revelation is the
a) use of the Greek words *logos* and *nikao*.
b) numerous quotations from the Old Testament.
c) fact that the Greek word *apokalupsis* is used in it.
d) apocalyptic character of the book use signs and symbols to convey spiritual truth.

4 To which of the following main divisions of the book of Revelation does the topic "All Things New" belong?
a) The Prologue
b) What You Have Seen
c) What Is Now
d) What Will Take Place Later
e) The Postscript

5 The purpose of a parenthetical enlargement in Scripture is to
a) introduce a subject not previously mentioned.
b) lengthen the space between two events of a similar nature.
c) shorten the space between two events of a similar nature.
d) give more information about a subject briefly mentioned elsewhere.

6 According to the *preterist* interpretation of the book of Revelation, the book describes
a) all of history up to the present time.
b) the triumph of good over evil in an allegorical manner.
c) the struggles of early Christians against Rome.
d) events of which most are yet to come.

7 The apocalyptic writings in the book of Revelation, as opposed to other apocalyptic writings, do NOT
a) include the intervention of angelic beings to explain events.
b) present a pessimistic view of the life of the godly.
c) future victory for the forces of God over those of Satan.

8 "The interpretation of a lamb to mean Jesus" relates most closely to which of the following principles of prophetic interpretation?
a) The use of signs and symbols
b) The Scriptures' interpreting themselves
c) Prophetic perspective
d) Double fulfillment

Short Answer. Briefly answer the following questions. Your answers may differ slightly from the wording we have given in the Student Packet, but they should be similar in content. Write your answer to each question in the space provided for it.

9 What were the three things about which Jesus instructed John to write in the book of Revelation?

....

....

10 Name four basic views of the meaning of the book of Revelation and state which one of them is presented in this course.

....

....

Answers to study questions

8 Your facts could include the following, in any order: a) the use of the Greek word *logos*; b) the use of the Greek words *nikao* and *ekkenteo*; c) the testimony of early church leaders, such as Justin Martyr, to John's authorship; d) the testimony of early church leaders as to the date the book was written; and e) the internal evidence of the book of Revelation concerning John's imprisonment on Patmos.

1 Your answer should be "the revelation of Jesus Christ."

9 He was told to write: 1) "what you have seen," 2) "what is now," and 3) "what will take place later."

2 a 1) The revelation of things to our understanding.
b 1) The revelation of things to our understanding.
c 2) The visible appearing of Jesus Christ.
d 1) The revelation of things to our understanding.

10 a 4) Main Division IV
b 2) Main Division II
c 2) Main Division II
d 5) The Postscript V
e 3) Main Division III
f 1) The Prologue I
g 3) Main Division III

3 Your answer should be similar to the following: The name of the book of Revelation is the *apokalupsis* of Jesus Christ. The word *apokalupsis* in this name means "the visible appearing" or "unveiling" of Jesus Christ. The theme of the book is the second coming of Christ. It is found in 1:7.

11 You should have circled **b**, **d**, and **e**.

4 a Verse 27 says "himself."
b Verse 27 indicates that it was the Old Testament Scriptures.

12 a 4) Futurist
b 1) Preterist
c 1) Preterist
d 3) Idealist
e 2) Historicist

5 You should have this list written in your notebook for further use.

13 You should have circled a), d), and f).

6 b) Jesus Himself, what He has done, is doing, and will do.

14 He stopped after the phrase "the year of the Lord's favor" because He knew it was not yet time for the fulfillment of the next phrase in Isaiah: "the day of vengeance of our God."

7 a John (1:1, 4, 9; 22:8).
b He was the servant of Jesus Christ (1:1).
c He was their brother and companion (1:9).

15 a 3) Principle of double fulfillment
b 4) Principle of the use of signs
c 2) Principle of prophetic perspective
d 1) Principle that Scriptures interpret themselves
e 2) Principle of prophetic perspective

What John Saw

In Lesson 4 we discussed some of the characteristics of the book of Revelation: name, theme, primary subject, author, and date of writing. We considered several systems of interpretation that are used to interpret the prophetic word. We also focused our attention on some very basic principles of interpretation. This preliminary study, we trust, will make the balance of the course easier to understand.

Now we move to chapter 5 and the second major part of the outline given in Lesson 4: *What You Have Seen.* Here we will encounter some vitally important topics. We will discuss, among other things, the source and purpose of the revelation, the beatitudes of Revelation, the Lord's Day, and the stars and lampstands. Finally, we will consider briefly the significance of death and Hades in the context of our Lord's position as Head of the church.

As you examine each part of the lesson, pray that the Lord will give you a special anointing to receive the truth He has for you. Pray also that you may apply this truth in an effective way in your Christian experience.

the activities...

- ◇ Work through the lesson development according to the procedures given in Lesson 1.
- ◇ Read chapter 1 of Revelation again before you turn to the lesson development.
- ◇ Go through the list of word pictures of Jesus Christ you recorded in your notebook in Lesson 4. Write the verse reference for each one that occurs in chapter 1. Before you read this lesson, write in your notebook what each of these pictures presented in this chapter should mean to you as a Christian.

the objectives...

5.1 *State the source of truth in the book of Revelation and the primary purpose of proclaiming that truth.*

5.2 *Describe what is meant by the term* quickly *as it pertains to the Lord's return.*

5.3 *Explain various ways in which the biblical word translated "angel" is used and identify what message the angel revealed to John in Revelation 1:2.*

5.4 *State the benefits associated with the first of the seven beatitudes of Revelation.*

5.5 *Determine the identity of the seven spirits mentioned in Revelation 1:4.*

5.6 *State the three things that Jesus is said to be in Revelation 1:5.*

5.7 *Recognize different meanings that the term translated "to see" has in the book of Revelation.*

5.8 *Explain why in Revelation 1:8 Jesus is called the "Alpha" and the "Omega."*

5.9 *State the meaning of the phrase "the Lord's Day" in Revelation 1:10.*

5.10 *Explain briefly the description of Jesus as John saw Him and the message that the seer was commanded to record.*

5.11 *Explain the term* paradise *and discuss its location.*

5.12 *Describe the symbolic meaning of the stars and lampstands in Revelation 1.*

the outline...

1 Source and Purpose of Revelation
2 Meaning of *En Tachei*
3 Meanings of *Angel*
4 Seven Beatitudes of Revelation
5 Seven Spirits of God
6 Threefold Description of Jesus
7 The Significance of the Word *See*
8 The Alpha and the Omega
9 The Lord's Day
10 Voice, Command, and Vision
11 Death and Hades
12 The Stars and Lampstands

State the source of truth in the book of Revelation and the primary purpose of proclaiming that truth.

Source and Purpose of Revelation

Revelation 1:1

The first verse of Revelation 1 makes known to us that God is the source of the truth contained in the book. It also shows us the purpose of proclaiming that truth in this book. Verse 1 shows that Jesus has the task of proclaiming this truth to servants of God on earth. Jesus is able to show His servants things which are going to take place to fulfill the truth that is prophesied in Revelation.

It is impossible for people who are not servants of God to understand the book of Revelation. It is foolishness to them just as "the message of the cross is foolishness to those who are perishing" (1 Corinthians 1:18). To those of us who are God's servants, however, Revelation is a great book of victory and rejoicing in Jesus Christ our Lord!

1 Who is the source of truth in the book of Revelation?

....

2 What is the primary purpose of proclaiming the truth that is given in the book of Revelation?

....

3 It is impossible for people who are not servants of God to understand the book of Revelation because

a) they do not know most of the words in the book.
b) they do not have enough human wisdom.
c) God has made foolish the wisdom of this world.
d) they do not have the necessary God-given wisdom.

Describe what is meant by the term quickly *as it pertains to the Lord's return.*

Meanings of *En Tachei*

Revelation 1:1

Revelation 1:1 reveals not only the nature and purpose of the book, but also the character of Christ's coming. The Greek phrase translated "soon" in this verse is *en tachei.* This phrase is translated "quickly" in Luke 18:8 and once again as "soon" in Romans 16:20. "Soon" in Revelation 1:1 refers to God's time—not ours. God's timing is not the same as ours. Second Peter 3:8 implies that God views everything as *now,* as *in the present.* The word *must* in Revelation 1:1 has led scholars who are not futurists to believe that the term *en tachei* indicates "certainty of fulfillment." Thus, they believe this indicates that the prophecies will certainly be fulfilled. However, the term *en tachei* can be translated by words other than "soon" or "quickly." For example, this Greek phrase can mean "suddenly"; therefore, it does not necessarily mean that "what must soon take place" had to take place immediately after Revelation was written. Finally, *en tachei* is used to mean "*imminent" which indicates the possibility of taking place at any time.

imminent
likely to happen soon, about to occur

In Lesson 4 we saw that the theme of the book of Revelation is the announcement of the coming of Jesus Christ (Revelation 1:7). His coming is "what must soon take place." As we have seen in the preceding paragraph, this five-word phrase in Revelation 1:1 strongly indicates that the *watchword of the Christian is to *be ready* for Jesus' coming! The coming of Christ includes more than one event; it introduces a series of events. This series of events begins in Revelation 4:1 and is described in some detail. Once these events begin, there will be no further delay in the consummation of God's redemptive program. The events that take place will no longer be intermediate, according to the law of prophetic perspective. They represent the final pages in God's plan of the ages.

watchword
a motto that embodies a principle or guide to action of an individual or group

4 What did Jesus send His angel to show His servant John?

....

5 What are the four English translations of the Greek phrase *en tachei* that are presented in this section of the lesson?

....

Explain various ways in which the biblical word translated "angel" is used and identify what message the angel revealed to John in Revelation 1:2.

Meanings of *Angel*

Revelation 1:1–2

Revelation 1:1 indicates that an angel revealed Jesus Christ to John, the author of the book of Revelation. Here we see that the word translated "angel" means "messenger." Elsewhere in the Bible the word translated "angel" sometimes refers to what we commonly call an angel, that is, a heavenly or spirit messenger (Genesis 19:1,15; Psalm 103:20; 148:2; Matthew 1:20; 2:13). At other times this word refers to a human messenger (Genesis 32:3; 1 Samuel 6:21; 1 Chronicles 14:1; Matthew 11:10; Luke 9:52). Since words translated "angel" can refer either to a human or a heavenly messenger, we must look at the context to determine which is meant. The important thing to remember here is that the focus is on the message, not the messenger. Whether he is human or heavenly is not our primary concern.

Notice two things in Revelation 1:2 that the angel revealed to John: "the word of God and the testimony of Jesus Christ." As we studied in Lesson 4, the angel communicated this message to John by means of signs and symbols. The message of the book of Revelation is thus communicated by a heavenly messenger and is recorded by John, a faithful witness of what he had heard and seen.

6 How does Revelation 1:1 show that the word *angel* means "messenger"?

....

7 What two kinds of messengers does the word *angel* refer to in the Bible?

....

8 The revelation was communicated or made known to John by an angel through what means? The angel

a) moved upon John through dreams to reveal divine truth.
b) communicated truths through the use of signs and symbols.
c) spoke through omens in the physical world.
d) inspired John to visualize the future based on Old Testament prophecy.

9 Two things revealed to John in Revelation 1:2 are the

a) word of testimony and the Son of God.
b) word of God and the testimony of Jesus Christ.
c) Father and Son in the Trinity of God.
d) word of Jesus and testimony of the Spirit.

State the benefits associated with the first of the seven beatitudes of Revelation.

Seven Beatitudes of Revelation

Revelation 1:3–5

beatitude
all of the declarations made in the Sermon on the Mount (Matthew 5:3–11) that begin with "Blessed are" or "Blessed is"

The best known *beatitudes are found in Matthew 5:1–12. After reading them, one should be able to explain why Revelation 1:3 is called a beatitude. It is the first of seven beatitudes of Revelation. The other six are found in Revelation 14:13, 16:15, 19:9, 20:6, 22:7, and 22:14. After locating them, write all seven of these beatitudes of Revelation in your notebook. They provide material for an excellent Bible study or sermon. Learn them well enough to write them out from memory on a test if you are asked to do so.

Observe especially the nature of this first beatitude of Revelation. First, a blessing is pronounced on the one who reads this prophetic book. Second, and most important, are the blessings promised to those who hear and *apply* what is written. That this prophetic word is important to believers is seen in the blessings promised to those who receive and apply its message to their Christian experience.

In Revelation 1:4, John begins to write to the churches. He begins with two commonly used New Testament greetings: *grace and peace.* We who are Christians are aware that a person must experience God's grace before he has real peace. *Why?* Notice in Revelation 1:4–5 the two persons and the group of beings from whom these greetings of grace and peace are extended to these churches. It is obvious that the first named person is the eternally existent God the Father because the other person is directly stated to be Jesus Christ.

10 Explain why Revelation 1:3 is called a beatitude.

....

11 Review the seven beatitudes of Revelation carefully. Then try to write a summary of them from memory in your notebook with the chapter and verse reference.

12 Why must a person experience God's grace before he has real peace?

....

13 The first of the seven beatitudes of Revelation concerns the
a) faithful who endure temptation and then enter eternal life.
b) diligent who persevere under difficult circumstances to extend the faith.
c) ones who read, hear, and apply the message of this prophecy.

Determine the identity of the seven spirits mentioned in Revelation 1:4.

Seven Spirits of God

Revelation 1:4

Let us present two opinions regarding the identity of the seven spirits mentioned in Revelation 1:4. *First,* since angels are called "ministering spirits" in Hebrews 1:14, some believe these seven spirits are angels. Some Jewish traditions indicate that seven angels stand in the presence of God. Luke 1:19 refers to an angel who

archangel
ruling angel; chief angel

stands in the presence of God. Some traditions hold that the *angels of the presence* are *archangels. But only one angel is called an archangel in the Word of God (1 Thessalonians 4:16 and Jude 9). Another popular opinion is that these seven spirits symbolize the completeness of the ministry of the Holy Spirit. Your writer holds this opinion because he sees no indication of or any reason for seven angels in Revelation 1:4. Furthermore, his views are influenced by the teaching of the sevenfold ministry of the Holy Spirit in Isaiah 11:2–3 and Zechariah chapter 4. Notice in Isaiah 11:2–3 the seven enablements which the Holy Spirit ministers to the Branch, that is, to Jesus the Messiah.

14 What are the seven enablements in Isaiah 11:2–3 that the Holy Spirit ministers to the Messiah?

....

15 According to your writer, what do the seven spirits mentioned in Revelation 1:4 symbolize regarding the ministry of the Holy Spirit?

....

State the three things that Jesus is said to be in Revelation 1:5.

Threefold Description of Jesus

Revelation 1:5–6

Notice the three descriptions of Jesus given in Revelation 1:5. Let us consider them one at a time.

affirmation
a positive statement, assertion

1. *He is the Faithful Witness*. A witness is one who gives evidence, one who testifies for a cause, one who has personal knowledge of something, one who gives public *affirmation by word or example. How can we understand God? As we behold Christ, hear His words, and witness His compassion, we see God (John 14:9). How can we know God's power? We know it by seeing Jesus as He heals the sick, raises the dead, and cleanses lepers. How can we know God's patience? We witness patience as we see Jesus in His longsuffering with His disciples. How can we know God's love? God's love is revealed in Jesus as He reaches out to every needy person and as He says "Father, forgive them; for they know not what they do" (Luke 23:34, KJV). Thus, Jesus is the perfect witness; He presents the character and attributes of God faithfully to His people.

Now, notice what Acts 1:8 indicates that the coming of the Holy Spirit upon believers would cause them to receive and be. They were to be baptized in the Holy Spirit, and the Spirit's indwelling presence would dramatically change their lives. Disciples of Christ would receive power to be witnesses for their Lord. The emphasis here is on what believers *are* rather than on what they *do,* for what believers *do* results from what they *are.* Just as people look at Jesus and see the Father, we are to be so filled with the Holy Spirit that people will see Jesus Christ in our lives and want to know Him as their Savior.

16 What does Acts 1:8 indicate that the coming of the Holy Spirit upon believers will cause them to receive and to be?

....

2. *Jesus is the Firstborn From the Dead.* Firstborn does not mean that Jesus was created at some point in time because God the Son has always existed (John 1:1–3, 14). The term *firstborn* is clarified in Colossians 1:18. By the phrase "the firstborn from among the dead" the apostle Paul refers to the resurrection of Christ from His earthly death, emphasizes that He is now alive, and points to the resurrection of others who sleep in Christ (1 Thessalonians 4:14).

17 The phrase "firstborn from among the dead" does NOT
a) indicate the way in which Jesus originally came into being.
b) stress the fact that Jesus is now alive.
c) refer to Jesus' resurrection from His death on the cross.
d) point to additional resurrections.

3. *Jesus is the Ruler of the Kings of the Earth.* He is in absolute control. Satan temporarily appears to be in control, but the book of Revelation shows who is really in charge!

In Revelation 1:5–6 we observe several important things. First, we see our Lord's attitude toward us: He loves us. Second, we note that this love is active; it moved Him to free us from our sins at the cost of His own life. Third, as a result of His redemptive love, He has elevated us from the status of alien sinners to occupy the role of citizens of His kingdom and priests of God. Thus, every believer is a priest and has access to God through Jesus Christ and no other mediators are needed (Hebrews 4:14–16).

18 Revelation 1:5–6 indicates that our Lord's attitudes and actions toward us have resulted in what status for us?
a) We have become eternally secure in Him regardless of the quality of our Christian life and service.
b) We have become citizens of His kingdom and priests to serve God.
c) We are assured that no temptation will overtake us that we personally cannot endure.
d) Slaves or property of low value.

Revelation 1:6 ends with the first exclamation of praise to God in the book of Revelation. One can make a very profitable Bible study on the praises to Him in this book. Write this one in your notebook, and as we come to the others, add them also. In addition, write the meaning of each word of praise and you will discover the things for which we need to praise God.

19 In summary of this section, state the three things that Jesus is said to be in Revelation 1:5.

....

....

Recognize different meanings that the term translated "to see" has in the book of Revelation.

The Significance of the Word *See*

Revelation 1:7

Several different Greek words are translated "see" by the author of Revelation. We pointed out in Lesson 1 that the announcement of the coming of Jesus Christ is the theme of the book of Revelation. "Every eye will see him"

(Revelation 1:7) is a statement that helps to describe the response of people on earth to Jesus' coming. The Greek word translated "see" in this statement suggests that the meaning intended here is on people's understanding rather than their physical sight. This emphasis is confirmed by the statement that "peoples of the earth will mourn" when they see Jesus coming. They will mourn because they understand what His coming means.

Another meaning of the word translated "to see" refers to physical sight. For example, John says "Mary . . . *saw* [italics added] that the stone had been removed" (John 20:1). A third meaning of the word translated "to see" occurs in John 20:6. Scripture says, "Peter . . . *saw* [italics added] the strips of linen lying there." Here the meaning stressed is Peter's theorizing, questioning, and wondering. In John 20:8 John sees with understanding. Thus, the expression *to see* may refer to "physical sight," emphasize "understanding," or stress "theorizing, questioning, and wondering."

Men see Jesus in different ways. Some mock Him; some neglect Him; and some refuse to come to Him when He calls. In Revelation 1:12, the word translated "see" suggests that John was merely turning to see with his eye. The word *saw* in Revelation 1:17, however, suggests that John saw with understanding and, therefore, fell down before Jesus. That is what every human being will do some day (Philippians 2:10–11).

20 In this section we have seen that the words translated "to see" in the book of Revelation include which of the following meanings? (Circle the letter preceding each correct choice.)

a) Physical sight
b) Superior human insight
c) Understanding
d) Wondering and questioning
e) The insight of a sorcerer

Our prayer is that as we progress through these lessons, each one will see Jesus *with understanding* as never before. Also, may we have the ability to share Him with others more effectively so that they may see and understand Him better.

Explain why in Revelation 1:8 Jesus is called the "Alpha" and the "Omega."

The Alpha and the Omega

Revelation 1:8

In Revelation 1:8 God refers to Himself as "the Alpha and the Omega." This figure of speech is like saying "the A and the Z" in English, because *alpha* and *omega* are the first and last letters of the Greek alphabet. Two further references to God as "the Alpha and the Omega" also contain the phrase: "the Beginning and the End" (Revelation 21:6 and 22:13). The Triune God is "the First and the Last" (Revelation 21:6). Both the Father and the Son are referred to in Revelation as the Alpha and the Omega, and in Hebrews the same quality is attributed to the Spirit (Hebrews 9:14). Revelation 22:13 refers more directly than do the other two verses to Jesus Christ as the Alpha and the Omega. God the Father created all things through His Son Jesus Christ (John 1:1–4, 10; Colossians 1:15–18; and Hebrews 1:1–4).

21 In your notebook explain briefly why Jesus is called the *Alpha* and the *Omega.*

State the meaning of the phrase "the Lord's Day" in Revelation 1:10.

The Lord's Day

Revelation 1:9

In Revelation 1:9 John tells us where he was and why he was there. Observe what John says in this verse about suffering. He indicates that he is "on the island of Patmos because of the word of God and the testimony of Jesus." The fact that he identifies himself as a brother and companion in suffering suggests that he was banished to this island because of his faith.

Tradition tells us the Roman emperor Domitian had tried to cook John in boiling oil, but John would not cook. Therefore, the emperor banished John to the island prison of Patmos. Moreover, the manner in which John discusses suffering indicates that this was a natural or common consequence of being a faithful witness of Jesus. The following Scriptures indicate that suffering for the cause of Christ is normal and to be expected (Hebrews 10:32–39; 11:35–38; 12:4–7; James 5:10; 1 Peter 1:6–7; 4:12–19; 5:8–10).

In spite of his isolation on the island, John declares that he was in the spirit (the Greek text says clearly that he *"became* in the Spirit") on the Lord's Day (v. 10). Though physically barred from the crowds, his spirit was free to soar into the presence of God. Moreover, this occurred on the Lord's Day.

What does the phrase "the Lord's Day" mean in Revelation? Some people believe that John was transported into the future and experienced the Day of the Lord which is another name for the Great Tribulation. The Greek phrase translated *the Day of the Lord,* however, is different from the phrase translated here as *the Lord's Day.* The latter Greek phrase refers to the first day of the week, Sunday. Thus, John's statement, "On the Lord's Day I was in the Spirit," indicates that it was on Sunday when John "became in the Spirit."

22 What does "the Lord's Day" refer to in Revelation 1:10?

....

....

Explain briefly the description of Jesus as John saw Him and the message that the seer was commanded to record.

Voice, Command, and Vision

Revelation 1:10–16

As John was in the Spirit, he heard a loud voice like a trumpet behind him (v. 10) Evidently the experience stirred the writer greatly. The voice commanded the seer to write on a scroll what he *saw* and to send it to the seven churches (v. 11). The seven churches were churches in seven cities of the Roman province of Asia, which we will discuss more completely in the next two lessons.

John turned to see who was speaking to him and he saw "seven golden lampstands" (v. 12). Among them was the person whose voice he had heard. Here, John had a vision of Jesus, the person who had just commanded him to write (vv. 13–16). We have listed the following information and symbolism of what John saw in this vision regarding Jesus' clothing and *physique.

physique
bodily makeup

1. Clothing: Jesus' dignity as prophet, priest, and king
2. Head and hair: Jesus' purity, wisdom, and eternity
3. Eyes: Jesus' omniscience and insight
4. Feet: Jesus' judgment of others
5. Voice: Jesus' power and strength
6. Right Hand: Jesus' concern, assistance, and control
7. Mouth: Jesus' completely authoritative word
8. Face: Jesus' glory, majesty, and holiness

John's vision was graphic, majestic, and utterly overpowering. To see the glorified Christ among the seven golden lampstands, the Lord with whom he had fellowshiped so closely for some three and one-half years during His ministry, must have overwhelmed the apostle. Believers in every period have been encouraged and inspired for service by a fresh vision of their Lord.

23 In your notebook give a brief description of Jesus as John saw Him in a vision and of the command Jesus gave John.

Explain the term paradise *and discuss its location.*

Death and Hades

Revelation 1:17–18

John's response to this marvelous vision is predictable. Daniel the prophet had responded in much the same way a few centuries earlier when he saw a similar vision (Daniel 10:4–12). Jesus placed His hand on John and said, "Do not be afraid" (Revelation 1:17). The touch of Jesus removes fear and brings assurance. We pray that as each one studies this course, the reality of Jesus' authority will so grip his life that he will know that the Christian has nothing to fear. Notice what Jesus told John in Revelation 1:18: "I am the Living One; I was dead, and behold I am alive for ever and ever! And I hold the keys of death and Hades." Since the word "keys" indicates authority, its usage here indicates Jesus' power over death.

When Old Testament people died, their spirits apparently went down into the earth, to *sheol* (a Hebrew word). The Greek equivalent in the New Testament is *Hades.* Jesus described what the Old Testament Hades was like in Luke 16:19–31. This passage indicates that Hades was divided into two parts. One part was a place of torment; the other part was called paradise, a place of comfort. Luke 23:42–43 and Matthew 12:39–40 suggest that Hades was *down in the earth* at this point. However, in 2 Corinthians 12:1–6 the apostle indicates that paradise is now located *above.* In Matthew 16:18, Jesus indicates His authority over Hades. Thus, Hades, that is, hell, cannot overcome the person who is in Christ.

Jesus Christ has authority over death and Hades (hell). When the Christian departs from this life, he does not go to Hades as godly people did who died in Old Testament times. What formerly was the paradise side of Hades is now empty. Second Corinthians 5:6–10 (especially v. 8) and Philippians 1:18–26 state that when the Christian dies, he goes immediately to be with the Lord. We will discuss what happens to those in the torment side of Hades later in the course.

24 On the basis of Scripture cited in this section, explain in your notebook the term *paradise* and discuss its location in Old Testament times and its location now.

Describe the symbolic meaning of the stars and lampstands in Revelation 1.

The Stars and Lampstands

Revelation 1:19–20

In this last section on the lesson, we will focus our attention on the last two verses of Revelation 1. We have already used the content of verse 19 as main points in an outline of the book of Revelation. Verse 20 identifies the seven stars and seven lampstands for us in a very clear and direct manner. The seven stars symbolize angels of the seven churches mentioned in Revelation 1:11. The seven lampstands symbolize the seven churches.

What is the significance of the lampstands and the Son of Man in their midst? It is clear that the function of a lampstand is to shine forth or enlighten. Clearly, the meaning is that the church has an obligation to radiate the light of the gospel to the world. Moreover, the angels here are messengers of the seven churches, and they are in the right hand of the Lord of the church. Those in charge of the church are thus seen to occupy a special place in the concern of the Lord.

25 The stars and lampstands of Revelation 1:20 symbolize
- a) the glory and power of God.
- b) seven churches and their angels or messengers.
- c) the beauty and purity of the church.

26 In your notebook give the symbolic meaning of the lampstands and stars that are pictured in verses 12, 13, and 16.

God help us always to remember our part in carrying out the purpose of the church. May we also remember that the kingdom, the power, and the glory belong forever to Jesus!

Self-Test

Multiple choice: Select t*he* best answer.

1 The primary purpose of the proclamation of truth in Revelation is to
a) remind angels of this truth.
b) challenge demons with this truth.
c) explain this truth to ungodly persons.
d) reveal this truth to servants of God.

2 Which one of the following words is NOT an English-word translation of the Greek phrase *en tachei?*
a) Soon
b) See
c) Quickly
d) Suddenly
e) Imminent

3 The two kinds of messengers that the word *angels* refers to in the Bible are
a) spiritual messengers and carnal messengers.
b) dependable messengers and undependable messengers.
c) human messengers and heavenly messengers.
d) official messengers and unofficial messengers.

4 The seven spirits mentioned in Revelation 1:4 symbolize the
a) completeness of the Holy Spirit's ministry.
b) complexity of the Holy Spirit's ministry.
c) simplicity of the Holy Spirit's ministry.
d) power of the Holy Spirit's ministry.

5 The golden lampstands are appropriate symbols of the church because
a) they speak of the usefulness of human institutions.
b) of their costliness and function as furniture.
c) their purpose is to enlighten or reveal.
d) they indicate the need for ornateness and costliness in church furnishings.

6 Jesus' presence among the lampstands implies that the purpose of the church is to reveal Him to
a) divine angels.
b) the Holy Spirit.
c) Satan.
d) people.

True-False. Write **T** in the blank space preceding each TRUE statement. Write **F** if the statement is FALSE.

. . . . **7** "Blessed are the dead who die in the Lord" is a quotation of part of one of the seven beatitudes of the book of Revelation.

. . . . **8** The threefold description of Jesus in Revelation 1:5 describes Him as the Ruler of the kings of heaven.

. . . . **9** The fact that God the Father created all things through Jesus Christ is a reason for calling Jesus the Alpha.

. . . . **10** This lesson has pointed out that the phrase "the Lord's Day" in Revelation 1:10 refers to the Great Tribulation.

. . . . **11** The angels or messengers of the seven churches are clearly identified as lay leaders over these churches.

. . . . **12** We find indication in Scripture that in Old Testament times paradise was down in the earth.

Answers to study questions

14 Wisdom, understanding, counsel, power, knowledge, fear, delight

1 God

15 The completeness of that ministry

2 To reveal this truth to servants of God

16 To receive power and to be witnesses for Christ

3 d) they do not have the necessary God-given wisdom.

17 a) indicate the way in which Jesus originally came into being.

4 What must soon take place

18 b) We have become citizens of His kingdom and priests to serve God.

5 "Soon," "quickly," "suddenly," and "imminent"

19 1) The Faithful Witness, 2) the Firstborn From the Dead, and 3) the Ruler of the Kings of the Earth

6 By indicating that Jesus Christ was revealed to John by an angel

20 You should have circled a), c), and d).

7 Human messengers and heavenly messengers

21 Jesus is called the Alpha and the Omega because these first and last letters of the Greek alphabet designate Him as the One through whom God the Father created all things and as the One through whom God the Father will bring an end to time. (You may have correctly presented additional things in your answer.)

8 b) communicated truths through the use of signs and symbols.

22 This phrase refers to the first day of the week, Sunday. John was in the Spirit on this day.

9 b) word of God and the testimony of Jesus Christ.

23 John saw Jesus in His glory: radiant, awesome, and majestic. The dignity, purity, power and compassion of the Son of Man were overwhelming. The message John received was to record what he saw on a scroll and to send it to the seven churches.

10 Because it points out and describes a specific blessing upon people.

24 Paradise refers to a place of comfort reserved for the saints in Old Testament times. It was located in the earth then, but now it is located up from the earth.

11 These quotations are from the NIV: (1) "Blessed is the one who reads . . . this prophecy . . . because the time is near" (1:3). (2) "Blessed are the dead who die in the Lord . . . they will rest" (14:13). (3) "Blessed is he who stays awake and keeps his clothes . . . so that he may not go naked" (16:15). (4) "Blessed are those who are invited to the wedding supper of the Lamb!" (19:9). (5) "Blessed . . . are those . . . in the first resurrection. The second death has no power over them" (20:6). (6) "Blessed is he who keeps the words of the prophecy in this book" (22:7). (7) "Blessed are those who wash their robes, that they may have the right to the tree of life" (22:14). (Practice writing these beatitudes from memory until you can do it easily.)

25 b) seven churches and their angels or messengers.

12 Because God's grace in his life is foundational to his having real peace.

26 The purpose of a lampstand is to enlighten, to show forth. The purpose of the church is to shine forth, to reveal Jesus Christ to people. These foregoing verses imply this purpose by presenting Jesus among the lampstands (that is the churches). His presence is among them and He holds the angels or messengers in His right hand.

13 c) ones who read, hear, and apply the message of this prophecy.

Letters to Ephesus, Smyrna, and Pergamum

We have completed our study of the first point of the outline given in Revelation 1. This point concerned "what John saw" in Revelation 1: the glorified Lord in the midst of the lampstands. This portrait revealed several significant facts: (1) the role of the church is to shine forth, (2) the Lord is near the church, and (3) the messengers of the churches are in the Lord's hand. The Lord's majestic presence had a singular effect on the prophetic writer, and a similar vision of the Lord will change each of us. Now we move to the second point of the outline: "What is now."

In the next two lessons the focus shifts to the seven churches. The Lord of the church addresses each of them in turn. In Revelation 2 and 3 He speaks specifically to conditions that exist in each. Nothing escapes His attention, for the all-knowing One walks in their midst. He points to elements worthy of praise and offers commendation; He sees aspects unworthy of His church which He sternly denounces. In these seven churches we see qualities that have characterized the church throughout history.

Jesus stands in these two chapters as the Judge of the church. His opinion matters much more than the opinions of others. What does He think of us as He looks into our hearts and observes our activities? Let us allow the words of Jesus to speak to our hearts and note the things He approves and the things He disapproves. Observe His promises to the overcomer and His warning to the one who does not overcome.

the activities...

- ◇ Study this lesson according to procedures given in Lesson 1.
- ◇ Be sure to look in the glossary for the meanings of any key words you do not know.
- ◇ As an optional, practical exercise, you may conclude the subsection on each of the seven churches by making a sermon outline or a Bible study outline of John's letter to the church studied in that subsection.
- ◇ Take the self-test on this lesson according to procedures given in Lesson 1.

the objectives...

6.1 *State the threefold purpose of the letters to the seven churches.*

6.2 *Recall the categories of things that the seven letters reveal regarding their source and purpose.*

6.3 *Select evidence from various sources presented to support the view that each of the seven churches represents a period of church history.*

6.4 *Identify characteristics of the church in Ephesus, including its historical background and problems.*

6.5 *Recall major features of the letter to the church in Smyrna, including its historical background and spiritual characteristics.*

6.6 *Discuss the leading characteristics of the letter to the church in Pergamum.*

the outline...

1 Threefold Purpose of the Seven Letters
2 The Outline of the Seven Letters
3 Church History Presented in the Seven Letters
  a The Letter to the Church in Ephesus
  b The Letter to the Church in Smyrna
  c The Letter to the Church in Pergamum

State the threefold purpose of the letters to the seven churches.

Threefold Purpose of the Seven Letters

We are given three reasons or a threefold purpose for the seven letters. First, the seven churches addressed were literal churches in the Roman province of Asia. Furthermore, the situations our Lord described were actually occurring in these seven churches, and they needed to be dealt with by the *Head of the church* Himself. Look at the map at the back of this lesson (Figure 6.1) and find the Roman province of Asia. Then find the location of all seven church cities of Revelation 2–3.

Second, these seven letters are messages of encouragement, warning, and rebuke for all members of the body of Christ. This is indicated by the exhortation to all such individuals that is found at or near the end of each of the letters: "He who has an ear, let him hear what the Spirit says to the churches." In these letters the Christian can see certain things to avoid and certain things which please the Lord. We can all examine ourselves in the light of these letters and the fact that Jesus is coming quickly.

Some scholars see the preceding two purposes as the only purposes of these seven letters, but many other scholars see more than two purposes in them. In Revelation 1:20 the word *mystery* is used in connection with the seven churches. This seems to indicate that there is more here than what seems to appear. So, third, we believe that the entire history of the church from its beginning on the Day of Pentecost in Acts 2 through its history to the Day of the Lord is pictured in the letters to the seven churches.

1 According to Revelation 1:20, the term *mystery* indicates
a) the inability of normal people to interpret spiritual truth.
b) that more is in the text than is at first apparent.
c) that special insight is required to interpret the implied symbolism.
d) a crime is about to be committed in the story.

Apparently these seven actual, local churches were not selected because they were more important than other churches in that area at this time. Evidently, they were chosen because certain situations that existed in them would characterize the church at various stages throughout its entire existence.

2 According to our chart of symbols in Lesson 4, the fact that the number of churches to which John wrote was seven indicates
a) political completion.
b) divine fullness.
c) final completion.
d) none of the above.

3 In your notebook write a summary of the threefold purpose of John's letters to seven churches in Revelation 2 and 3.

Recall the categories of things that the seven letters reveal regarding their source and purpose.

Outline of Seven Letters

Each of John's letters to the seven churches in Revelation 2 and 3 contains the following parts, with the exception of things noted in the outline below. Sometimes the order of these parts varies slightly from letter to letter:

I. Greeting to the Angel (leader) of Each Church
II. Characteristics of Jesus, Each Letter's Source
III. What Jesus Knows About Each Church
IV. What Jesus Approves in Each Church (Except Laodicea)
V. What Jesus Disapproves in Each Church (Except Smyrna and Philadelphia)
VI. Special Exhortation and/or Promise to Each Church
VII. Instruction to Each Church to Hear
VIII. Promise to Overcomers in Each Church

4 Study John's letters to the seven churches in Revelation 2 and 3. Then analyze them carefully, following the above basic outline. Write from memory in your notebook the main categories of things that the letters reveal about the source and the subject of the letters.

Select evidence from various sources presented to support the view that each of the seven churches represents a period of church history.

Church History Presented in the Seven Letters

Some Bible prophecy expositors, your writer included, believe that each of the seven letters presents characteristics that relate to a certain period of time in church history. Those who see the entire spectrum of the church age reflected in these seven letters, however, accept somewhat different dates for the various periods. The dates we have given are approximations only and simply represent the broad outline of church history, we believe the things that characterize the last four churches will still exist at the time of the Rapture.

pristine
as it was in its earliest form or state; original; primitive

The church at Ephesus appears to us to represent the *pristine state of the apostolic church from its birth to about the end of the first century. Near the end of the first century, however, a marked change occurred in the cultural circumstances of the church that seems to begin a second period. A hostile world initiated a series of persecutions that lasted for a little over two hundred years. Again, a marked change occurred in the church's outward circumstances and was reflected in its internal life. We associate this with the third period of church history. These types of changes in various periods appear to us to justify associating the characteristics of each church with a respective period of church history.

5 According to our discussion, the messages to the seven churches present characteristics in seven local churches in Asia that seem to correspond to

a) conditions that characterize the church within a certain period, as well as throughout her history.
b) conditions in the first-century church only.
c) specific times and events in history that are clearly defined.
d) the ministry problems facing seven specific apostles.

We will study the letters to the seven churches in this lesson and Lesson 7 based on the respective periods of church history each represents. As an optional, practical exercise to conclude the study of each church, we urge you to use the material in the questions and answers to make an outline for a sermon or Bible study.

Identify characteristics of the church in Ephesus, including its historical background and problems.

The Letter to the Church in Ephesus

Revelation 2:1–7

Artemis
a goddess in Greek mythology, identified by the Romans with Diana, apparently regarded in earliest times as a nature goddess, and especially worshiped by women as presiding over childbirth

Ephesus was the leading city in the province of Asia. It had an ample harbor and it was located in a rich farming area. Moreover this city was exceedingly wealthy. The temple of *Artemis stood in the city. It was one of the seven wonders of the ancient world. Ephesians honored Artemis, the many-breasted goddess of fertility, and they believed this image "fell from heaven" (Acts 19:35). They were proud that their city was called *The Temple Warden of Artemis.* Many priests were dedicated to Artemis, and as many as 3500 priestesses were committed to serve the goddess. We know that idolatry always produces immorality; therefore, it is not surprising that the city was filled with immorality and debauchery, as well as religion, philosophy, and culture.

6 Read the historical background material in Acts 18:18–20:38 about how the gospel was introduced in power at Ephesus. Pay special attention to the persons named, the length of time Paul stayed in Ephesus, and the major events that occurred. Then answer in your notebook the following questions.

a Who introduced the gospel to Ephesus?
b How did the people of Ephesus respond to the gospel?
c How long did the apostle Paul minister in Ephesus?
d Who helped the apostle establish the work at Ephesus?
e What major public response to the preaching of the gospel led to a riot?

Characteristics of Jesus that are implied symbolically in Revelation 2:1 indicate that He is active in the church at Ephesus. He walks in the midst of His people there and He is acquainted with their activity and service. This is an excellent picture of the early church, where the presence of the Lord was seen constantly in power to save souls and perform other miracles. Our Lord still desires to be present in such power in church services today. It is one thing to know He is there; it is another thing to allow Him to manifest Himself in our church services. Our pattern ought to be to fit into His program—not to ask Him to fit into ours. He knows exactly what needs to be done and how to do it. *As we learn to depend on our Lord's guidance, He will continue to build His church through us* (see Matthew 16:18).

7 In Revelation 1:20, reread the definitions of the stars and lampstands. In your notebook explain the meaning of the two characteristics of Jesus that are mentioned symbolically in Revelation 2:1.

In each of John's letters to seven churches in Revelation 2 and 3, Jesus states something He knows about the church. In five of them he states, "I know your deeds." *He knows our activities also, and the motives behind them.*

In Revelation 2:2 and 6, Jesus approves five things in the church at Ephesus. The statement "I know your deeds" indicates that the Ephesian church was an active church. While *good deeds* do not save a person, they are an indication of his spiritual vitality. We do well to remember that one is not saved by faith *and* works, but by faith *that* works. *Hard work*, which is singled out as a commendable virtue, sometimes means work to the point of exhaustion. *Perseverance*, another of this church's virtues, means determination to keep on going in spite of opposition.

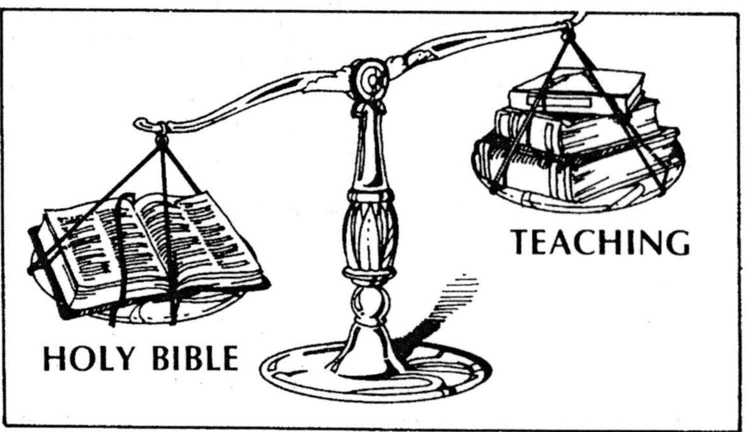

orthodox
having generally accepted views or opinions, especially in religion

The Ephesian believers were a perceptive group of people. They held a standard of uprightness, and they were careful to weigh every teaching against the Bible standard. They were an *orthodox group and would not tolerate false teaching. It is possible, though, that orthodoxy had become their highest priority;

consequently, their love had grown cold (v. 4). Their need was not to become less discerning and less committed to sound doctrine. Rather, they needed to demonstrate love in all their relationships—even with those whose teachings were contrary to the Word of God. God does not love what the sinner does, but He loves the sinner. We too must love those who do not know Jesus Christ, and we must do our best to reach them with the message of the gospel. Meanwhile, Christians are to test those who claim to be sent from God. The Word of God is the standard for such testing. We may be sure that a person sent from God does not have a message contrary to the Word of God (2 Corinthians 4:5; 10:17–11:4; Galatians l:6–10; 1 John 2:18–27). The Ephesian believers were correct to measure ones doctrine by a scriptural standard, but they were not to abandon their love in the process.

Nicolaitans
may have been those who supported the idea of elevating the clergy above the laity; may have been people in the first century AD who claimed one could be a Christian and practice all kinds of immorality

Ephesian believers were also commended for their attitude toward the *Nicolaitans, whose deeds they detested. There are two interpretations of the meaning of *Nicolaitans*. First, the word comes from two Greek words which mean "people conquerors." These words may represent the beginning of the idea that priests and ministers are to be elevated to a special place above other Christians. We might say that this represented the beginning of the institutional church ministry with a separate clergy and laity. There certainly is an authority connected with the ministry, but this authority is described in 1 Peter 5:1–4 as one connected with humility and service. Second, there is some indication that the name *Nicolaitans* referred to a group of people who claimed one could be a Christian and practice all kinds of immorality. Ignatius, a disciple of the apostle John, referred to these people as "impure Nicolaitans . . . who are lovers of pleasure . . . corrupters of their own flesh." We do not know precisely what their doctrines were, but we know that the Lord hated their practices and commended this church for its stand against them.

8 State briefly five things Jesus approved in the church at Ephesus.

....

....

While most of the letter *commends* this church, verses 4 and 5 give our Lord's *condemnation* of one feature of the church's life and practice. He warns believers regarding the loss of their *first love* and He tells them what will happen if they disregard His warning. Love here is translated from the Greek word *agape*. It is defined for us in John 3:16 and 1 Corinthians 13:1–8. *Agape* is the total giving of one's self, holding nothing back from God. The Ephesian church had forsaken this vital ingredient of that relationship. Believers' love for God had not remained fresh and alive; therefore, the Lord of the church issues a sinister, simple warning: "repent!" *Repent* simply means to change your mind and as a consequence, your direction. If the relationship is to remain intact, we must purpose to live as close to Jesus as we once did. Our relationship demands that fervent love.

9 In your notebook state a condition in the church at Ephesus of which our Lord disapproved, the warning He gave as a result, and what would happen if the church ignored His warning.

10 In your notebook list some of the things which cause one's love for the Lord Jesus to grow cold and some things that can help it to stay fresh. If you are married or are planning to be married, list some things which could cause your love for your spouse to grow cold. Also, list some things that can help it.

overcomer
one who surmounts or prevails over obstacles or enemies

In Revelation 2:7 the *overcomer is promised a blessed place in the paradise of God. Who are *overcomers*? To some people overcomers are those Christians who have reached an advanced degree of maturity in Christ. To others, *overcomers* represent those who live very narrow lives—those whose lives are characterized by "do's" and "do nots." The Bible, however, is its own best interpreter. The word *overcome* means "to win the victory over" (1 John 5:5 and Revelation 15:2). It refers to those who overcome external pressure and temptation as well as internal thoughts, motives, and attitudes that are inconsistent with the Lordship of Christ in their lives.

The characteristics of the church at Ephesus—zeal for the right doctrine, diligent service, and vigorous action—indicate the early church period. These characteristics were generally true of the church from its beginning until the latter part of the first century.

11 Circle the letter preceding each TRUE completion. The church in Ephesus is characterized

a as part of a rich port city in a wealthy farming area that was noted for its idol worship.
b by its initial spiritual fervor and the work of the one who established the gospel there.
c by its lukewarmness, weariness in service, and compromise with evil doers.
d as a body which totally opposed the wicked Nicolaitans.
e by its doctrinal orthodoxy and its ability to perceive false teaching.
f by the fact that it had never forsaken its first love.

As an optional, practical exercise, review the questions and answers in this section on Ephesus and use this material to make a sermon outline or Bible study outline of John's letter to the church in Ephesus.

Recall major features of the letter to the church in Smyrna, including its historical background and spiritual characteristics.

The Letter to the Church in Smyrna

Revelation 2:8–11

Smyrna was described in its day as the "most beautiful city in the world." Smyrna was located on a bay of the Aegean Sea and it was called the "crown of Ionia, the ornament of Asia." The city was rich in architecture and culture. *Smyrna* comes from the word used for the spice *myrrh*, which was used to embalm the dead. You may recall that the wise men brought myrrh to Jesus at His birth, perhaps as a prophecy of His death for all mankind.

This period is associated with the persecution in the Roman Empire that became widespread and, at times, intense from the end of the first century until about AD 313. John is writing to a suffering church. What does one write to such an audience? Normally, one seeks to encourage those undergoing such severe tests to persist in their faith and to take courage by looking at heroic models—others who have overcome. Thus, in verses 8 and 9 several facts are given to inspire confidence. First, our Lord knows where His people are, what they are undergoing, and their limits of endurance. He urges them to labor on in faithfulness. Second, the One who encourages sufferers has Himself faced the ultimate test and overcame. In Him, every believer is a potential victor.

12 What two characteristics of Jesus are revealed to the church in Smyrna in Revelation 2:8?

....

....

Not only are the people of this church afflicted, they are also poor. However, their Lord says that their poverty is only apparent; actually, they are rich. The best and enduring riches are not material; they are spiritual. In this sense, then, the believers in Smyrna were rich. Christians in general have undergone persecution throughout the church's history. The apostle Paul indicated that the common lot of true Christian discipleship involves hardship (Acts 14:22). Indeed, hardship aptly describes his own experience (2 Corinthians 6:4–10, 11:22–33), but it did not lessen his desire to persist in his faith and be a true overcomer (Romans 8:18).

13 Considering our comment in the previous paragraph, the first sentence of Revelation 2:9 clearly implies what about the suffering of the church at Smyrna? Use your notebook for this response.

Messiah
Jesus, the expected King and Deliverer of the Jews and Savior for all mankind

Believers in the church of Smyrna are said to be suffering slander from certain false Jews (v. 9). These so-called Jews may have been Jews by virtue of their race and religion, but they were not truly Jews, for they rejected Jesus as their *Messiah and persecuted His church. It is also possible that these false Jews were Judaizers who demanded that all Christians keep Old Testament rules (such as circumcision, feast days, and not eating certain foods). Whoever they were, they were not God's people. Actually, they are identified as Satan's, and they slandered the people of God in Smyrna.

14 Supposed members of the religious community in Smyrna were guilty of doing what to true believers?

a) They slandered them.
b) They imprisoned these faithful ones.
c) They persecuted them.
d) On occasion they killed these believers.

The church now receives two special exhortations and a general notion of what the immediate future holds (v. 10). First, the Lord of the church says in effect, "Fear not! Conflict is coming, and the devil will test you to the limit. Prison and persecution are coming. Be ready to defend the faith—even to death!" Second, the Conqueror—our Conqueror—exhorts: "Be faithful!" Then follows the blessed promise "I will give you a crown of life."

A clear look at the approaching storm reveals that the testing and persecution is apparently limited to a specific period of time: ten days. Some scholars believe that the number *ten* in Revelation 2:10 referred to an extended, although impermanent, condition of persecution. Other scholars feel that this ten-day persecution "indicated a full and complete period, either long or short, which will eventually end." Still other scholars believe this ten-day persecution represented ten distinct periods of persecution which the church suffered under imperial Rome from the end of the first century until the year AD 313. Whatever the ten-day persecution means, we know it pointed to an *impending test, and those who successfully overcame would receive "the crown of life." Of course, the ultimate reward for faithful believers is the crown of life—eternal life in His presence.

impending
about to happen or take place

15 Read each of the following Scriptures. Beside each, state the type of crown mentioned, and from the context, indicate for what reason each is given.

a 1 Corinthians 9:25..

b 1 Thessalonians 2:19..

c 2 Timothy 4:8..

d James 1:12..

e 1 Peter 5:4..

16 Circle the letters preceding statements that reflect accurate facts we have studied relating to the church at Smyrna.

a Smyrna was an inland agricultural community which suffered extreme poverty.
b The name of the city is related to the spice called myrrh.
c The Lord of the church addressed the saints of Smyrna in His role as Eternal One—the First and the Last.
d Smyrna's believers were slandered by those who may have been racial and religious Jews but who denied the Messiah and rejected His people.
e The Lord promised to keep believers from all trials because trials indicate one is out of God's will.
f Persecution is both allowed and foretold by the Lord, but the indication is that the trial will not be unending.

The mention of "persecution for ten days" in John's letter to the church at Smyrna could represent the time of ten major persecutions of Christians by the Roman Empire from the latter part of the first century until AD 313. It was certainly a period marked by intolerance of Christianity, and it did end with the *Edict of Milan* which brought peace to the whole of Rome's imperial domain. Moreover, it introduced a new period that was marked by extremely different conditions. Whereas the suffering church in the second period fought for its life, the next period was set apart by extreme toleration in which the church gradually blended in with the secular world of which it was a part. Thus, it lost its distinctive purity and vision in the process, as we shall see in our next section of study.

As an optional, practical exercise, review the questions and answers in this section on Smyrna and use the material to make a sermon outline or Bible study outline of John's letter to the church in Smyrna.

Discuss the leading characteristics of the letter to the church in Pergamum.

The Letter to the Church in Pergamum

Revelation 2:12–17

The city of Pergamum, although not as important commercially as Ephesus and Smyrna, was more important as a political and religious center. On its acropolis, Pergamum had dedicated a high altar to Zeus and a temple to Athena. Pergamum was also the first city of Asia to support the imperial cult. Here citizens were required to worship the emperor; to refuse was to invite the charge of treason. Some scholars associate the phrase "where Satan has his throne" (v. 13) with the prominence of Pergamum as the center of the imperial cult. There was a large medical center in Pergamum named after the serpent god Asclepius, and the city was well-known for her college of medical priests. These things help us to see why Pergamum was called the place "where Satan has his throne . . . where Satan lives" (v. 13). Pergamum had a large library containing 200,000 volumes. Like other cities, this city was a place of pagan religion, immorality, philosophy, and education.

In our approach to the interpretation of Revelation 2 and 3, we have emphasized that each church corresponds to a period of church history. This third period, in our view, includes the period from AD 313 until about AD 600. After a sustained period of religious intolerance, the Roman Empire reversed its stand and finally accepted Christianity. Under persecution, the church thrived and spread rapidly, but under the smile of official acceptance the faith lost its vitality and vision. Under the patronage of the Emperor Constantine, Christianity was popularized. Superficial religion was substituted for reality, and ceremony replaced personal experience with God. Large numbers of pagans were baptized without ever having a personal relationship with Christ. The first love that had been forsaken temporarily in the first period now began to suffer a radical decline in its life and witness for Christ.

The Lord who addresses this church is characterized as having a sharp, double-edged sword (v. 12). The sword here is a symbol of the Word of God that is used to denounce false teachings that the church permitted. The Word of God is still the standard by which church teachings are to be measured. Those teachings which do not measure up to this standard are to be rejected.

17 Circle the letter preceding each TRUE statement.

- **a** Pergamum was the political and religious center of Asia Minor.
- **b** The Roman imperial cult flourished in Pergamum, and it made emperor worship a test of loyalty.
- **c** Since Pergamum was a center of superstition, learning and culture were relatively unimportant here.
- **d** During this period, the church grew rapidly both in numbers and in spiritual maturity.

18 What does the characteristic of Jesus pointed out in verse 12 symbolize?

....

....

In verse 13 we observe things of which our Lord approves. First, the church at Pergamum was true to our Lord's name. His name stands for everything He is. To be true to His name means to recognize that Jesus is the Son of God, that we must worship God only, and that we must approach God through Him (John 14:6 and 1 Timothy 2:5). The reference to Antipas implies our Lord's special approval of the faith in Him that characterized the people in this church in a time of great trial. *Do not forget that our Lord always approves when we keep our faith in Him especially when our faith is greatly tried.*

19 Of what things mentioned in verse 13 does our Lord approve in the church at Pergamum?

....

....

Having commended the church for qualities worthy of praise, the Lord of the church now pointed to two items that He strongly condemns (vv. 14–15). This first thing He condemns is idolatry and sexual immorality. There is another possibility here. Balaam, who is mentioned in this context, promoted compromise with idolatry and immorality in Old Testament times. He is undoubtedly the forerunner of all who promote compromise with the world. Verse 14 clearly implies that when one eats knowingly "food sacrificed to idols," he is guilty of an act of idolatry. Such eating indicates support for the belief that those idols supply one's spiritual as well as physical needs.

During the Pergamum period, images of saints were placed in increasing numbers of churches. These images were said to be in the churches to remind people to worship God, but there always has been a danger that the presence of such images will cause people to worship them or the saints they represent rather than God. Nothing must ever detract from Him as the object of our worship. The second thing Jesus condemns is holding "to the teaching of the Nicolaitans" (v. 15). Both physical appetite and spiritual discernment appear to be undisciplined in this church which exists in a time of spiritual laxity.

In verse 16, Jesus warns people in Pergamum to repent of these things that He has condemned. If they do not repent, He will fight against them with the sword of His mouth—the Word of God. *Jesus still gives this entire warning to us today when we do things of which He disapproves.* How dreadful it would be to have the Savior of the church become its Destroyer. The key to restored spiritual balance is genuine repentance.

20 In your notebook list two major things in the church at Pergamum (vv. 14–15) that Jesus condemned.

In verse 17, overcomers in the church at Pergamum are promised certain rewards: hidden manna and a white stone. The hidden manna is the spiritual food one now receives as He partakes of Christ. The white stone is thought to represent acquittal in contrast to a black stone, which would indicate condemnation that one on trial received as the verdict of the judicial tribunal. The overcomer is justified by faith in Christ in a manner that makes him entirely free of guilt from sin. He stands justified by faith in Christ and is acquitted of his sins before the throne of God.

21 What two things does our Lord promise to overcomers in the church at Pergamum?

....

....

The characteristics of the church at Pergamum seem to represent the church in the period from AD 313 to about AD 600. We emphasize again that this is a rough approximation of the time frame each church period occupies.

As an optional, practical exercise for your personal use, review the questions and answers in this subsection on Pergamum and use the material to make a sermon outline or Bible study outline of John's letter to the church in Pergamum.

Self-Test

Multiple choice: Circle the letter preceding the best answer..

1 All of the following but one represent the threefold purpose of the letters to the seven churches. Which one is NOT a stated purpose?
- a) The situation described existed in the churches and needed to be dealt with by the Head of the church.
- b) The content is intended for all members of the body of Christ.
- c) The situations described in the letters are hypothetical incidents and do not relate to actual conditions in the church of Jesus Christ.
- d) The entire history of the church from its beginning to the Day of the Lord is pictured in the letters.

2 Of the letters to the seven churches we can say most accurately that
- a) they are all generally the same in structure, having slight variations from letter to letter.
- b) each letter is unique in structure, content, and style.
- c) they follow the same identical pattern from beginning to end.
- d) there is an evolution in the letters which reflects the passage of time and the maturity of the church.

3 The notable exception to the spiritual performance of the church at Ephesus concerned
- a) its tolerance of wicked people.
- b) the forsaking of its first love.
- c) her lack of spiritual discernment.
- d) the inability of the people to withstand hardship for Christ's name.

4 From our study of the Nicolaitans we learn that this group may have emphasized
- a) Christian liberty more than Christian responsibility.
- b) the compromise of Christian values in order to gain the world's favor.
- c) that the legal requirements of the Old Testament were binding on all Christians.
- d) elevation of the clergy above the laity in the church.

5 The church at Smyrna was informed that the Lord knew of and permitted what in order to develop Christian character?
- a) Poverty
- b) Sickness
- c) Slander
- d) Afflictions

6 While the "ten days of persecution" are interpreted variously by different Bible scholars, generally this time element indicates that
- a) a short period of time is meant.
- b) an indefinite time is indicated.
- c) a period of time, short or long may be meant, but it will come to an end.
- d) the church will suffer limited persecution.

7 The symbolism of our Lord with a sharp, double-edged sword refers to the
- a) Word of God.
- b) offensive armor of the believer.
- c) instrument by which He will judge the wicked.
- d) vengeance He takes on enemies of the church.

8 According to our study, the teaching of Balaamism which the church at Pergamum tolerated may well have involved the
a) compromise of the Christian standard regarding sin and holiness.
b) introduction of teaching on ways to make the church prosperous.
c) move by leaders to make Christianity acceptable to the world.
d) reappearance of Judaizers in the church.

9 Of the three churches we have discussed in this lesson which one was situated in the city where the temple of Artemis was located?
a) Smyrna
b) Pergamum
c) Ephesus
d) Alexandria

10 Which church existed in a city where a medical center was dedicated to the serpent god?
a) Ephesus
b) Pergamum
c) Smyrna
d) Appolonia

Map Containing the Roman Province of Asia

Figure 6.1

Answers to Study Questions

11 **a** True
b True
c False
d True
e True
f False

1 b) that more is in the text than is at first apparent.

12 Jesus is eternal, the First and the Last, and He is resurrected from temporal death to eternal life

2 b) divine fullness.

13 It appears that our Lord approves of affliction. He uses affliction as a means of developing strong Christian character, patience, and trust in Him. The writer to the Hebrews comments briefly on this (Hebrews 12:1–11).

3 Your answer should include the following facts. John wrote to give Jesus' message of encouragement, warning, and rebuke to seven actual, local churches, all members of the body of Christ, and the entire church from its beginning throughout its existence.

14 a) They slandered them.

4 (1) Things that Jesus is, (2) things that Jesus knows about particular churches, (3) things that Jesus approves in particular churches, (4) things that Jesus disapproves in particular churches, (5) things such as exhortations, promises, and instruction that Jesus communicates to particular churches.

15 **a** Incorruptible or imperishable crown. Given for faithful service in winning the lost.
b Crown of glory or in which we glory. Given for faithful ministry.
c Crown of righteousness. Given to those who love His appearing for faithful service.
d Crown of life. Given for faithful service under trial to those who love their Lord.
e Crown of glory. Given for faithful leadership to those who oversee God's flock.

5 a) conditions that characterize the church within a certain period, as well as throughout her history.

16 You should have circled **b**, **c**, **d**, and **f**.

6 **a** Paul introduced this gospel there (Acts 19:1–5).
b Many people believed it there (Acts 19:17–18).
c The apostle ministered there for three years (Acts 20:31).
d Priscilla and Aquila helped establish the church (Acts 18:18–28).
e Many people burned their sorcery scrolls publicly. This represented a great victory for the gospel, but it angered those who made their living by making and selling idols. The reaction of the craftsmen to the gospel produced a major riot in Ephesus (Acts 19:23–41).

17 You should have circled **a** and **b**.

7 First, His presence among the churches indicates His concern for them, care of them, and commitment to their spiritual welfare. Second, the fact that the leaders of the churches are in His hand indicates that He guides the church through them and that they are important to Him.

18 That Jesus is the possessor and user of the Word of God. Here it seems to indicate that the purpose is to correct false doctrine.

8 Hard work, perseverance, intolerance of wickedness, testing of false claims, and hatred of Nicolaitans' practices

19 He approves of believers' faithfulness to His name. He also approves of their steadfastness in a time of great trial.

9 The condition was the forsaking of first love. This warning was to do what they formerly did. The result for ignoring His warning was isolation from God.

20 He condemned: (1) the teaching of Balaam regarding idolatry and sexual immorality and (2) the teaching of the Nicolaitans.

10 Your answer. One thing is common to all relationships: maintaining them. One sure way to kill a relationship is to neglect it. Our relationship with the Lord must be our highest priority and that with our spouse should follow it closely.

21 He promises "hidden manna" and a "white stone." These indicate spiritual nourishment and the believer's acceptance before God's throne.

Letters to Thyatira, Sardis, Philadelphia, and Laodicea

In Lesson 6 we began our study of the letters to the seven churches. We examined the purposes for these letters and their structure as well. Then we moved to the specific study of each church of the first three church periods. Hopefully, this introduction has given us some helpful insights into the kinds of problems each church faced and how it responded to the challenges of its time. Now we continue with our study of the remaining four churches.

As we continue to consider both positive and negative traits in these churches, remember that the distinctive characteristics of the respective churches did not end with that period. The Ephesian problem of forsaking her first love is a potential problem for every church and believer of the church age. Worldliness and compromise that Pergamum struggled with are still major problems in the church. The names of the specific problems—Balaamism, Nicolaitanism, Jezebelism—may change, but the underlying spiritual problems remain. These principles that underlie our Christian experience must be understood and addressed if we are to fulfill our calling and complete God's work on earth.

As you study this lesson, stay open to the voice of the Spirit. Permit Him to help you recognize potential problems in your experience that could limit your effectiveness as a believer. As you do, He will open your eyes to behold greater challenges in the world around you, to which you can respond in His power.

the activities...

◇ Study the lesson according to the usual procedures.

◇ You may use your Bible to answer study questions and the questions in the self-test.

◇ Review the lessons in this unit in preparation for your unit progress evaluation (UPE). Read the instruction page in your Student Packet, then turn to Unit Progress Evaluation 2. When you have completed the UPE, check your answers with the answer key provided in your Student Packet. Review any items you may have answered incorrectly. (Although UPE scores do not count as part of your final course grade, they indicate how well you learned the material and how well you may perform on the final examination.)

the objectives...

7.1 *Choose from various statements those that characterize correctly the church in Thyatira.*

7.2 *Identify facts concerning major elements of the letter to the church in Sardis.*

7.3 Recognize important features of the letter to the church in Philadelphia.

7.4 Identify significant features of the letter to the church in Laodicea

the outline...

1 Introduction

2 The Letter to the Church at Thyatira

3 The Letter to the Church at Sardis

4 The Letter to the Church at Philadelphia

5 The Letter to the Church at Laodicea

Introduction

As we saw in Lesson 6, the general structure of the letters to the seven churches is the same. Differences occur in the characteristics of the Lord which are revealed to each church. Of course, things commended, condemned, or both, differ from church to church. However, the underlying message to the church universal is that the Lord has called the church to be His witness in the world. This witness is to be carried on both by active proclamation and consistent Christian living—the things that give real substance to the message. Observe carefully the status of each church from His perspective as we consider the details of His message to each one.

Choose from various statements those that characterize correctly the church in Thyatira.

The Letter to the Church in Thyatira

Revelation 2:18–29

Thyatira was an inland city which had a long military history. Thyatira was located in a rich agricultural area, and it was important as an industrial center. This city was famous for purple dye, and it was supported by a purple cloth industry that was manufactured under the control of well-organized trade guilds. Thyatira was not a religious or political center and it was not a strong supporter of emperor worship. You may recall that "Lydia, a dealer in purple cloth from the city of Thyatira" (Acts 16:14) was converted under Paul's ministry in Philippi.

1 In your notebook describe briefly the setting of the city of Thyatira and historical, geographic, and economic facts that concern the city.

Verse 18 gives three further characteristics of our Lord. First, this is the only place in the book of Revelation where Jesus is called the Son of God. It is our privilege to worship Him because of who He is. Second, His eyes that are like blazing fire see beyond our outward appearance into our hearts. They can also flash with anger at flagrant sin. Third, His feet of brass will trample upon all His enemies.

2 What three characteristics of Jesus are pointed out in verse 18?

....

....

Our Lord singles out four things of which He approves in the church at Thyatira. *Remember that He also approves these same things when He finds them in us.* In the original text, Jesus specifically mentions *deeds* twice: at the beginning and at the end of the verse. Although this is an area of approval, the implication may be that the church is depending too much on works. As we noted earlier, we are not saved by works; we could never merit salvation. Furthermore, works are no substitute for love of the Lord and faithfulness to His purpose.

3 State the four things indicated in verse 19 that Jesus approves in the church at Thyatira.

....

As you read Revelation 2:20, you may recall that the major things which Jesus condemned in the church at Pergamum are again disapproved in the church at Thyatira. We learn that the foreign woman Jezebel was outstanding in the promotion of idolatry in Israel from the fact that Ahab, Israel's king, began to serve and worship Baal when he married her (1 Kings 16:29–34). Beginning about AD 600, the church began to use images, worship Mary and saints, and consider that *extra-biblical literature was as authoritative as the Bible. This church thus began to demonstrate characteristics of tolerance for much that was neither biblical nor helpful to the spiritual life of believers. These characteristics will exist throughout the Church Age and on into the Great Tribulation.

The church in this period went into a period of deep spiritual decline. It attempted to join the Christian faith with pagan philosophy and heathen religious practices. The prominence of the risen Christ, which had so characterized the apostolic church, gave way to the prominence of the mother of Jesus. She tended to be held on a level with God, and her role as man's mediator with God became prominent in the teaching of the *medieval church. The *icons, relics, and doctrines of men which crept into the church were symptoms of spiritual idolatry. The church no longer resembled the joyful force of believers that had all things in common at Pentecost (Acts 2:44).

A closer look at the specific problem of the church at Thyatira, however, reveals that the church tolerated a false prophetess, of whom Jezebel was a *prototype. The early church was indeed accustomed to inspired teaching through prophetic utterance, and the office of *prophet* was given due honor (1 Corinthians 12, 14, and Ephesians 4:11). In fact, before the New Testament appeared, apostles and prophets mediated the revelation of divine truth (Ephesians 3:5). However, strict rules were given to regulate spiritual gifts, and the church was urged to test the spirit behind prophetic utterance (1 John 4:1–3). Thyatira, however, had a false prophetess whom church members recognized, but they refused to take action against her (see verses 20-27). Though she was a threat to the spiritual vitality of the body through openly advocating sexual immorality and idolatry, she was allowed to coexist in the church with true believers. Jesus saw her as an infectious disease, threatening the life of the entire church. This condition called for radical means.

Paul's warning, "a little yeast works through the whole batch of dough," (Galatians 5:9) is truly to the point here. Having been warned—a warning she ignored—and being unwilling to change, Jesus says, He will judge her forthwith (vv. 22–23). Those who have become her children, accepted her wicked doctrines, will be killed. Then, when believers of other churches see her judgment, they will know it is divine *retribution—that God will not tolerate a low view of sin.

extra-biblical
non-biblical material; that which goes beyond scriptural authority

medieval
of, having to do with, or belonging to the Middle Ages (the years from about AD 500 to about AD 1450)

icons
pictures or images of Christ, an angel, or a saint, usually painted on wood or ivory, and venerated as sacred

prototype
the first or primary type of anything

retribution
a deserved punishment; return for evil done

4 State the two major things that Jesus had disapproved in the church at Pergamum and disapproves again (v. 20) in the church at Thyatira.

....

5 In verses 24–25 Jesus addresses a group which is not involved with Jezebel's doctrines and gives them a special exhortation. That special exhortation is to

a) try to convert Jezebel and her followers.
b) denounce the doctrines and practices of Jezebel
c) hold on to what they have.
d) pray for strength to resist Jezebel's teachings.

Those of Thyatira's believers who were unaffected by false teaching are encouraged to persevere—to hold on firmly to their faith (vv. 24, 25). Those who persist until the end—victorious Christians—are promised a share in Christ's rule over the nations (v. 26). They are also promised "the morning star" (v. 28), which may refer to the promise of glory that awaits the victor (see Daniel 12:3) or to a place of prominence in glory (Job 38:7).

6 Circle the letters preceding TRUE statements that characterize facts about the church in Thyatira.

a Thyatira was known primarily as a political and religious center.
b The industry of Thyatira was based on its purple dye and purple cloth trade.
c Believers in Thyatira were known for their deeds of love, faith, services, and perseverance.
d The spiritual problems of Thyatira against which our Lord spoke chiefly was its tolerance of wickedness.
e Jezebel's problem in the church arose from the fact that she was a prophetess, and women did not have biblical warrant to prophesy.
f The sins of sexual immorality and idolatry of which our Lord warned Thyatira's church were unknown in other churches.
g In our system of identifying each of the seven churches with a period in church history, we believe Thyatira represents characteristics of the church from AD 600 to the Great Tribulation.

The characteristics of this church are like those that existed in the church from about AD 600 onward. That is, the church was generally tolerant of much that was neither scriptural nor spiritually beneficial, and these traits will characterize the "*professing church" on into the Great Tribulation.

professing
laying claim to; pretending; claiming to be; often used to contrast those who "claim to be Christians" with those who are actually Christians in life and behavior

As a special optional exercise, review the questions and answers in this subsection on Thyatira, and use the material in them to make a sermon outline or Bible study outline of John's letter to the church in Thyatira.

Identify facts concerning major elements of the letter to the church in Sardis.

The Letter to the Church in Sardis

Revelation 3:1–6

The city of Sardis was built on a hill over 1000 feet above the surrounding plain. Citizens here had a strong sense of security because they believed their city was too strong to be conquered by an enemy. Sardis was considered to be a wealthy city, and was known for jewelry, textiles, and dye. A temple dedicated to the goddess Artemis was located here, making it a strong pagan religious center. Moreover, the city lay on an important trade route down the Hermus valley. Sardis was less powerful under Roman rule than she had been previously.

7 In your notebook write five details of historical background for Sardis that are mentioned in the above paragraph.

Revelation 3:1 gives us two characteristics by which the Lord reveals Himself to the church in Sardis. He possesses the seven spirits of God and the seven stars. These reveal His complete wisdom and complete control of the messengers or leaders of the church. Jesus is aware of the deeds of the church; He is never misled by her profession and so-called reputation. As we saw in 1:20, the stars represent *messengers* or leaders of the seven churches. Because the leaders are in Christ's hand, we gather that they are responsible to Him and that their leadership is authoritative.

8 What do the two characteristics of Jesus revealed to the church in Sardis suggest?

....

....

In the last sentence of verse 1 we observed what Jesus condemns in the church at Sardis. This church had a good reputation before people. Indeed, it may have been a model of organization and good programming, but a church's reputation before men is not what counts most! What counts most is what our Lord thinks of us. Many churches that were born in a great move of the Spirit of God are now only social-welfare agencies. It is good to help people materially, but it is far more important for a person be saved—to know Christ personally. Notice the five verbs that Jesus uses in verses 2 and 3 to command the church to get rid of what He disapproves. *Through the Holy Spirit, Jesus speaks to us in this same commanding manner when He sees in us what He disapproved of in the church at Sardis.*

The last sentence of verse 3 sounded a great warning to most of the people in the church at Sardis because they no longer accepted the Bible as God's Word. In a terse, unmistakable warning the Lord of this church advises believers in Sardis. The door of mercy is open, but they must respond while the offer is extended; otherwise, heedless people will suffer eternal loss. If a person does not accept the truth of the Bible which tells him about the return of the Lord, he cannot know anything about the time of His coming. Jesus indicated that neither people nor angels know the day or the hour: "No one knows. . . that day or hour. . . but only the Father" (Matthew 24:36). However, we can tell from things which are happening in our world—the signs of the times—that the time is near: "As it was in the days of Noah, so it will be at the coming of the Son of Man" (Matthew 24:37).

9 Based on the discussion in the two preceding paragraphs, the condition that aroused our Lord's disapproval in verse 1 was

a) social unawareness.
b) the lack of a humanitarian spirit.
c) refusal to carry on spiritual activities.
d) spiritual deadness.

As we stated previously, many of the Spirit-born churches of the Reformation have fallen away from biblical Christianity. Even so, there are some today in every Spirit-born church denomination who are still preaching the gospel of Christ! Likewise, there were a few people in the church in Sardis who had not fallen away from God. These are singled out for special recognition by the

Lord of the church (v. 4). They will be dressed in white, which symbolizes purity. Moreover, their names will remain forever in the Book of Life and be acknowledged before God and His angels.

10 Circle the letter preceding each TRUE statement.

a Sardis was thought to be secure from any enemy attack.
b Jesus is revealed to this city as one who held "the seven spirits of God and the seven stars.
c The church in Sardis was singled out for several points which her Lord felt were worthy of praise.
d The problem with the Sardis church lay in the fact that she appeared to be what she really was not.
e In the midst of general spiritual deadness, some believers in Sardis lived lives of purity and devotion to Jesus Christ.

The apostasy in the church at Sardis, which is described in the letter to this church, seems to correspond to characteristics in the church from about AD 1517 and into the Great Tribulation. At the point in history indicated by the beginning date, there was a widespread spiritual awakening, but it was soon followed by a steady drift into dead orthodoxy. The church, while still carrying some of these characteristics, was awakened from its slumber by the modern missionary movement which gained momentum in the 1800s. The characteristics of the various church periods we have discussed seem to indicate principles of spiritual life that do not dramatically begin and end at a given date. Therefore, the loss of love of Ephesus, the compromise of Pergamum, the tolerance of evil seen in Thyatira, and the spiritual deadness of Sardis pose problems the church must combat until the Rapture.

As a practical optional exercise, review the questions and answers in this section on Sardis and use this material to make a sermon outline or Bible study outline of John's letter to the church in Sardis.

Recognize important features of the letter to the church in Philadelphia.

The Letter to the Church in Philadelphia

Revelation 3:7–13

The city of Philadelphia was built by a king of Pergamum, Attalus Philadelphus, who named it after himself. It was a place of major earthquakes, and the city was destroyed twice in the first century AD It was a center of pagan worship and was known as "Little Athens." This indicates that the philosophy, religion, and immorality of the large city of Athens were present in Philadelphia.

11 In your notebook list five details of historical background for John's letter to the church in Philadelphia based on the above paragraph.

In verse 7, we see the characteristics by which our Lord reveals Himself to this church. The passage in Isaiah 22:21–22 sheds light on this present verse. It was considered by Jewish scholars as a prophecy of the Messiah who would have the glory (throne) of and key to (authority of) the House of David.

12 What are the characteristics of Jesus that John's letter to the church in Philadelphia points out in verse 7?

....

The open door placed before the church in Philadelphia suggests to us the opportunity to spread the gospel (v. 8). There are various open doors to the church of our day. List in your notebook as many of them as you can think of. Then ask yourself: "What am I doing to take advantage of these open doors for service to Jesus Christ?" You may want to see what this idea of the "open door" indicates in other Scriptures we have listed also (1 Corinthians 16:9; 2 Corinthians 2:12).

The second sentence of verse 8 reveals what Jesus commends in the church at Philadelphia. He commends this church for having "a little strength" (KJV). Isaiah 40:28–31 explains how God's people of all eras have experienced spiritual victory by depending mainly on the strength that God gives them rather than on their own strength. While believers in Philadelphia demonstrated strength by recognizing and accepting Jesus' word and name for what His word and name really are, they depended mainly on divine strength to maintain the attitudes toward Jesus' word and name for which He commends them here. We, like Paul, "can do all things through Christ" (Philippians 4:13, KJV) if we depend on Christ's strength in the measure that Paul did.

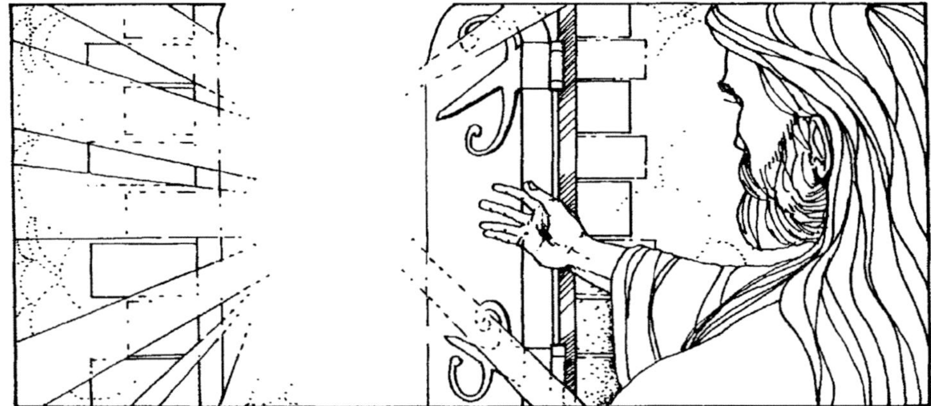

13 State three things in the second sentence of verse 8 that Jesus commends in the church at Philadelphia.

....

....

There is nothing of which Jesus disapproves in the church at Philadelphia. The word *philadelphia* means "brotherly love." It is an appropriate description for a church whose people are patient, faithful to their calling, and diligent in service.

Verse 10, which we will discuss in greater detail in Lesson 8, commends Philadelphian believers for their faithful obedience under trial. The indication is that believers will be kept from the hour of trial that will come on the world (the coming worldwide Great Tribulation).

14 In your notebook tell what is the significance of the special promise in verse 10 and the special exhortation in verse 11.

15 In your notebook name the four things Jesus promises in verse 12 that He will do for overcomers in the church at Philadelphia.

16 Circle the letter preceding each TRUE statement about important features of the church in Philadelphia.

- **a** Philadelphia was a city which was subject to major earthquakes.
- **b** The "open door" set before Philadelphian believers may indicate opportunity for the proclamation of the gospel.
- **c** This church was commended for its great strength and its rigid orthodoxy.
- **d** Philadelphians were condemned mainly because of their "little strength."
- **e** Patient endurance shown by Philadelphian believers will be rewarded by protection from the worldwide test that is coming upon all earth's people.

Jesus' special promise in verse 10 to the church at Philadelphia and His special exhortation in verse 11 seem to indicate that this church represents the true Bible-believing church in the last part of the church era which is ready for the coming of the Lord.

As a practical optional exercise, review the questions and answers in this subsection on Philadelphia and use this material to make a sermon outline or Bible study outline of John's letter to the church in Philadelphia.

Identify significant features of the letter to the church in Laodicea

The Letter to the Church in Laodicea

Revelation 3:14–22

The city of Laodicea was named after the wife of King Antiochus II, Laodice. It was a wealthy business center. The city was famous for its medicines, an ear ointment, and an eye powder. Since Laodicea had no water supply, water from hot springs six miles south of the city was brought through aqueducts to serve community needs. By the time this water reached the city, it was lukewarm. Laodiceans could easily identify with the Lord's reaction to their lukewarm condition, for they knew how sickening lukewarm water could be to the thirsty. When the city suffered a destructive earthquake in AD 60, its leaders, speaking with one voice, refused assistance from Rome, replying: "I have grown rich and am in need of nothing."

17 In your notebook list five details of historical background that are mentioned in the above paragraph.

The first of the three characteristics that John attributes to Jesus in verse 14 is that He is the *Amen*. *Amen* means "true" or "truly." The emphasis seems to be on the accuracy of Jesus' judgment. One Bible scholar says that the *Amen* as a title for Christ "indicates His sovereignty and the certainty of the fulfillment of His promises."

18 What are the three characteristics of Jesus that John's letter to the church in Laodicea points out in verse 14?

....

....

Jesus does not commend anything in the church in Laodicea. The word *laodicea* means "popular judgment" or "popular approval." In the church this kind of approval often manifests the will of the people rather than the will of God. It implies that ministers and spiritual leaders consider it more important to please the people than to please God. Observe especially a condition in verses 15–19 that Jesus condemns in the church at Laodicea. Church members were neither cold nor hot in their spiritual condition. *Cold* meant "to be away from God but to be aware of the need to get right with Him." *Lukewarm* suggests "being away from God without realizing it." Laodicean believers are counseled to buy "gold refined in the fire" (v. 18), which refers to the spiritual wealth that Christians receive through tests and trials of their faith. Job 23:10 and 1 Peter 1:7 teach us that such tests and trials produce purity in God's people in the manner that gold is purified by fire. Obviously, this is what Laodiceans desperately needed. Jesus' statement in verse 19, "Those whom I love I rebuke and discipline," is evidence that God's people receive blessing in *adversity, and it indicates God's concern for our spiritual growth and development. But this statement is followed by an exhortation which indicates the Laodicean need to act on His advice: "Be earnest, and repent."

adversity
condition of being in unfavorable circumstances; misfortune; distress

19 In verses 15–19 that which Jesus condemns in the church at Laodicea is believers'
a) awareness of their need of spiritual riches.
b) lack of awareness of their need of spiritual riches.
c) material riches.
d) material poverty.

Our Lord's statement in the first part of verse 20, "I stand at the door and knock," shows us that He is outside the door of the church in Laodicea. He is not in this church at all. Your writer is convinced that this church represents many of the false churches of these last days—churches which claim to be Christian but have nothing to do with Jesus Christ. Their teachings come from the opinions of men—not from the Word of God! Many of them deny the deity of Jesus Christ. He is still knocking, for He wants all to be saved (2 Peter 3:9). In the last sentence of verse 20 Jesus makes a special promise to individuals in the church in Laodicea. "If anyone hears my voice and opens the door, I will go in and eat with him, and he with me." This is a spiritual feast that will satisfy the longing of every seeking heart.

God feasts on man's love and fellowship. The Bible is primarily the story of God seeking man (Luke 19:10). In Genesis 3:9 God called to man, "Where are you?" In John 4 in the story of Jesus and the woman of Samaria, Jesus asked as He approached the woman: "Will you give me a drink?" (v. 7) He was not seeking the water in the well; He was seeking a response that indicated her spiritual love and fellowship. This explains why Jesus did not want to eat when His disciples came back with food. This is why He said: "I have food to eat that you know nothing about" (v. 32). *He wants your love and fellowship in the same way.* This spiritual love relationship is a feast for us and for Him too!

20 In your notebook give the special exhortation that Jesus makes in the last sentence of verse 19 to the lukewarm church in Laodicea and the special promise He makes to individuals in the last sentence of verse 20.

21 What does Jesus promise in verse 21 to overcomers in the church at Laodicea? In light of what has been presented earlier in this lesson, what does this promise mean?

....

....

22 Circle the letter preceding each TRUE statement that identifies significant features relating to the church in Laodicea.

a Laodicea was served by a lukewarm water supply that was piped to the city from an outside source.

b We can assume from the attitude of Laodicean believers that they were self-satisfied, spiritually immature, and sadly lacking in vision.

c Laodicea, like other churches, had good points and bad points; being worthy of both praise and blame.

d The fact that Jesus is on the outside knocking at the door indicates how far the church had slipped from its original purpose and commitment.

e Laodicea pictures the last period of church history and involves apostasy to the very end.

As a practical optional exercise, review the questions and answers in this subsection on Laodicea and use this material to make a sermon outline or Bible study outline of John's letter to the church in Laodicea.

Self-Test

We are including a comprehensive review of chapters 6 and 7 in this self-test. You may want to examine the objectives and self-test of Lesson 6 and review the objectives for this lesson before you take this self-test.

Short Answer. Briefly answer the following questions in the spaces provided.

1 State the threefold purpose of John's letters to seven churches in Revelation chapters 2 and 3.

....

....

2 Name two important things that John's letters to seven churches in Revelation chapters 2 and 3 reveal pertaining to Jesus, the ultimate source of the letters.

....

....

3 Write from memory the names of the seven churches noted in Revelation chapters 2 and 3 in the order that John recorded. Also, list with each church at least one of its chief characteristics.

....

....

....

Matching. Follow specific instructions for each matching question.

4 Match each letter to the church (right) with the characteristic of Jesus it mentions either literally or symbolically (left).

. . . . **a** Jesus is resurrected.

. . . . **b** Jesus possesses and uses God's Word.

. . . . **c** Jesus walks among churches.

. . . . **d** Jesus gives the Holy Spirit to believers.

. . . . **e** Jesus has all-seeing eyes.

. . . . **f** Jesus is the Amen.

. . . . **g** Jesus is the Messiah.

1) Letter to Ephesus
2) Letter to Smyrna
3) Letter to Pergamum
4) Letter to Thyatira
5) Letter to Sardis
6) Letter to Philadelphia
7) Letter to Laodicea

5 Match the number of each letter (right) with the item, characteristic, or belief associated with it (left).

. . . . **a** Great altar of Zeus	1) Letter to Ephesus
. . . . **b** Belief that Artemis' image fell from heaven	2) Letter to Smyrna
. . . . **c** Known as the ornament of Asia	3) Letter to Pergamum
. . . . **d** Water supplied by aqueducts	4) Letter to Thyatira
. . . . **e** Known as "Little Athens"	5) Letter to Sardis
. . . . **f** Situated on a high hill	6) Letter to Philadelphia
. . . . **g** Made weapons, dye, and cloth	7) Letter to Laodicea

6 Match each number (right) with each thing Jesus disapproves either literally or symbolically (left). (Note: You must write two of the numbers from the right column in one of the six blank spaces in the left column.)

. . . . **a** Jezebel's teaching on idolatry and sexual immorality	1) Letter to Ephesus
. . . . **b** Spiritual condition of death in most people	2) Letter to Smyrna
. . . . **c** Nothing	3) Letter to Pergamum
. . . . **d** Lack of awareness of need of spiritual riches	4) Letter to Thyatira
. . . . **e** Forsaking of first love	5) Letter to Sardis
. . . . **f** Balaam's teaching on idolatry and sexual immorality	6) Letter to Philadelphia
	7) Letter to Laodicea

7 Match the appropriate letter (right) with each thing Jesus approves either literally or symbolically (left).

. . . . **a** Nothing commended	1) Letter to Ephesus
. . . . **b** The keeping of His Word	2) Letter to Smyrna
. . . . **c** The unsoiled clothing or faithfulness of a few people	3) Letter to Pergamum
. . . . **d** The giving of service	4) Letter to Thyatira
. . . . **e** The keeping of faith in Him through great trial	5) Letter to Sardis
. . . . **f** Spiritual riches in the midst of material poverty	6) Letter to Philadelphia
. . . . **g** The testing of false claims	7) Letter to Laodicea

8 Match each letter (right) with each promise which Jesus makes to overcomers either literally or symbolically (left).

. . . . **a** Jesus will never erase their names from the Book of Life.

. . . . **b** Jesus will give them authority over the nations.

. . . . **c** Jesus will give them the right to sit with Him on His throne.

. . . . **d** Jesus will make them pillars in the temple of His God.

. . . . **e** Jesus will give them the right to eat from the tree of life.

. . . . **f** Jesus promises them they will not be hurt by eternal death.

. . . . **g** Jesus will give them spiritual food and freedom from guilt.

1) Letter to Ephesus
2) Letter to Smyrna
3) Letter to Pergamum
4) Letter to Thyatira
5) Letter to Sardis
6) Letter to Philadelphia
7) Letter to Laodicea

Unit Progress Evaluation 2

Now that you have finished Unit 2, review the lessons in preparation for Unit Progress Evaluation 2. You will find it in your Student Packet. Answer all of the questions without referring to your course materials, Bible, or notes. When you have completed the UPE, check your answers with the answer key provided in your Student Packet, and review any items you may have answered incorrectly. Then you may proceed with your study of Unit 3. (Although UPE scores do not count as part of your final course grade, they indicate how well you learned the material and how well you may perform on the final examination.)

Answers to study questions

12 That Jesus (1) is holy and true, (2) is the Messiah, (3) has all power and authority

1 (1) Thyatira had a military history. (2) Its industries were prominent. (3) It supported trade guilds. (4) Dye and cloth were its chief products. (5) Lydia, a convert under Paul, was from this city.

13 He commends (1) the little strength they do have, (2) their having kept His word, and (3) their having not denied His name.

2 Jesus is the Son of God, He has all-seeing eyes, and He has crushing feet for His enemies.

14 The special promise: "I will . . . keep you from the hour of trial that is going to come upon the whole world" may refer to the church's being protected from the Great Tribulation. The exhortation Jesus gives, seen against the background of His soon coming, notes the importance for believers to maintain their relationship with Christ so that they may obtain their reward for service.

3 Love, faith, service, and perseverance

15 He will (1) make them pillars in the temple of God, (2) write on them the name of God, (3) write on them the name of the city of God, and (4) write on them His new name.

4 He disapproved of sexual immorality and idolatry.

16 **a** True
b True
c False
d False
e True

5 c) hold on to what they have.

17 The city of Laodicea was (1) named after Queen Laodice, (2) wealthy, (3) famous for its medicines, (4) supplied water by aqueducts, and (5) the victim of a destructive earthquake.

6 **a** False
b True
c True
d True
e False
f False
g True

18 Jesus is the *Amen*, the faithful and true Witness, and the Ruler of God's creation.

7 The city of Sardis was (1) situated on a high hill, (2) situated on an important trade route, (3) a powerful fortress, (4) wealthy, but (5) less powerful under Rome than previously.

19 **b)** lack of awareness of their need of spiritual riches.

8 They suggest our Lord's complete knowledge of the deeds of the church. Ministers are responsible to Him and their leadership is authoritative.

20 The exhortation is to be earnest and repent. The promise is that if anyone will open his heart to Jesus, that person and the Lord will enjoy a spiritual feast together. (Notice here that Jesus gives the exhortation in literal language, but that He gives the promise in figurative language.)

9 **d)** spiritual deadness.

21 Jesus promises the right to sit with Him on His throne. This means that they will rule with and under Jesus during the Millennium.

10 **a** True
b True
c False
d True
e True

22 **a** True
b True
c False
d True
e True

11 The city of Philadelphia was (1) built by a king of Pergamum, (2) given its builder's name, (3) a place of earthquakes, (4) a center of pagan worship, and (5) called "Little Athens."

THE CONTINUATION OF END-TIME EVENTS

Lessons...

8 The Church and the Great Tribulation

9 The Beginning of the Seventieth Seven

10 Midtribulation Events

11 Progress in the Prophetic Panorama

Procedures...

1 Observe the objectives for key points.
2 Reflect on the headings and subheadings.
3 Study the content identifying key points (highlight, underline, etc.) as you read.
4 Answer the self-study questions.
5 Do the self-test to reinforce key concepts.
6 Review the lessons in this unit in preparation for the Unit Progress Evaluation.

The Church and the Great Tribulation

We have completed the first two points of the outline given by Jesus in Revelation 1:19. The first point you studied, John's great vision of Jesus Christ which reveals His glory and majesty, concerned "What you [John] have seen." Then you examined Jesus' words of encouragement, promise, warning, and judgment to the church in point 2 which concerned "What is now." Now we are ready to move on to point 3, "What will take place later," to observe how God is going to complete His plan. This lesson presents the view of many Bible scholars that *the church will be kept out of the Great Tribulation*. Revelation chapter 4 and other passages of Scripture will be discussed in support of this view.

In Ephesians 1:9–10 the apostle Paul indicates that God has made known the mystery of His will to bring all things in heaven and on earth together under one Head, Christ. The remaining events and messages in the book of Revelation will help to explain how what God has "made known to us" concerning His plan will "be put into effect." The remainder of this book will help you to understand how the bringing of "all things in heaven and on earth together under . . . Christ" will take place. As you study this lesson, you should know more assuredly that God is in full control of His universe. We pray that this study will make you more determined to be what Jesus Christ wants you to be and to do what He wants you to do in these closing hours of time.

the activities...

◇ Read Revelation chapter 4, Matthew 24:1–25:13, and Thessalonians 2:1–12 before you study this lesson.

◇ Study this lesson and take the self-test on it according to procedures given in Lesson 1.

◇ You may use your Bible to answer study questions and the questions in the self-test.

◇ Be sure to look in the glossary for the meanings of any key words you do not know.

the objectives...

8.1 *Recognize the statement which gives the significance of the Greek phrase* meta tauta.

8.2 *Explain the view that John's going from earth through an open door into heaven relates to the rapture of the church.*

8.3 *Explain why the Great Tribulation is a unique experience in the history of people on earth.*

8.4 *Explain the way in which the words* church *and* out of *affect the interpretation of the church's role during the Great Tribulation.*

8.5 *Identify the meanings of the Greek words* parousia, harpadzo, *and* epiphaneia.

8.6 *State the significance of the three end-time questions that Jesus' disciples asked Him as recorded in Matthew 24:3.*

8.7 *Identify from Scripture what or who will restrain the apostasy and the Antichrist and explain how this will he done.*

the outline...

1 Meaning of the Phrase "After These Things"
2 An Open Door in Heaven
3 Uniqueness of the Great Tribulation
4 Use of the Words *Church* and *Out Of*
5 The Coming of Jesus in 1 Thessalonians 4:13–5:11
6 The Meanings of Words Which Relate to Jesus' Coming
7 Discussion of Three End-Time Questions
8 The Restrainer of Apostasy and the Antichrist

Recognize the statement which gives the significance of the Greek phrase meta tauta.

Meaning of the Phrase "After These Things"

Revelation 4:1

In the outline given to you for the book of Revelation in Lesson 4, part IV deals with what will take place "after these things." "After these things" is a literal translation of the Greek phrase *meta tauta*. Part IV of this outline thus describes the things which must take place *after* the *things which John had seen* and the *things which are now*. Since we believe that Lessons 6 and 7 describe the Church Age, the things which follow appear to be after the Church Age. Revelation 4:1 begins with the Greek phrase translated "after these things" and ends with this same phrase. In our view this wording is important because of Jesus' use of this phrase in the outline He gave in Revelation 1:19. Moreover, in Revelation 4:1 our Lord uses the word "must" to indicate that it is necessary for more things to take place. And the time when they are to take place is *meta tauta* or after the events described in Revelation chapters 2 and 3.

1 According to our discussions, the significance of the Greek phrase *meta tauta* is that it suggests

a) a specific outline for future events.
b) what took place during John's day.
c) what will occur after the Church Age.
d) specific events in church history.

Explain the view that John's going from earth through an open door into heaven relates to the rapture of the church.

An Open Door in Heaven

Revelation 4:2

In addition to the time sequence we examined in Revelation 4:1, another subject is introduced here and in the following verse which, we believe, is a key to the interpretation of end-time events. John sees an open door in heaven and hears the voice which he had first heard speaking to him like a trumpet (Revelation 1:10–18). This time, however, the voice calls him to "come up" to heaven. Then John is caught up from earth by the Spirit through the open door into heaven. While the clause, "At once I was in the Spirit," has been seen by some as an indication that John fell into a trance, it must be remembered that the prophet was already "in the Spirit" (1:10). The indication is that John was caught up because in verse 2 he is "before . . . a throne in heaven." The rest of Revelation chapter 4 is a description of this throne in heaven and the activities associated with it. We will return to chapter 4 in our next lesson, but for the balance of this lesson we will discuss the church in relation to the Great Tribulation.

In our study of Revelation, chapter 4:1–2 brings us to a particular vantage point. Since we have expressed the view that characteristics of the church throughout the entire course of the church age are represented in chapters 2 and 3, we now consider events which appear to follow the *rapture of the church as symbolized by John's going into heaven described above. We believe that the church will be raptured when the Church Age ends. This seems to be symbolized by John's rapture into heaven *after* the events that characterize the Church Age. This symbol—John's being caught up into heaven—seems to suggest to us that the church will not be on earth during the Great Tribulation which begins in Revelation 6:1.

rapture
a carrying away or being carried away in body or spirit; as used in Bible prophecy, refers to the "catching away of the church, the bride of Christ, at the Second Coming"

2 Identify, giving chapter and verse, whose voice John heard in Revelation 4:1.

....

3 In your notebook tell what John is commanded to do in Revelation 4:1 and what is the significance of this command.

4 Based on our comments in this section, explain in your notebook how John's going from earth through an open door into heaven may be interpreted by some to relate to the rapture of the church and how this relates to the church and the Great Tribulation.

selectively protected
refers to the way God protects His own in the midst of judgment on the wicked. For example, while the plagues affected Egyptians, they did not affect Israelites, leading us to say they were selectively protected

Before we move on to the next point in the study, let us add that many godly men and women hold different views on the time of the Rapture. Some believe that the church will be on the earth for at least part of the Great Tribulation. Others believe that the church will be on earth during the entire tribulation period, being *selectively protected from God's wrath as Israel was protected from the plagues that destroyed Egypt (Exodus 7–12). Those who hold such views are men and women who love the Lord Jesus Christ, and they have an honest opinion. However, we ask that you do consider carefully the information given in this lesson on this subject.

Explain why the Great Tribulation is a unique experience in the history of people on earth.

Uniqueness of the Great Tribulation

The title for this lesson mentions the church in relation to the Great Tribulation. If you have not previously studied biblical prophecy, you may not be familiar with this term. Looking forward to events that will take place after the church has been caught away, we see that the wicked—individuals, nations, and the collective, worldwide institutions and associations of ungodly people—will face the wrath of God. As this time of collective reckoning comes, it is referred to as the great day of the wrath of God (6:17) and as "the great tribulation" (7:14). The focus here is on the *consummation of God's redemptive program as it concerns those who have rejected His grace and attempted to hinder His work on earth.

consummation
bring to completion; fulfillment

Seen in the light of the previous paragraph, the Great Tribulation does not concern the victorious church. We do not believe that the church will experience God's wrath as it is revealed in the Great Tribulation. Others, however, argue that Christians have endured tribulation throughout the church's history. They say, "Why should the church of the last days be spared physical and mental suffering, or even martyrdom?" The Bible does indicate that hardships and tribulation (Acts 14:22, KJV) are the lot of believers in this world (2 Timothy 3:10–13; John 16:33), but this tribulation does not represent the wrath of God. Only in the context of the *end time is the accumulated wrath of God poured out. It is described as "the wine of God's fury, which has been poured full strength into the cup of his wrath" (Revelation 14:10). In the Great Tribulation, therefore, "God's wrath is completed" (15:1).

end time
as an adjective it relates to the end of the present world system or the events associated with it in religious expectation

Obviously, no other judgment in history since the flood will touch so many people, and no other means of punishment has been described in Scripture as the great day of God's wrath (6:17). The Great Tribulation is therefore unique in history in terms of its nature, purpose, and scope. Many Christians today are suffering terribly and many more will undoubtedly suffer before Jesus comes; however, this suffering is not to be compared with the Great Tribulation.

5 Why is the Great Tribulation a unique experience in the history of people on earth?

....

Explain the way in which the words church *and* out of *affect the interpretation of the church's role during the Great Tribulation.*

Use of the Words *Church* and *Out Of*

The word *church* is used seven times and the word *churches* twelve times in the first three chapters of the book of Revelation. After John is caught up in 4:1, however, neither word is used again until the reference to *churches* in 22:16. None of these references indicates that the church will be on earth during the Great Tribulation period. The absence of any reference to the church during this critical period seems to indicate that the church will not be on earth during this time.

The Greek word *ek* is a preposition. Prepositions show relationship or position. They are words such as *in, under, through, from, upon, and beside*. The preposition, *ek* means "out of." The promise to the people of the church of Philadelphia was that Jesus would keep them *ek* (out of) "the hour of trial that is going to come upon the whole world to test those who live on the earth" (Revelation 3:10). The church is not told here that it will be kept in the midst of this worldwide tribulation nor taken out of the middle of it. Rather, the sense of the Greek word *ek* indicates that the church will be kept out of it.

6 State in your notebook how the words *church* and *ek* are used in the book of Revelation to indicate that the church will not be on earth to experience any of the Great Tribulation.

7 Read carefully Luke 21:34–36 in which Jesus speaks to His disciples about the Great Tribulation. How many people will this day of Great Tribulation come upon? How much of this Great Tribulation should Christians pray that they may be able to escape?

....

....

Identify elements that will characterize the event when Jesus comes down from heaven with a loud command.

The Coming of Jesus In 1 Thessalonians 4:13–5:11

In 1 Thessalonians 4:16, the apostle Paul describes our Lord's coming "with a loud command." Your writer believes that this is apparently the trumpet-like call of Jesus to John, "Come up here" (Revelation 4:1). It seems evident to him that this call catches away or raptures not only John, but also at the same moment, the entire body of Christ. After this call, the body of Christ, the true church, is evidently no longer on earth. In 1 Thessalonians 4:13–5:11 Paul gives the order in time for the rapture of the church and the beginning of the Day of the Lord, which is another name for the Great Tribulation.

First, notice who will be "with Jesus" (4:14) when He comes "down from heaven, with a loud command" (4:16). Paul promises that two things will happen when the Lord comes in this manner. Next, observe in 4:16–17 what they are and the order in which they will happen. Verse 18 explains how Christians should act toward each other because of their blessed hope. Finally, note the event that will come "like a thief in the night" (5:2). This passage indicates that the rapture of the church will precede the beginning of the Great Tribulation. Remember: there were no chapter divisions in this passage when Paul wrote it.

In 2 Corinthians 5:1–10 Paul refers to the Christian's physical body as a tent (v. 1). In verses 6–8 he clearly indicates *where* the nonphysical part of a Christian goes at the time of his physical death. Now answer the following questions based on the passages from 1 Thessalonians and 2 Corinthians.

8 Who will be with Jesus when He comes down from heaven with a loud command?

....

9 What two things will happen when Jesus comes down from heaven with a loud command? Which one of these things will happen first?

....

....

10 Based on our discussion in this section, at the event known as the Rapture, Jesus will bring
a) Christians' bodies with Him to join their resurrected spirits.
b) Christians' bodies and spirits with Him.
c) neither Christians' bodies nor their spirits with Him.
d) Christians' spirits with Him to join their resurrected bodies.

Identify the meanings of the Greek words parousia, harpadzo, *and* epiphaneia.

The Meanings of Words Which Relate to Jesus' Coming

parousia
Greek word which means "a personal arrival or coming"

Armageddon
in the Bible, the great and final conflict between forces of good and evil at the end of this age

harpadzo
Greek word which, in relation to our Lord's coming, means "to snatch away by force"

It has been customary for those who believe that the rapture of the church will take place before the Great Tribulation to call the Rapture the **parousia*, a word that has come into English from Greek. In Greek, *parousia* means "a personal arrival or coming." In the New Testament it is used to refer to the coming of various persons (1 Corinthians 16:17). However, when parousia is used of Jesus' coming in the future, it is never used alone to describe His return at the conclusion of the Tribulation period as King of Kings and Lord of Lords. It is used alone, though, to describe His coming for the church at the Rapture.

The *Rapture* and the *Second Coming* or revelation of our Lord are separated by a period of seven years—the *seventieth seven* of Daniel's prophecy. During this time, we believe that the church will be with the Lord. This entire seven-year period is sometimes referred to as the *parousia*. Thus, the *parousia* begins with the Rapture and ends with Jesus' return at the Battle of *Armageddon (Revelation 16:16–19:2). In the Greek New Testament *parousia* is used in 1 Thessalonians 2:19, 3:13, 4:15, and 5:23 in connection with the Rapture.

While the word *rapture* is not in the King James Version of the Bible, the concept is. The word *rapture* comes from the Latin word *repare*, which means to "snatch up with force." The Greek word **harpadzo* in 1 Thessalonians 4:17 means the same thing. It is translated "caught up."

epiphaneia
Greek word which in relation to Christ's coming means ''brightness'' or "splendor"

Second Thessalonians 2:8 calls Jesus' coming at Armageddon the "splendor of his coming." The Greek text calls this the **epiphaneia* of His *parousia*. In this case, *parousia* is used with another word to explain what part of the *parousia* is in view. Peter uses a similar word *ephanes* in Acts 2:20. It is translated there as "glorious." It seems obvious that Peter is referring to the same event as that noted in 2 Thessalonians 2:8, the coming of Jesus at Armageddon. Literally, *epiphaneia* means "brightness" or "splendor." It is used of Jesus' appearance as a man on earth in 2 Timothy 1:10, of the Rapture when Christians will see Jesus in His brilliance, and of His coming at Armageddon when the world will see Him in His brilliance.

11 Match each Greek word (right) with its meaning or definition (left).

.... **a** To snatch away with force	1) *Parousia*
.... **b** Brightness or splendor	2) *Harpadzo*
.... **c** A personal arrival or coming	3) *Epiphaneia*

State the significance of the three end-time questions that Jesus' disciples asked Him as recorded in Matthew 24:3.

Discussion of Three End-time Questions

Matthew 24:1–25:13

We trust you read Matthew 24:1–25:13 as recommended in the learning activities before you began studying this lesson. The "Olivet Discourse" is a fascinating passage, and it has challenged the abilities of generations of able Bible scholars. Many of these scholars believe that this passage refers exclusively to Israel. We believe, however, like many others that the church is in view as well as Israel in this scriptural setting. We will examine the entire segment briefly, starting with Matthew 24:1–3.

After Jesus and His disciples came from the temple to the Mount of Olives, the disciples called attention to the temple's beauty and magnificence. Jesus responded by noting that the entire structure would be totally destroyed. The disciples were troubled by this word and asked three specific questions: (1) When will the temple be destroyed? (2) What will be the sign of your coming? (3) What will be the sign of the end of the age? Matthew does not record Jesus' answer to the first question, but Luke records it in the parallel passage in Luke 21:20-21. Matthew lists Jesus' responses to the other questions in the balance of chapter 24 and in the early part of chapter 25. We shall focus our attention now on question 3, which is discussed in Matthew 24:4–31.

Question 3 relates to the sign of the end of the age. The end of the age will come at Armageddon when Jesus comes back as King of Kings and Lord of Lords. Let us consider some specific facts that are detailed in verses 4–31.

1. Verses 4–14 give us a preview of the experience of God's people throughout history on earth before the end of the age. Notice, among other things, that worldwide proclamation of the gospel is to occur before the end comes.
2. Verses 15–25 speak of the last three and one-half years of the Great Tribulation. You should notice especially the reference to the "abomination that causes desolation" (v. 15). Jesus' words here reinforce the prophecy in Daniel 9:27

about what will take place in the middle of the final seven years. We will see more details of the final three and one-half-year period later on in our study.

3. Verses 26–28 warn about the danger of responding to false christs at any time, now or during the Great Tribulation. This warning suggests that when Jesus comes, those who are following false christs will be like *vultures gathered around and feeding on a dead carcass. The use of the word lightning here refers to the "splendor" of Jesus' coming, as we noted above (2 Thessalonians 2:8). As we will see later in our discussion of Revelation, the nation of Israel will not have to hunt for Jesus following the Battle of Armageddon. *He will go where His people are and reveal Himself to them.*

vultures
any of certain large birds of prey related to eagles, falcons, and hawks that eat the flesh of dead animals

4. Verses 29–31 describe the end of the age. You should observe the similarity between verse 30 and Revelation 1:7. You may recall from Lesson 4 in which we mentioned that the content of this verse is the theme of the book of Revelation. Here our Lord says He will send His angels to "gather His elect . . . from one end of the heavens to the other" (v. 31). It appears that the *elect* here in heaven represent another bit of evidence that the church will not go through the Great Tribulation.

We now turn to Question 2, "What will be the sign of your [Jesus'] coming?" This question is the focus of Matthew 24:32–25:13. Let us examine some of the specific facts that relate to this discussion.

1. Verses 32–33 compare the budding of a fig tree to fulfillment of signs that announce the approach of Jesus' coming. The fig tree's budding shows that summer is near, and the signs of the times presented in this discourse indicate that Jesus' coming is near also.
2. Verse 34 suggests that "this generation" will not pass until all that has been prophesied comes to pass. Admittedly, this statement raises some questions. Was Jesus referring to the things He discussed in Question 1, concerning the destruction of the temple, or Question 3, concerning the tribulation period? Or are we to understand that the word translated "generation," which may also be translated "race," refers to the Jewish race? Regardless of the view we take of this question, we do see in this verse the certainty of the prophetic fulfillment.
3. Verses 36–25:13 concern the suddenness of the Lord's coming at the beginning of the *parousia*. (The Greek word *parousia* is used in verses 37 and 39 to refer to the Lord's coming.) The comparison with the days of Noah shows that the Lord's corning will take place suddenly and without warning.
4. Verses 42–44 focus on the suddenness and secrecy of the *parousia*. This event will be as unexpected as the coming of a thief for unbelievers (1 Thessalonians 5:1–9). By contrast, when Jesus comes to earth at the Battle of Armageddon at the end of the age, every eye will see Him. He will not come then as a thief. In fact, the armies of the world will know that He is coming, and they will make war with Him. In the parable of the Ten Virgins (25:1–13), Jesus teaches about His sudden appearing at the beginning of the *parousia*.

From our study of the "Olivet Discourse," we see much detail about the course and consummation of the age. The signs of the times seem to indicate that very soon we will hear the cry: "Here's the bridegroom! Come out to meet him!" (25:6). Are you ready for this summons?

12 Circle the letter preceding each TRUE statement.

a Matthew does not record Jesus' response to Question 1, but Luke does record it.

b The course of the age is to be characterized by betrayal, false christs, hatred, and the persecution of believers.

c Alongside the apostasy of many, the gospel will be preached throughout the world.

d The parousia is described in one set of terms: it is a private, secret affair that will catch everyone by surprise.

13 In your notebook state the significance of the three end-time questions Jesus' disciples asked Him in Matthew 24:1–3.

Identify from Scripture what or who will restrain the apostasy and the Antichrist and explain how this will he done.

The Restrainer of Apostasy and the Antichrist

2 Thessalonians 2:1–12

As we approach the study of the final section of the lesson, let us list from Paul's teaching in 1 Thessalonians 4:13–5:11 the order of end-time events. First, the rapture of the church will take place. Then, the Day of the Lord, that is, the tribulation period, will begin. From our reading of 2 Thessalonians 2:1–12, we learn that believers in Thessalonica had become troubled about the coming Day of the Lord. Apparently, some false reporters had told Thessalonian Christians that the Day of the Lord had already come. This word caused them to believe that the Rapture had taken place and that they had missed it. In response to their anxiety, Paul called their attention to end-time events, setting them in the order in which they will occur.

In verse 1, when the apostle refers to "the coming of our Lord Jesus Christ and our being gathered to him," he is speaking of the rapture of the church. In this verse he uses the Greek word *parousia* which is translated "coming." After reassuring these believers a bit, Paul notes two things that must happen before the Day of the Lord can begin (v. 3). First, a rebellion will occur. *Rebellion* is translated from a Greek word that means "apostasy." Apostasy refers to departure from the faith—false Christianity. We believe that it refers to a great, worldwide religious system which is called "the great prostitute" in Revelation 17:1. This religious system will exercise tremendous power in the last days until it is cast aside by the man of lawlessness (Revelation 17:15–18).

The second thing that must occur before the Day of the Lord can begin is the revelation of "the man of lawlessness . . . the man doomed to destruction" (v. 3). This man is none other than the Antichrist whom we have considered in our studies in Daniel. He will oppose everything associated with God and exalt himself over God, demanding the worship that rightly belongs to God. Moreover, he will in arrogance set himself up in God's temple, declaring that he is God. This irreverent, arrogant, powerful man will be revealed, then, *before* the Day of the Lord begins.

You might ask, "How can one man expect to dethrone God and demand the worship that is rightly His? How could a person come to a place of international prominence, win the confidence of the masses, and attain such vast power?" In verses 9–12, the apostle outlines this man's rise to power. He will display all kinds

charisma
a mysterious power to fascinate and attract; great personal magnetism or glamour

of miracles, signs, and wonders, noting that he will be a master of deception, working every sort of evil. People will be drawn to him not only because of his evil *charisma, but also because they have willfully rejected the truth and light God has given them. Falling into this error, they will suffer eternal condemnation.

The apostle indicates in verse 6 and following that the principle of evil is already working in the world. He notes *what* is holding back or hindering the revelation of the Antichrist and the onset of unrivaled apostasy. In verse 7 Paul uses the pronoun *he* to describe *who* is restraining apostasy. Consider in the first sentence of Revelation 22:17 the two-part agency that calls people to God. The Holy Spirit is the invisible part of God's agency on earth; the church, or bride, is the visible part of it. It appears that the combination of the *what* and the *he* refers to the operation of the Holy Spirit through the church. This indicates that presently the Holy Spirit working through the church is the force that restrains unparalleled apostasy and the Antichrist. When the church is raptured, however, the Holy Spirit's operation through the church that has restrained evil will be removed and evil will rapidly envelop the earth. This view does not imply, however, that the Holy Spirit, who is everywhere present, will be removed from the earth. The fact that many people on earth will be saved during the Great Tribulation is proof that the Holy Spirit Himself will be on earth at this time. Since it is the Spirit who gives life (John 6:63), no person could be saved during that time unless the Holy Spirit were present to draw that person to Jesus. Nevertheless, the church, that unique redemptive instrument God has chosen and through which the Spirit operates to evangelize the world, will be removed. Then, the Day of the Lord will begin.

14 What, briefly, had some false reporters been telling the Thessalonian Christians?

....

15 What are two things that must happen before the Great Tribulation can begin?

....

....

16 Who is restraining apostasy and the Antichrist and how is this being accomplished?

....

....

17 Circle the letter preceding each TRUE statement.

a The restraining influence in the world today appears to be the Holy Spirit who works through the church to lead people to Christ.

b Following the rapture of the church, the Holy Spirit's presence will be removed from the earth.

c The man of lawlessness will come to power on the basis of deception and miracle-working; however, people will receive him more readily because they have willfully rejected the truth.

d As the world moves onward toward the last days, a rise of lawlessness and evil can be expected that will reach its climax under the rule of Antichrist.

Self-Test

Multiple choice: There is one best answer for each question. Circle the letter preceding your choice of the best answer.

1 John's going from earth through an open door into heaven represents the rapture of the church in a way that indicates that the church will be kept
- a) through the Great Tribulation.
- b) out of the last half of the Great Tribulation.
- c) through nearly all of the Great Tribulation.
- d) out of all of the Great Tribulation.

2 The fact that the Great Tribulation is the great day of God's wrath makes it
- a) different from all other tribulations.
- b) different from most other tribulations.
- c) similar to all tribulations.
- d) identical to all other tribulations.

3 When Jesus comes to catch up the true church, He will bring
- a) Christians' bodies with Him to join their resurrected spirits.
- b) Christians' spirits with Him to join their resurrected bodies.
- c) with Him Christians who have not experienced physical death.
- d) with Him no Christian of any description.

4 In relation to Jesus' coming, the Greek word *parousia* means
- a) brightness.
- b) to snatch up with force.
- c) a personal arrival or coming.
- d) glory.
- e) splendor.

5 The second coming of Christ at the Battle of Armageddon is described clearly by the Greek word *epiphaneia* which means
- a) a personal appearing.
- b) to come with great strength.
- c) to snatch away with force.
- d) brightness or splendor.

6 The doctrine of the Rapture is suggested to us by the Greek word *harpadzo* which meant to
- a) come with great power.
- b) make a personal appearance.
- c) snatch away with force.
- d) come with splendor and brightness.

True-False. Write **T** in the blank space preceding each TRUE statement. Write **F** if the statement is FALSE.

. . . . **7** "With these things" is a literal meaning of the Greek phrase *meta tauta.*

. . . . **8** The fact that no use of the words *church* or *churches* is made in the book of Revelation during the Great Tribulation indicates that the church will not be on earth to experience any of it.

. . . . **9** During the Great Tribulation the Holy Spirit will operate through the church on earth to restrain apostasy and the Antichrist.

Short Answer. Briefly answer the following questions in the space provided.

10 According to this lesson, what does John's Rapture before the events of the Great Tribulation began symbolize?

....

....

11 List the three end-time questions that Jesus' disciples asked Him that are recorded in Matthew 24:3.

....

....

12 How must the occurrence of the great end-time apostasy and the revealing of the Antichrist relate in time to the period of the Great Tribulation?

....

....

Answers to study questions

9 First, the dead in Christ will rise. Then the living in Christ will be caught up with these resurrected dead to meet Jesus.

1 c) What will occur after the Church Age.

10 d) Christians' spirits with Him to join their resurrected bodies.

2 It is apparently the voice of Jesus Christ as indicated in Revelation 1:10–18.

11 **a** 2) *Harpadzo*
b 3) *Epiphaneia*
c 1) *Parousia*

3 John is told to "come up here." The significance is that the immediate scene changes to heaven.

12 **a** True
b True
c True
d False (It has a public part also in which at the end of the Tribulation every eye will see Him.)

4 This *rapture* of John in Revelation 4:1–2 seems to represent the rapture of the church. This is seen to indicate that the church will be kept out of the Great Tribulation.

13 You should have noted that in responding to these three questions, Jesus summarized both the immediate and long-term historical experience of the Jews. He covered the destruction of the temple and the city of Jerusalem. He also spoke of the characteristics of the age that would lead up to the conclusion, and He noted specific signs that would precede the end of the age and His coming. This message gives us good insight into God's plan for the church and for the Jews also.

5 Because it is the only tribulation which can be correctly called the great day of God's wrath.

14 False reporters had been telling them that the Day of the Lord had come and this caused them to believe they had missed the Rapture.

6 The fact that neither the word *church* nor the word *churches* is used in the biblical narrative which describes the Great Tribulation indicates that the church will not be on earth to experience any of the Great Tribulation. In Revelation 3:10 *ek* is used in a manner which indicates that the church will neither be kept in the midst of the Great Tribulation nor taken out of the middle of it. Rather, it will be kept "out of" it.

15 The great end-time apostasy must occur, and the Antichrist must be revealed.

7 It will come upon the people of the entire earth. Believers should pray for an escape from all of it.

16 The Holy Spirit operating through the church is restraining apostasy and the Antichrist.

8 Those who have experienced physical death in Christ

17 **a** True
b False
c True
d True

The Beginning of the Seventieth Seven

After our brief introduction to Revelation 4 in Lesson 8, we addressed the matter of events from the rapture of the church to the conclusion of God's plan. Our study exposed us to the doctrine of the Rapture, the location of the church during the tribulation, the Great Tribulation itself, the Restrainer, and some other important end-time questions. Now we return to chapter 4 where we view the scene that John saw in heaven, and we consider in chapters 4–6 events that proceed from the throne of God as He begins to bring His plan to an end.

The sight John saw in heaven was certainly overwhelming. Put yourself in his place as he saw one amazing scene after another. In these scenes God revealed to Him the events which will occur in the future. In the midst of all the things John saw and heard in his vision, however, one person fills the scene with glory. That person is the *Lion-Lamb* who is introduced in Revelation 5:5–7.

The splendor, majesty, and awe surrounding the entire scene in chapter 4 results in heavenly worship of the Lord God Almighty. In addition, Christ the Lamb receives universal praise in chapter 5 as His saving grace is recounted. The entire universe seems to bow in adoration to God for Who He is and what He has done in these scriptural settings. May your study of this lesson help to increase your understanding of why every redeemed person should, like David in Psalm 34:1, praise God always.

the activities...

◇ Read Revelation chapters 4–6 before you study this lesson. As you read, please take note of the Person who is sitting on the throne in chapters 4 and 5. Read any other Scripture passages that are assigned in the lesson development.

◇ You may use your Bible to answer study questions and the questions in the self-test.

◇ Study this lesson and take the self-test according to the instructions given in Lesson 1.

the objectives...

9.1 *Identify and describe the occupant of the throne in heaven.*

9.2 *Describe and identify the twenty-four elders, giving four scriptural indications from Revelation 4:4.*

9.3 *Identify and give the significance of the persons represented by the four living creatures in Ezekiel chapter 1 and Revelation chapter 4.*

9.4 *Identify the seven-sealed scroll and indicate what this scroll contains.*

9.5 *Demonstrate why it will be as a slain Lamb rather than a Lion that Christ will open the seven-sealed scroll.*

9.6 *Identify things that take place at the opening of each of the first six seals.*

the outline...

1 Occupant of Heaven's Throne
2 Identity of the Twenty-four Elders
3 Identity of the Four Living Creatures
4 The Seven-Sealed Scroll and the Redeemer
5 Christ the Lamb Greatly Praised
6 The Opening of the First Six Seals

Identify and describe the occupant of the throne in heaven.

Occupant of Heaven's Throne

Revelation 4:3

The Person whom John sees on the throne in heaven is not only its occupant, but also its permanent possessor because He created it (Revelation 4:11). This Person is the Lord God Almighty (4:8). In Colossians 1:15 He is said to be invisible, but here in John's vision in chapters 4 and 5 we see that He has taken on visible characteristics. While various verses here describe the regal majesty of the throne, Revelation 4:11 gives the warrant or justification for His position as occupant of the throne. The prophet most certainly found it difficult to explain the glory of God's appearance, but he does compare God's glory to the dazzling splendor of rare jewels (4:3).

The clearness of jasper suggests purity, while the redness of carnelian speaks of redemption and judgment. Moreover, we have an indication that God is eternal (4:9–11), that He exercises will (v. 11), and that He cared enough about people's redemption to make the supreme sacrifice: giving His Son (5:9–10). Verse 3 tells us what encircled the throne, and a comparison with Genesis 9:12–16 suggests what is symbolized.

1 The occupant and permanent possessor of the throne in heaven is the
- a) preincarnate Lord Jesus Christ.
- b) Lord God Almighty.
- c) risen and triumphant Christ.

2 Which one of the following aspects describes most accurately the occupant of the throne in Revelation 4:4–5?
- a) He is awe-inspiring, surrounded by instruments of judgment, and all Creation flees from His presence.
- b) He is viewed as recently crowned, served by fearful subjects, and living in mists of eternal darkness.
- c) He is presented as living in glory, surrounded by worshipful subjects, and attended by awe-inspiring natural phenomena.

3 The rainbow which encircled the throne (4:3) symbolizes God's
a) visibility.
b) invisibility.
c) promises.
d) judgment.

Describe and identify the twenty-four elders, giving four scriptural indications from Revelation 4:4.

Identity of the Twenty-Four Elders

Revelation 4:4

The specific number of elders mentioned in Revelation 4:4 seems to indicate that these elders are a group which represents something. In Old Testament times the many priests were divided into twenty-four different orders, each order having a representative. When these representatives came together, they represented all the priesthood. Some scholars of the Bible believe that these elders are angels. Usually such scholars believe the church will go through the Great Tribulation, but nowhere in the Bible are angels called elders. However, in Acts 20:17–28 we see an example of those who are called elders, and they are not angels.

In Revelation 4:4 observe what the twenty-four elders are sitting on, how they are dressed, and what they have on their heads. Now reread the promises Jesus gave to the churches in Revelation 2:10 and 3:4–5, 18, and 21. It is evident from these Scriptures that the twenty-four elders of 4:4 have received what Jesus promised to victorious, overcoming church people in chapters 2 and 3. Redeemed people with white garments are mentioned again in Revelation 6:11 and 7:9 and 14. As concerns their crowns, two kinds of crowns are mentioned in Scripture. The crowns mentioned in 4:4 are *stephanos* or victors' crowns which may be compared to the medals that are given to winners in today's Olympic Games. The other kind, the *diodemata* (Revelation 19:12), are kingly crowns. The crowns of gold worn by the twenty-four elders in 4:4 have evidently been awarded to them as redeemed people on the basis of their victory over sin and Satan.

4 In Revelation 4:4 what are the twenty-four elders sitting on, how are they dressed, and what do they have on their heads?

....

....

5 In your notebook give four indications that the twenty-four elders of Revelation 4:4 are redeemed people rather than angels, based on what we have said in this section.

Who do the twenty-four elders of Revelation 4:4 represent? Many Bible scholars believe they represent only the church. They believe that no Israelite has any part in this group because at this point Israel as a nation will not yet have accepted Jesus Christ as Savior. These scholars often use Daniel 12:2 to show that the righteous people of the Old Testament will not be resurrected until just before or just after the Battle of Armageddon. We do not agree that such a conclusion can be based on this verse. Some men and women of God in the Old Testament were not Israelites (Noah, for example). According to the argument that no Israelite is represented by the twenty-four elders, Noah should be resurrected when the church is raptured, but not King David. This argument does not, therefore, seem valid.

In contrast to the preceding view, we and many other Bible scholars believe the number twenty-four in Revelation 4:4 represents all the righteous people of the Old Testament and all the righteous people of the New Testament. Why? As we read Hebrews chapter 11, we see that it is the story of God's Old Testament heroes of faith. Some of these heroes were Israelites; some were not. Verses 39 and 40 indicate that the righteous of the Old Testament are made perfect or complete together with New Testament believers, the church. Now examine the description of the New Jerusalem, the home of the bride of Christ, in Revelation 21:12–14. A comparison of these Scriptures indicates that the righteous of the Old Testament are represented together with the righteous of the New Testament in the New Jerusalem by twenty-four representatives: twelve tribes and twelve apostles.

6 According to Revelation 21:12–14, the significance of the wall around the New Jerusalem is that the

a) gates and foundations will be named for tribes of Israel.
b) gates and foundations will be named for apostles of Christ.
c) gates will be named for apostles of Christ and the foundations for tribes of Israel.
d) gates will be named for tribes of Israel and the foundations for apostles of Christ.

7 Explain in your notebook how Hebrews 11:39–40 and Revelation 21:12–14 seem to indicate that the twenty-four elders of Revelation 4:4 represent all the righteous of the Old Testament and all the righteous of the New Testament.

Before going on to the next section of the lesson, examine the symbols in Revelation 4:5 which indicate that God's throne is set for judgment.

Identify and give the significance of the persons represented by the four living creatures in Ezekiel chapter 1 and Revelation chapter 4.

Identity of the Four Living Creatures

Revelation 4:6–11

Four living creatures are described in Revelation 4:6–8, and four living creatures are also pointed out to us in Ezekiel 1. As one reads both of these passages, he may see that the description in Ezekiel differs from that in Revelation. However, the use of the words lion, ox, man, and eagle, in each description seems to indicate that what is represented or symbolized is the same in each of the two passages.

Ezekiel, at the point of this prophecy, is in his thirtieth year, the year he is to begin his priesthood. God wants to let this young priest and future prophet know through a vision of four living creatures that God still rules in the affairs of people. Ezekiel sees a man on a throne who has fire going up and down his body. This One is surrounded by dazzling light, and the glory which surrounds Him is like a rainbow on a rainy day (vv. 27–28). We believe the rainbow suggests that all of God's promises will be summed up in a man, while the fire shows that this Man will purify and judge. The whole scene is *resplendent with the glory of God.

resplendent
very bright; shining; splendid

8 In verse 28, how does Ezekiel relate his vision of four living creatures to God?

....

....

God's glory represents everything He is: His nature, power, and character. Anything one can say about God can be summed up by the word *glory*. Hebrews 1:3 indicates that the Son shares this infinite glory.

You have seen the lion, ox, man, and eagle in Ezekiel chapter 1. Now let us consider them here in Revelation 4:7. Remember the title of this book? It is *The Revelation of Jesus Christ* (Revelation 1:1). It occurs to us that since Ezekiel's vision was a vision of God's glory, and Jesus is God's glory, these four living creatures represent characteristics of Jesus Christ in both Ezekiel and Revelation. This representation is not new; some of the early church writers of the second century had the same opinion. They believed that the four Gospels pictured characteristics of the life of Jesus, which are indicated by the lion, ox, man, and eagle. One of these characteristics of Him is emphasized in each of the four Gospels. The following chart (Figure 9.1) on the four living creatures of Revelation 4:7 will help us to see this truth more clearly.

NAME	NATURAL MEANING	SPIRITUAL MEANING	EMPHASIZING GOSPEL
Lion	King of wild animals	Lion of the tribe of Judah	Matthew: Jesus as King of Israel
Ox	King of serving animals	Suffering servant of God	Mark: Jesus as obedient, active servant of God
Man	King of all of God's creation	Last Adam and perfect man	Luke: Jesus as sinless man
Eagle	Mysterious king of the birds	God-man beyond our understanding	John: Jesus as divine-human giver of eternal life

Figure 9.1

9 Whom does Scripture indicate as the radiance of God's glory?

....

....

10 Based on our discussion in this section, the person who seems to be characterized by the four living creatures in chapter 4 is

a) Almighty God.
b) Jesus Christ, the Son.
c) Moses, the initiator of the Law.
d) either Gabriel or Michael.

11 Review the preceding chart and then match each living creature characteristic (right) with the description of Jesus Christ (left) to which it relates.

. . . . **a**	Sinless perfection	1) Lion
. . . . **b**	King of Israel	2) Ox
. . . . **c**	God-man combination	3) Man
. . . . **d**	Obedient servant	4) Eagle

As an optional exercise, you may want to write in your notebook an outline of the worship found in Revelation 4:8–11. This would make an excellent study outline for you to share with others. Worship and service must accompany each other in our relationship with God (Matthew 4:10). Satan's self-exaltation (Isaiah 14:12–15) and desire to be worshiped (Matthew 4:9) caused his downfall, but Jesus always did His Father's will! May this be our prayer, "God, help us to have you on the thrones of our hearts instead of ourselves—not our will, but yours be done in our lives."

Identify the seven-sealed scroll and indicate what this scroll contains.

The Seven-Sealed Scroll and the Redeemer

Jeremiah 32:1–44, Revelation 5:1–5

As we read Revelation 5:1–5, let us observe in the description of the seven-sealed scroll these things: (1) the location of the writing on the scroll, (2) the question the angel asks, and (3) the answer to the angel's question. Remember, the Bible is its own best interpreter. In order to shed some light on the scroll in question, let us read all of Jeremiah 32 carefully to see if we can identify this seven-sealed scroll.

In the Old Testament we find a Hebrew term, *go'el*, which may be translated "kinsman redeemer" or "nearest relative." Its use is associated with the ownership of property and how property was passed on from one generation to another. Property during this period of time was protected by certain legal statutes. In the event that one mortgaged his property and later could not redeem it, his *go'el* could redeem it for him.

Leviticus 25:8–55 gives these details of property ownership for the people of Israel, including conditions of sale and terms of redeeming one's rights of ownership. This scriptural setting also includes terms of *indenture, that is, the conditions under which poor persons might contract to work for others for given periods of time.

indenture
a written agreement, such as a contract or deed; contract by which a servant or apprentice is bound to work for someone else

In the story of Ruth in the Bible we have the practical application of the *go'el* principle in what Boaz did when he married Ruth (Ruth 3:9–12; 4:1–12). He redeemed, or bought back, Ruth's property for her. The terms of these property transactions were written on the inside of scrolls and stated what had to be done to redeem the property (see v. 11 in Jeremiah 32). The scroll was signed on the back side with the names of the witnesses and the name of the *go'el*. It was rolled up and sealed so that the details of the agreement were on the inside and the names of the witnesses and the *go'el* on the outside. In the event a person lost his property and could not redeem it, only his *go'el* could open the seals and see what had to be done to redeem the property.

With the brief background of the scroll in biblical history and the related matter of the kinsman-redeemer in view, let us read Revelation 5:1–5 once again before we answer the following questions. As you reflect on the very moving scene in heaven portrayed here, imagine John's feelings (v. 4) as the impact of this moment dawned on him. He may have suddenly seen that the whole human race was in bondage to sin until the great Kinsman-Redeemer came to buy back all people at a very great cost. Perhaps the true significance of the cross and its necessity for our redemption flooded in on the prophet with new force. Christ was our near relative, He was willing to redeem us, and He was able. Thank God He redeemed us!

12 The writing on the seven-sealed scroll in Revelation 5 is located
- a) only on the inside of the scroll.
- b) on the inside, but some signatures are on the outside.
- c) on the outside where all can view its contents.
- d) on both the inside and the outside of the scroll.

13 The question the angel asked regarding the scroll was
- a) "Who is the nearest relative?"
- b) "Are there any near relatives?"
- c) "Who is worthy to break the seals and open the scroll?"
- d) "Who is willing to break the seals and open the scroll?"

14 One of the elders responded to the angel's question, saying
- a) "No one in all the universe is worthy to break the seals and to open the scroll."
- b) "The Lion of the tribe of Judah . . . is able to break the seals and open the scroll."
- c) "God will find one who is both willing and worthy to break the seals and open the scroll."
- d) "A search will be made to find a suitable *go'el* for this occasion."

15 According to our discussion in this section and our study of the supporting Scriptures, the Hebrew term *go'el* means
- a) any one who is able and willing to redeem another.
- b) one who is a near relative, a kinsman-redeemer.
- c) those who are in sympathy with people in need.
- d) one who is moved by the dismal conditions in society.

The seven-sealed scroll is a symbol that represents the results of sin that separated people from the eternal life that they were created to enjoy. The opening of this scroll represents the act of making eternal life available to people. The seven-sealed scroll here represents the terms for the redemption of people so that they may inherit God's provision: eternal life. First Corinthians 15:20-21 tells us that in Adam all people die and are separated from eternal life; it also says that in Christ, the Kinsman-Redeemer, eternal life is made available to all who will accept His redemption. Adam was created to be the head of the human race and to live in perfect fellowship with God, to love Him, and to be loved by Him. But Adam and Eve turned their backs on God (Genesis 3:1–6). In 1 John 2:15–17 we see a brief definition of *love for the world* and how it separates people from eternal life.

16 The seven-sealed scroll here represents the
a) terms for the redemption of people from slavery to sin so that they may inherit eternal life.
b) sins of people which will be used as a basis for condemning them.
c) symbolical catalogue of all people's sins.
d) list of those who have accepted God's salvation.

17 The significance of the seven-sealed scroll of Revelation 5:1–5, according to our study, is that
a) without Christ's work of redemption, which is symbolized here, people would have remained under the slavery of sin.
b) Christ's work of atonement would not have been accomplished without a symbolic scene.
c) all biblical symbolism must be acted out in real life.
d) the artistic symmetry of odd-numbered decorations.

To summarize this scene, then, John wept in Revelation 5:4 because he knew what this seven-sealed scroll meant. He knew that unless someone could open the way to the eternal inheritance Adam lost, mankind would continue in his lost condition without hope. Satan would continue as a roaring lion, and sin, pain, misery, war, hatred, prejudice, and suffering would also continue. John knew that people could never be freed from the curse of sin and that God's kingdom would never come on earth unless someone could open this scroll, redeeming people from their lost estate. Thank God, One was found!

18 Match each term or phrase (right) with its appropriate description (left).

. . . . **a** Must be near of kin, willing and able to redeem one in need

. . . . **b** Contained terms of redemption

. . . . **c** Term used to describe one who is a near relative, a kinsman-redeemer

. . . . **d** Act which symbolized voiding the terms of the contract, thus freeing one from its requirements

. . . . **e** Symbolized that the contract was in force until terms were fulfilled by the one who made it or his *go'el*

1) Scroll
2) *Go'el*
3) Seals
4) Breaking seals
5) Qualifications of a redeemer

Demonstrate why it will be as a slain Lamb rather than a Lion that Christ will open the seven-sealed scroll.

Christ the Lamb Greatly Praised

Revelation 5:6–14

In the book of Revelation Christ is first mentioned as a Lamb in 5:6. Earlier John the Baptist and Peter had referred to Christ as a lamb. John the Baptist had said of Jesus that He was, "The lamb of God who takes away the sin of the world" (John 1:29). Referring to our spiritual redemption, Peter indicated that we are saved by "the precious blood of Christ, a lamb without blemish or defect" (1 Peter 1:19). Boaz indeed redeemed Ruth's property, but Christ has redeemed, spiritually and eternally, those who believe in Him. *Remember always that you are *ransomed*

ransomed
delivered, especially from sin or ignorance

from the effects of sin by the blood of Christ the slain lamb! "Without the shedding of blood there is no forgiveness" (Hebrews 9:22). Jesus poured out His entire sinless life for you, me, and all other people, including those who have not yet heard about it. *Remember also that to have our sins forgiven does not remove us from temptation to sin again.* Christ, however, overcame all temptation to sin (Luke 4:1–12), lives in us (Galatians 2:20), and can enable us through our faith in Him to overcome all temptations (1 Corinthians 10:13).

In Revelation 5:6–7 John sees a Lamb take the seven-sealed scroll from the Occupant of the throne. Obviously, Christ the Lamb is taking the scroll in order to open it. Since John had been told about the lion aspect of Christ in verse 5, he may well have expected to see the scroll taken by the Lion rather than the Lamb. However, since the opening of this scroll represents the act of making eternal life available once again to people, Christ the slain Lamb will open it. Thus Christ, God's Son and our *Go'el*, proceeds to lake the scroll out of the Father's hand (v. 7). No one else can or ever could have done so or even dared to try.

19 Explain how we are enabled to overcome all our temptations.

....

20 Why is the slain-lamb aspect of Christ rather than His lion aspect emphasized as He opens the seven-sealed scroll?

....

Now carefully examine Revelation 5:8–14. This passage expresses great praise for Christ the Lamb. We observe that each one of the four living creatures and twenty-four elders is praising Him with a harp, and each has a bowl of incense (v. 8). Moreover, we see that every creature in the universe is praising Him (v.13). Musical instruments are frequently used to praise God in the Psalms. We believe that the prayers of the righteous must be, "Your kingdom come," as in Matthew 6:10. As an optional exercise, write an outline in your notebook of the details of this great praise in 5:8–14. It will make an excellent sermon or Bible study outline.

21 Describe in your notebook the vast extent of praise in Revelation 5:8–14 for Christ the Lamb.

What a great day of praise that is going to be for those who know Jesus Christ. From what is happening in our world, it appears that this day will soon come. We must tell people about Jesus, for the time is drawing near when He is coming to take us to be with Him forever.

Identify things that take place at the opening of each of the first six seals.

The Opening of the First Six Seals

Revelation 6:1–17

In Revelation 6 Christ the Lamb opens the first six seals of the seven-sealed scroll. As He does so, one of the four living creatures says "Come." The word translated *come* in verses 1, 3, 5, and 7 can also be translated *go*. It appears that *go* is used here because *go* shows more clearly that nothing can move from heaven without permission.

In response to the summons, John looks at the unfolding scene which follows. As the first seal is broken, John sees a white horse ridden by one who holds a bow. Moreover, the rider is given a victors crown, and he goes forward as a conqueror bent on conquest. There are varieties of opinions about the identity of this white horse rider under the first seal (v. 2). Some believe it is Jesus; some interpret this rider as representative of the Christian age; some feel he represents the Word of God going forth.

The majority of those who believe the church will *not* go through the seven years of the tribulation period, however, believe that this rider is the Antichrist. Why? First, the word *anti* does not always mean *against*; sometimes it means *instead of*. The Antichrist is going to be the man the world and Israel accept as their Christ instead of the true Christ. Second, we have seen from 2 Thessalonians 2 that the Antichrist will come on the scene to begin the tribulation period. When Jesus comes back in Revelation 19, He too will be on a white horse; however, here in Revelation 6:2 the white horse rider appears to be an imitation. Thirdly, Jesus will have the **diadems* or kingly crown On His head. Fourth, the bow is a military weapon which may represent the military power of the Antichrist. The only weapon Jesus will need is His Word, the sharp double-edged sword. A final item regarding the identity of the white horse rider is that it seems rather inconsistent for Christ the Lamb to be shown opening the seals while He is at the same time the contents of the first one.

diadems
kingly power or authority; the victor's crown or crowns

The opening of the seals marks the beginning of the Great Tribulation. Thus the first major event concerns the unveiling of the man who will be responsible for so much that will occur during this *turbulent period. You probably noticed that we used the term *Great Tribulation* to denote the entire seven-year period of tribulation. Some call only the second half of the seven years the Great Tribulation, but we will see when we get to chapter 7 that the entire seven-year period should probably be called the *Great Tribulation*. The Great Tribulation is also called the *Day of the Lord*. It is a special period of time in which we believe God will accomplish His goals for Israel and the nations of the world.

turbulent
causing disorder; unruly; violent

Scriptures which we feel indicate that the period in view is longer than would be indicated by just half the seven-year period are Isaiah 2:12–21, 13:9–16; Joel 1:15–2:11, 2:28–32, 3:9–12; Amos 5:18–20; Obadiah 15–17; and Zephaniah 1:7–18. Zechariah chapters 12–14 emphasize both God's judgment of the nations and His restoration of Israel. Jeremiah 30:7 calls it "the time of Jacob's trouble" (KJV), while Daniel 12:1 indicates that it will be the greatest time of trouble in history. The Great Tribulation is the time of the wrath of God. We will see this as we go on through the book of Revelation. As we have endeavored to point out and as 1 Thessalonians 5:9 clearly states, Christians are not appointed to suffer wrath.

22 Most people who do not believe that the church will go through the seven years of the Great Tribulation believe that the rider of the white horse is the
- a) Antichrist.
- b) Lord Jesus Christ.
- c) Word of God.
- d) Christian age personified.

The Antichrist, as we have seen, is called by many names in the Bible. Various portions of Scripture have referred to him as:

- The Antichrist (1 John 2:18).
- A little horn (Daniel 7:8, 23–26).
- A stern-faced king (Daniel 8:23).

- The prince that shall come (Daniel 9:26–27, KJV).
- The worthless shepherd (Zechariah 11:15–17).
- The lawless one (2 Thessalonians 2:1–12).
- The man doomed to destruction (2 Thessalonians 2:3).

Other descriptions of the Antichrist are found in Scripture. He has the characteristics of a:

- Boastful speaker (Daniel 7:8).
- Military man (Daniel 8:24).
- Master of intrigue (Daniel 8:24).
- Successful man (Daniel 8:24).
- Proud person (Daniel 8:25).
- Man who corrupts with flattery (Daniel 11:32).
- One who magnifies himself above God (Daniel 11:36).

We will discuss the Antichrist further in connection with Revelation 13 and 17. For a time he will probably bring peace and straighten out the world's economy. Some Bible scholars interpret the fact that he arrives with a bow and no arrows as evidence that his early conquests represent diplomatic and therefore bloodless achievements. However, before long he will have to implement his program for world peace and economic unity, and this will undoubtedly bring about serious loss of life. For the present, however, we must consider the circumstances that will follow his unveiling.

As the second seal is opened, a fiery red horse emerges. He is ridden by one who carries a large sword. This rider has power to take peace from the earth (vv. 3–4). His emergence symbolizes war which will follow. Next, under the opened third seal, is a black horse whose rider carries a pair of scales. This quite clearly represents a shortage of food (v. 5). In the wake of war, as masses of men are diverted from food production to fighting, famine frequently follows. However, with the world's rapidly increasing population, the inability of the world's people to produce enough to feed themselves will doubtless make this matter worse. Food will be very costly as the shortage progresses (v. 6); however, some people even in these difficult times will seek oil and wine which are luxuries. People will sell their souls for luxuries. They will not understand what Jesus meant when He told the woman of Samaria, "Everyone who drinks this water will be thirsty again, but whoever drinks the water I give him will never thirst" (John 4:13–14). Jesus was explaining that satisfaction comes from what one has on the inside. Happiness works from the inside out—not from the outside in! What good will luxuries be when there is not enough food?

personified
represented or regarded as being a person

As the fourth seal is broken, a pale horse emerges ridden by one called *Death* who is followed closely by *Hades*. Here Death and Hades are *personified, that is, they are referred to as persons. Personification is common in the Old Testament. For example, in Proverbs wisdom is treated as if it were a woman (1:20). This scene speaks of the devastating loss of life that will take place in the Great Tribulation. Hades always follows death for the non-Christian.

Under the fifth seal John sees a host of martyrs. Some Bible scholars believe these slain represent the martyrs of the Christian faith throughout history. Those who believe that the church will go through the Great Tribulation see them as Christian believers who are killed during this final period. We believe that these slain people are those who accept Jesus Christ during the first half of the Great

Tribulation period who will be killed because of their faith in God. They will be "under the altar" (v. 9) because God will consider their deaths as a sacrifice.

Under the sixth seal (vv. 12–14) we see one of the most dramatic pictures in God's Word. Some of the descriptions are similes or comparisons that use the words *like* or *as* to make the word pictures more vivid. The other descriptions make use of direct, literal language.

In rapid order John sees a mighty earthquake, something like an eclipse of the sun, an ominous change in the moon in which it appears to earth dwellers to be blood red (which might be the result of volcanic ash or dust in the atmosphere brought about by the earthquake). Moreover, he sees many stars, probably*meteorites, fall to the earth, while the sky above suddenly disappears even as the mountains and islands of the planet are moved from their places. Verses 15–17 give us people's reaction to these frightful scenes. Fear grips the hearts of all people as they realize that this is a time unlike any other in human history. People have seen the wrath of nature on occasion, and they have felt the wrath of man at times. However, with the sky removed, they now seem to be able to see directly to God's throne, and they realize that they face the wrath of the God of the universe.

meteorites
masses of rock or metal that enter the earth's atmosphere from outer space with great speed and reach the earth without burning up

This is just the beginning of the Great Tribulation, the day of the Lord. Keep in mind that God is a God of such great love that He sent His Son to die for all people of the world. God loved us so much that He sent His Son to pay the penalty for our sin—to die in our place. Yet God is also a God of holiness and justice. He cannot tolerate sin which separates people from Him. His very nature requires Him to punish the sin of those who will not accept the forgiveness He has provided through the sacrifice of His Son. Therefore knowing what lies ahead, Christians must exert every effort to make God's salvation known to all people. This is the task of the church collectively in the world, and it is the personal responsibility of each Christian as well.

23 Identify some things that take place at the opening of each of the first six seals by matching each seal (right) with the things (left) which take place when it is opened.

. . . . **a** Appearance of horse rider in which Death and Hades are personified

. . . . **b** Great earthquake and related physical and heavenly disturbances

. . . . **c** Appearance of horse rider who takes peace from the earth

. . . . **d** People killed because of their Christian faith

. . . . **e** Appearance of horse rider with a bow

. . . . **f** Appearance of horse rider with a pair of scales

1) First seal
2) Second seal
3) Third seal
4) Fourth seal
5) Fifth seal
6) Sixth seal

Self-Test

Multiple choice: Circle the letter preceding the best answer..

1 The person who is the permanent possessor of the throne in heaven is the
- a) Lion of the tribe of Judah.
- b) slain Lamb of God.
- c) Lord God Almighty.
- d) Angel of the Lord.

2 The vast praise for Christ in Revelation 5:8–14 comes from
- a) the four living creatures and the twenty-four elders.
- b) myriads of angels.
- c) all other creatures in the universe.
- d) all of the above.
- e) both a) and b) above.

3 The person who seems to be represented by the four living creatures in Ezekiel 1 and Revelation 4 is
- a) God the Father.
- b) Jesus Christ.
- c) a mighty angel.
- d) Ezekiel himself.

4 The Hebrew word *go'el* means
- a) "victor's crown" or "kingly crown."
- b) "come" or "go."
- c) "against" or "instead of."
- d) "kinsman-redeemer" or "nearest relative."

5 Revelation 6 indicates that a great earthquake will take place at the opening of the
- a) sixth seal.
- b) fifth seal.
- c) fourth seal.
- d) third seal.
- e) second seal.

True-False. Write **T** on the blank space preceding each TRUE statement. Write **F** if the statement is FALSE.

. . . . **6** The ox aspect relates more closely to Jesus as a God-man combination.

. . . . **7** The lion aspect of Christ rather than the lamb aspect is in view when He opens the seven-sealed scroll.

. . . . **8** The significance of the seven-sealed scroll of Revelation 5:1–5 is that without Christ's work of redemption, which is symbolized here, people would have remained forever under the slavery of sin.

Short Answer. Briefly answer the following questions in the space provided.

9 Explain how Hebrews 11:39–40 seems to indicate that the twenty-four elders of Revelation 4:4 represent all the righteous of the Old Testament and all the righteous of the New Testament.

....

....

10 State Christ's relationship to eternal life for human beings.

....

Answers to study questions

12 d) on both the inside and the outside of the scroll.

1 b) Lord God Almighty.

13 c) "Who is worthy to break the seals and open the scroll?"

2 c) He is presented as living in glory, surrounded by worshipful subjects, and attended by awe-inspiring natural phenomena.

14 b) "The Lion of the tribe of Judah . . . is able to break the seals and open the scroll."

3 c) promises.

15 b) one who is a near relative, a kinsman-redeemer.

4 They are sitting on thrones, they are dressed in white, and they have crowns of gold on their heads.

16 a) terms for the redemption of people from slavery to sin so that they may inherit eternal life.

5 (1) Nowhere in the Bible are angels called elders. (2) The twenty-four elders of Revelation 4:4 have received what Jesus promised to victorious, overcoming church people in Revelation chapters 2 and 3. (3) White garments are mentioned later in the book of Revelation as the clothing of redeemed people. (4) The crowns of gold in Revelation 4:4 have evidently been given to redeemed people for their victory over sin and Satan.

17 a) without Christ's work of redemption, which is symbolized here, people would have remained under the slavery of sin.

6 d) gates will be named for tribes of Israel and the foundations for apostles of Christ.

18 **a** 5) Qualifications of a redeemer
b 1) Scroll
c 2) *Go'el*
d 4) Breaking seals
e 3) Seals

7 Hebrews 11:39–40 seems to suggest this by showing that the righteous of the Old Testament will be made perfect together with the righteous of the New Testament, the church. Revelation 21:12–14 seems to indicate this by its connection of the twelve tribes of Israel, who refer to the righteous of the Old Testament, with the twelve apostles of the Lamb, who refer to the righteous of the New Testament, with the home of the bride of Christ, the New Jerusalem.

19 By our faith in Christ who lives in us

8 He indicates that this vision is "the likeness of the glory of God."

20 Because the opening of this scroll represents His redemptive act of making eternal life available to people.

9 The Son, Jesus Christ

21 This vast praise is from the four living creatures and twenty-four elders, many multiplied thousands of angels, and every creature in the universe. It starts as a mighty anthem of praise and gains in extent until it seems to reverberate throughout the universe.

10 b) Jesus Christ, the Son.

22 a) Antichrist.

11 **a** 3) Man
b 1) Lion
c 4) Eagle
d 2) Ox

23 **a** 4) Fourth seal
b 6) Sixth seal
c 2) Second seal
d 5) Fifth seal
e 1) First seal
f 3) Third seal

Lesson 10 Midtribulation Events

In our last lesson, we addressed matters of concern related to the beginning of the Great Tribulation. We observed the unveiling of the Antichrist and the rise of unequaled war, famine, and disease. Death like a hungry animal followed these three, claiming countless victims and filling Hades. Meanwhile, amid all this trouble creation was *convulsed with its greatest natural disasters. Fear gripped the hearts of people as they looked toward the Sovereign to whom every living creature must give account. Now we move beyond this initial preview of the Day of the Lord to events which seem to be associated with the mid-point of the Great Tribulation period.

convulsed
what has been shaken violently

Two companies of people are in view in chapter 7: the 144,000 and a vast multitude of white-robed, palm-bearing people. We will examine each and its significance in end-time events. Following this review, we will see how the trumpet judgments wreak havoc on the earth and its people. While we might expect people to respond to the fearful events that follow the opening of the six seals by repenting, we learn that most do not. Rather, they become hardened because they love their sin. They are caught in its clutches and are slaves to its devices. Unless they consciously will to have these chains of sin broken by the power of the gospel, they will remain victims of their filthy habits, appetites, and carnal nature. Our task is to share the good news that true life—"life . . . to the full" (John 10:10) is available to them now in Jesus Christ. He can satisfy their every desire, longing, and purpose.

the activities...

- ◇ Read carefully Revelation chapter 7, 8, and 9 before you study this lesson.
- ◇ You may use your Bible to answer study questions and the questions in the self-test.
- ◇ Be sure to look in the glossary for the meanings of any key words you do not know.
- ◇ Remember to write your own answers to the study questions before looking up the answers at the back of this lesson. This procedure will help you to learn the material more quickly.
- ◇ Study this lesson and take the self-test on it according to procedures given in Lesson 1.

the objectives...

10.1 *Relate major events in Revelation chapters 4–22 to the time segment in which they will occur.*

10.2 *Identify the purpose of the sealing of the 144,000.*

10.3 *Explain who the 144,000 people from twelve tribes of Israel represent.*

10.4 *Explain why certain tribes of Israel are omitted from the list of the tribes of Israel given in Revelation 7:5–8.*

10.5 *Identify and give the significance of the great white robed multitude of Revelation 7.*

10.6 *Explain the symbolism of the angel with the golden censer.*

10.7 *Identify things that will take place when each of the first six trumpets is sounded.*

the outline...

1 Introduction

2 Overview of Revelation Chapters 4–22

3 Four Angels and the Sealing Angel

4 The 144,000

5 The 144,000 Identified

6 The Great Multitude in White Robes

7 An Angel With a Golden Censer

8 The Sounding of the First Six Trumpets

Introduction

As our lesson title indicates, we are concerned with events that occur during the tribulation period. As you will see, however, there is some question about when this point is reached, that is, what scriptural events mark its beginning. Some scholars believe that Revelation 12 marks its arrival, while others think it begins during the bowl judgments in chapter 16. Still others are convinced that the middle point of the Tribulation is reached at the opening of the sixth seal in Revelation 6 because the destruction there is similar to that given in Matthew 24:29. In our view and that of many other Bible teachers, the events described in chapter 7 take place at the middle of the seven years. We might add that even those who place the middle point of the Tribulation at a different place in the book of Revelation agree that the events described in chapter 7 seem to be at or near the midpoint.

The events that occur in chapter 7 seem to suggest that the final half of the tribulation period begins between the opening of the sixth and seventh seals. In a broader sense, however, we believe that all the material we will study in chapters 7–9 concerns the middle of the seven-year period. Our approach to these things will therefore reflect this underlying belief.

Relate major events in Revelation chapters 4–22 to the time segment in which they will occur.

An Overview of Revelation Chapters 4–22

Before we begin our study of midtribulation events in Revelation chapters 7–9, let us examine the following chart (Figure 10.1) on Revelation chapters

4–22. Our purpose in doing this is to help you understand better the order of events you study in this course. Examine the following chart carefully before you move on to do Study Question 1.

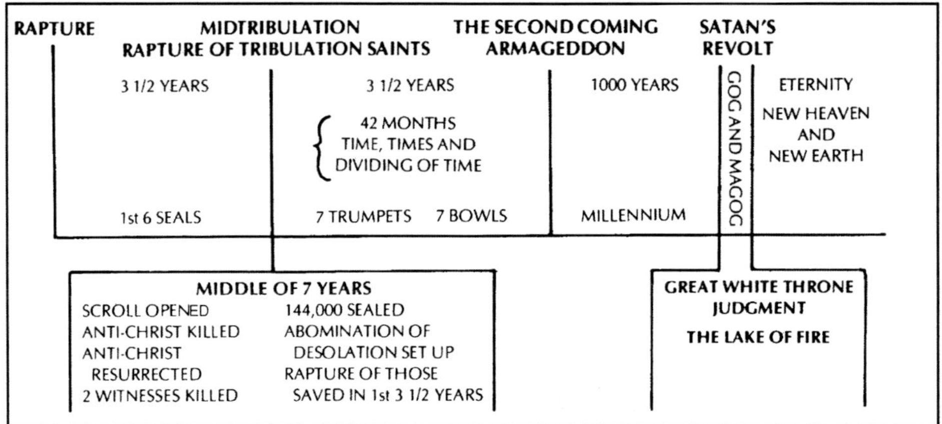

Figure 10.1

1 Match each of the five time segments considered in this section (right) with the event or events (left) which are associated with each one.

. . . . **a** White throne judgment and Lake of Fire
. . . . **b** Opening of first seal
. . . . **c** Last two bowls are poured out
. . . . **d** New heaven and new earth
. . . . **e** Midtribulation rapture of the righteous
. . . . **f** Millennial reign of Christ

1) First 3 ½ years
2) Between the two 3 1/2–year periods
3) Second 3 ½ years
4) 1000 years
5) Eternity

In this lesson we will focus our attention primarily on the part of the foregoing chart that concerns the midtribulation rapture of the righteous and other midtribulation events. We must hasten to add that some of the major events noted on the chart occur at the very beginning or end of a given period. For example, the last two bowls and the Battle of Armageddon occur at the end of the second three and one-half years before the Millennium begins. With the general time frame in view, let us move on to examine midtribulation events in Revelation chapters 7–9.

Identify the purpose of the sealing of the 144,000.

Four Angels and the Sealing Angel

Revelation 7:1–3

John now views four angels who stand strategically at the four corners of the earth, holding back the four winds from blowing on the earth. Verse 1 does not tell us whether these are winds of blessing or judgment. However, we readily see in verses 2 and 3 that they are destructive. At this point, another angel comes into focus who has the seal of the living God. He calls out to the four angels to postpone their mission of judgment until "we put a seal on the foreheads of the servants of our God" (v. 3).

In the immediate and larger context (chapters 7–9), it appears that the seal is protective because judgment is about to be poured out. In chapter 9:3–4 it is obvious that the seal serves to protect those who are sealed from the ravages of the fifth trumpet judgment. Here the process of judgment is restrained while the 144,000 receive a seal which provides protection for them. It is *obvious* for it is put on their foreheads.

2 Four angels in Revelation 7:1–3 hold back the four winds which are intended to
   a) renew the earth.
   b) harm the earth.
   c) revive the earth's people.
   d) bring storms on earth.

3 While four angels restrain the four winds, another angel comes into focus whose mission is to
   a) restrain judgment while the gospel is proclaimed.
   b) encourage the angels of judgment to complete their task soon.
   c) determine which servants of God are worthy to be sealed.
   d) place a seal on the foreheads of the servants of God.

4 The purpose of the sealing of the 144,000 is to
   a) enrich the lives of those who are sealed.
   b) empower those who receive the seal of God for service.
   c) provide protection for them in the midst of judgment.
   d) inspire them to do mighty deeds during the period of judgment.

Explain who the 144,000 people from twelve tribes of Israel represent.

The 144,000

Revelation 7:4

There are different viewpoints concerning the identity of the 144,000. Some people believe that the 144,000 have already gone to heaven, while the rest of God's people work to inherit the earth. There is absolutely no biblical basis for such a belief. Other people teach that the 144,000 are Christians who keep the Old Testament Sabbath Day as part of their salvation. Again, our response is that there is no scriptural evidence for such teaching. Two major viewpoints are held about the identity of this group. They are usually divided between those who believe that the church will go through the Great Tribulation and those who do not hold this view.

Those who believe that the church will go through the Great Tribulation tend to think that the number 144,000 is representative of all God's people in this present period of time. They feel that this representative body is made up of Jews and Gentiles alike who accept Jesus Christ as Savior.

These people believe that the 144,000 represent the church. Some of these people, however, believe that Israel will be restored and *coexist with the church on earth.

coexist
to exist together or at the same time; to live in peace with each other

Those who believe the 144,000 represent all the people who will be saved during the Great Tribulation base their belief on certain Scriptures which they believe point out that the church receives blessings which God originally promised to Abraham. Some of the Scriptures they use are Romans 2:28–29, Romans 4 (especially verse 16), and Galatians 3:6–9. They state also that many of the prophecies in the Old Testament which are given to Israel are given again in the New Testament with reference to the church. They say that an example of this type of repetition is the quotation of Jeremiah 31:31–34 in Hebrews 8:8–12.

However, notice Paul's remarks in Romans 9:1–5 and try to decide whether he is speaking of *the church as spiritual Israel or of the physical race of Israel.* The following points from Romans chapters 9–11 might help further to determine who these 144,000 sealed people from twelve tribes of Israel represent.

1. Not all of Abraham's children will inherit the promises God gave Abraham; these promises must be inherited by faith (9:6–9).
2. God chose Israel on the basis of His will—not the people's works (9: 10–18).
3. The majority of Israelites have fallen from God because of unbelief (9:27–33).
4. The only way anyone can be saved, Jew or Gentile, is by faith in Jesus Christ (10:6–13).
5. Believing Gentiles have been grafted into the root of a cultivated olive tree (11:11–24).
6. The spiritual blindness of Israel will be removed when "the full number of the Gentiles has come in" (11:25).
7. Israel as a nation will be saved and grafted back into the righteousness of God (11:26–32).

The phrase "all Israel" (Romans 11:26) refers to what the Old Testament calls "the remnant of Israel," for example, see Isaiah 10:20-21. It is the nation of Israel of the last days which will turn to Jesus Christ during the Great Tribulation. This does not mean that every Jew will accept Jesus Christ as Savior any more than every Gentile accepts Him now. However, those who do accept Him will be considered "the remnant." The naming of specific tribes in Revelation 7:5–8 seems to refer to people from the nation of Israel that will have turned to God in faith and become spiritual Israel also. So in these verses, 12, the number that is seen by some to symbolize final completion, times 12 shows that the remnant of Israel accepts Christ. We believe that this acceptance will bring in the final half of the Great Tribulation period, a view that will be supported in Revelation 12 and in Daniel 12. We might add that some view the 144,000 as the first fruits of the whole nation that will turn to God. That is, the 144,000 are just the *earnest* of the total harvest from the nation of Israel that will eventually be saved. While we are not indicating that this is so, it is an interesting suggestion that we may ponder as we study.

5 In Romans 9:1–5 Paul is evidently speaking to
- a) neither the church nor the nation of Israel.
- b) both the church and the nation of Israel.
- c) the nation of Israel rather than the church.
- d) the church rather than the nation of Israel.

6 In your notebook explain who the sealed 144,000 people from twelve tribes of Israel represent.

Explain why certain tribes of Israel are omitted from the list of the tribes of Israel given in Revelation 7:5–8.

The 144,000 Identified

Revelation 7:5–8

We move now to a discussion of which tribes of Israel are included in the 144,000 and why some of those mentioned earlier in Scripture are omitted in Revelation 7:5–8. Genesis 35:23–26 gives us an initial list of the sons of Israel. Later on, Israel pronounced a special blessing on the sons of Joseph, Ephraim and Manasseh (Genesis 48:11–20), giving Joseph a "double portion" by including his sons as heirs among the tribes of Israel. A further change occurred in the list of Israel's heirs when God chose the tribe of Levi instead of the firstborn sons of all the tribes of Israel. Thus, the tribe of Levi did not have an inheritance in the land. In the list of sealed tribes given in Revelation 7:5–8, however, it appears that Levi has been inserted for Dan and Joseph for Ephraim.

You may ask, "Why are Dan and Ephraim not mentioned?" We believe that clues to this question are to be found in Old Testament history. For example, it appears that Dan was the first tribe to go into idolatry (Judges 18:30-31). Moreover, when the kingdom of Israel was divided following the death of Solomon, Jeroboam, the king of the northern kingdom, established two official centers of idolatry for his people: one was located in Dan; the other was located in Bethel, a city in the land of Ephraim. A quick review of Exodus 20:34 and Deuteronomy 16:21–22 reminds us that God hates idolatry. Looking ahead to the Antichrist's rule, we see that he will attempt to lead Israel once again to forsake God and worship an idol made in his own image. He will forbid lawful worship and require all people to worship him and his image. This is the abomination that Daniel mentions (9:27) and to which Jesus refers (Matthew 24:15). This latest expression of idolatry, like all others before it, will bring about the judgment of God upon the Antichrist and his kingdom. We thus believe that the omission of Dan and Ephraim are directly related to God's feelings about idolatry.

7 According to our study in this section, explain why the names of Dan and Ephraim are omitted from the list of sealed tribes of Israel in Revelation 7:5–8.

....

....

Identify and give the significance of the great white robed multitude of Revelation 7.

The Great Multitude in White Robes

Revelation 7:9–17

John now describes the great multitude in white robes that appears in his vision at the middle point of the Great Tribulation period. He indicates that this multitude is made up of countless people. He views them as they stand before the throne in front of the Lamb. They are wearing white robes and are holding palm branches in their hands. John observes as they lift their voices in a mighty anthem of praise to God, and he hears the angels, the elders, and the four living creatures respond to affirm God's worthiness to receive universal praise.

As an optional exercise, write in your notebook a detailed outline of the praise found in Revelation 7:10–12 as you were encouraged to do with the worship found in Revelation 4:8–11 and the praise in 5:8–14.

Following the great and glorious expression of praise, John learns from one of the elders that the great multitude of people in white robes "have come out of the great tribulation" and "have washed their robes . . . in the blood of the Lamb" (7:14). Obviously, this group of people has been redeemed out of the Great Tribulation. These are the facts we shall address shortly.

We have already discussed the identity of the twenty-four elders who serve in the presence of God. In this section we are introduced to another group. For purposes of comparison, we have prepared a chart (Figure 10.2) that shows a few important differences between the twenty-four elders of Revelation 4:4 and 5:8 and this white-robed multitude of 7:9. We note especially that the elders serve in the immediate presence of the throne; the multitude stands rather than sits in God's presence. The elders wear crowns; whereas, the multitude does not. The elders have harps and bowls of *incense which indicate their service; the multitude is a joyful band of the redeemed who praise God.

incense
any substance producing a pleasant odor when burned

24 Elders	***White-Robed Multitude***
Sit on thrones around God's throne	Stand before God's throne
Have crowns	No crowns are mentioned
Have harps and hold bowls of incense	Hold palm branches

Figure 10.2

We have discussed the description of this vast multitude and where it came from. Now we must attempt to identify the group and its significance in our overall scheme of end-time events. In this regard, there are three basic views about the identity of this group. Some Bible scholars believe that the rapture of the church takes place in the middle of the seven-year tribulation period. They base their belief on verse 14, which says that these are redeemed ones who have come out of the Great Tribulation. A second view is held by some who say that this great multitude is composed of *martyrs who are not yet resurrected bodily. Our view and that of many other Bible teachers is that this multitude represents those who have been caught up in a "second rapture" at the midpoint of the tribulation period. From the facts given here it seems obvious that the people in this white-robed multitude have accepted Jesus Christ during the first half of the Tribulation. We are probably safe in assuming that some members of this group have been killed for their faith. However, there is no hint that all of them are martyrs. We learn from this multitude that people will apparently be saved during the Tribulation and that they will be caught up to the presence of the Lord, where they will remain forever.

martyrs
persons killed because of their beliefs

8 Circle the letter preceding each TRUE statement.

a The multitude in view is not involved with service in God's presence.
b Robes washed in the blood of the Lamb indicate martyrdom.
c Our study to this point and the immediate context indicate that this multitude represents the raptured church.
d We learn from our study of this numberless multitude that people will be saved during the tribulation period and caught up into God's presence.
e From the scriptural reference, we see that the great multitude comes from every nation, people, tribe, and language.
f The destiny of the white-robed multitude is not stated clearly in John's vision.

9 In your notebook identify the great white-robed multitude of Revelation 7:9–17 and give its significance.

Explain the symbolism of the angel with the golden censer.

An Angel with a Golden Censer

Revelation 8:1–5

With the opening of the seventh and final seal, the seven-sealed scroll is now entirely open (8:1). Strangely, however, nothing takes place. Instead, there is silence in heaven for about half an hour. Why? This silence may emphasize the desire of all created beings in heaven to find out what remains inside the seven-sealed scroll. All these beings are probably wondering how people are going to receive their inheritance, how this age is going to be completed, and how all things are going to be put in their proper places.

John now sees seven trumpets given to "the seven angels who stand before God" (v. 2). However, before these angels begin to sound their trumpets, a parallel sequence of activities occurs: another angel comes on the scene. He is given incense to offer with the prayers of the righteous on the golden altar before the throne. John observes as the smoke of the incense ascends with the prayers of the righteous into God's presence.

We are convinced that this other angel in verse 3 is another picture of the person and ministry of the Lord Jesus Christ in the book of Revelation. You may recall that in the Old Testament the golden *censer was used to offer incense within the Most Holy Place on the Day of Atonement (Leviticus 16:12–13). Hebrews 4:14–16 teaches us that Jesus is our Great High Priest. Second, the prayers of the saints are given to this other angel in Revelation 8:3 to offer up to God with the incense. This portrays the ministry of Jesus who is the "mediator between God and men" (1 Timothy 2:5), interceding for them and presenting their petitions to God. Incense carries with it the thought of a pleasing smell to God. The sweetness of the odor of the burning incense rising as an offering to God suggests the spiritual pleasure that God receives from this offering of incense and prayers.

censer
an ornamented container in which incense is burned, especially during religious services

10 The silence in heaven for about half an hour probably emphasizes the desire of all heaven's created beings to know how

a) man is going to receive his inheritance.
b) this age is going to be completed.
c) all things are going to be put in their proper places.
d) all of the above.
e) both a) and b) above.

11 In your notebook give two reasons why it seems evident that the angel in Revelation 8:3–4 with a golden censer is a symbol of Jesus Christ.

Before moving on to the next section, notice in Revelation 8:5 that the angel who has the golden censer uses this censer in a way that differs from the way he has used it in the two preceding verses. At first he used it in behalf of God's people, but in verse 5 he uses it in connection with judgment which is to be outpoured on the earth. As John watches, no doubt in wonder, the angel fills the censer with fire from the altar and hurls it to the earth. At once, peals of thunder, rumblings, flashes of lightning, and an earthquake follow. It is not difficult to see a connection between the prayers of the righteous, such as those cries to God in Revelation 6:10 which call for judgment of the wicked, and the onset of judgment that follows as the trumpets are sounded. In other words, the prayers of the righteous here appear to result in God's judgment of the wicked.

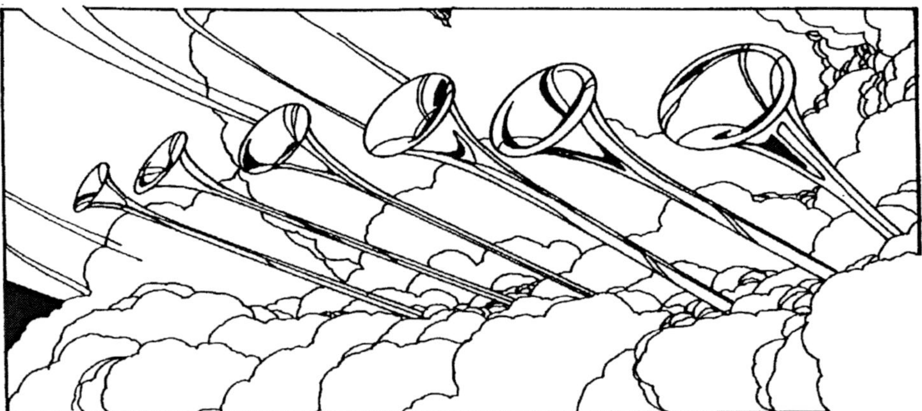

Identify things that will take place when each of the first six trumpets is sounded.

The Sounding of the First Six Trumpets

Revelation 8:6–9:21

While the effects of the rolling thunder, quaking earth, and vivid flashes of lightning are still fresh in his mind, John sees the drama begin to unfold. With their trumpets ready, the seven angels prepare to sound their trumpets, and the prophet witnesses the onset of *dire judgment. As we shall see, some of the judgments are described at length while others are introduced, their effects described, and their impact noted more briefly.

dire
causing great fear or suffering; dreadful

As the first angel sounded his trumpet, hail and fire mixed with blood were hurled upon the earth. One third of the earth was burned as well as one third of all trees and all the green grass. A judgment such as this will tend to produce not only fear, but also a grave effect upon earth's ability to produce oxygen.

The process of photosynthesis, the earth's ability to produce life-giving oxygen, depends on trees and green plant life.

At the second trumpet blast, a huge burning mountain was thrown into the sea. It caused one third of all the sea to turn to blood, one third of all marine life to die, and one third of all ships to be destroyed. The third angel's trumpet sound brought a giant star to the earth. This star, called Wormwood, corrupted one third of the fresh waters on earth, and many people died because of the bitter water. The fourth trumpet sound brought a bad effect on the sun, moon, and the stars so that their light was withheld from earth one third of the time. This judgment will obviously reach beyond planet earth to the solar system and the universe.

Few people would deny the effect these four trumpet judgments will have on those who live on earth. The impact of these disasters is not local; it will touch the planet and the universe as well, as we have seen. Man will be powerless to do anything to prevent these cosmic and natural disorders. Like Pharaoh's magicians who were powerless before God's judgments, unsaved people will have to admit: "This is the finger of God" (Exodus 8:19). However, at this point another sobering announcement is made. John hears an eagle call out in a loud voice as it flies in midair, "Woe! Woe! Woe to the inhabitants of the earth, because of the trumpet blasts about to be sounded by the other three angels" (v. 13).

12 Circle the letter preceding each TRUE statement.

- **a** The background of the trumpet judgments leads one to conclude that earth's people are due to experience fearful times.
- **b** The first trumpet, which brings hail, fire, and blood to the earth, is symbolic only of corrective or minor punishment that is intended to change people's behavior.
- **c** When the terms *stars* or *mountains* are used in Scripture, as in the second and third trumpet judgments, they refer symbolically to the destruction of important people.
- **d** The impact of the first four trumpet judgments will extend to a widespread area of the earth and also the solar system.
- **e** The announcement following the first four trumpet judgments seems to indicate that the next judgments will be severe.

Revelation 9:1–12 indicates that when the fifth trumpet sounded, John saw a star that *had fallen* from the sky to the earth. The star was given the key to the shaft of the Abyss (v. 1). From our study of Revelation 1:20, we learned that stars in that setting were identified as angels or messengers. Scripture indicates in many places that angels are personal beings, that is, they have all the qualities of personality. Moreover, the fact that this *star* is referred to in verse 2 by the pronoun "he" is evidence that he is a personal being. The fact that he is referred to as having fallen previously, that is, before the sounding of the fifth trumpet, leads us to suspect that this angel is none other than Satan. Jesus, you may recall, said that He "saw Satan fall like lightning from heaven" (Luke 10:18). In addition, the fact that this fallen star is given authority symbolized by the key to the shaft of the Abyss supports the notion that this fallen star is Satan. As to the *Abyss*, Luke 8:30-31 implies that it is a place where demons are confined (compare Luke 8:31 with 2 Peter 2:4 and Jude 6).

As the *star* opened the Abyss, John saw smoke rise from the pit, and out of the smoke a demonic army emerged on the earth. In Luke 8:32–33 demons possessed pigs, but here demons seem to possess locusts. These locusts have power like that of scorpions of the earth, and they have a specific mission: to torture people five months. The pain they cause will bring agony to all those who do not have the seal of God on their foreheads. In those days people will seek death in order to escape their agony, but they will be required to undergo the judgment God has decreed.

The description of these demonic locusts and their numbers is awesome. Their leader is said to be "the angel of the Abyss" (v. 11). His name, *Abaddon* in Hebrew and *Apollyon* in Greek, means "destruction" and "destroyer," and in the wake of this infernal army there is only pain and the desire for death. This judgment represents the first woe; consequently, two more fearful woes await the people of the earth.

13 Circle the letter preceding each TRUE statement.

- **a** The *star* that had fallen from the sky to earth, who was given the key to the Abyss, may be identified as Satan.
- **b** The "angel of the Abyss" is thought to be a personal being because he has a normal body.
- **c** The pronoun *he* used in reference to the angel of the Abyss, is an indication of personality.
- **d** The *Abyss* is referred to clearly in Scriptures we have studied in this section as the place of dead people.
- **e** The fifth trumpet judgment will last for five months.
- **f** Abaddon and Apollyon mean literally "anointed one."

14 The fifth trumpet judgment brings forth a multitude of demonic locusts whose task is to

a) destroy earth's people.
b) hurt people who are not sealed with the seal of God.
c) torture those who resist the judgment of God.
d) repay some wicked people for certain evil deeds.

15 List three things which suggest that the "fallen star" of Revelation 9:1 is Satan.

....

....

Revelation 9:13–21 describes the sounding of the sixth trumpet. As the scene unfolds, John hears a voice coming from the horns of the golden altar. This voice commands the sixth trumpet angel to release the four angels who are bound at the Euphrates River. Earlier, you may recall, four angels were holding back the winds of judgment (7:1). These angels were not bound, but here in verse 14 the angels are bound. In our view, angels who are in bondage are evil (Jude 6). Here they appear to be leaders of the great army that is mentioned in verse 16 which will be released to kill one third of mankind (v. 15). The "river Euphrates" (v. 14) is considered to be the dividing line between the east and the west (Revelation 16:12). This verse might refer to the movement of armies from the Orient against the Antichrist. There is a hint in Daniel 11:44–45 that eastern armies will move westward for battle in the land of Israel and interrupt the conquests of the Antichrist. This scriptural passage may also refer to the same military action as Revelation 16:12.

This massive host of two hundred million cavalrymen is prepared for this specific time and purpose (v. 15). Awesome in appearance and deadly in operation, this demonic cavalry will kill on a scale unknown in human history. Fire, smoke, and sulphur will combine to wipe out one third of earth's people. Yet, even in the face of this awful judgment John observes that the balance of earth's people are so entrapped by sin that they neither repent nor amend their ways (v. 20). They continue to worship demons and idols, senseless to the peril they face (vv. 20-21).

The word *senseless* we have used leads us to consider especially what part "magical arts" (v. 20) play in dulling the senses of the wicked. The term *magical arts*, you see, comes from a Greek word that describes witchcraft that is associated with the use of drugs. Our word *pharmacy*, in fact, comes from this word. Can it be that as the Great Tribulation comes upon people, they become increasingly committed to the use of drugs? This may explain why they seem to ignore the disasters that befall them and continue in their sin.

16 According to our study in this section, the angels in Revelation 9:14–15 appear to be demons because they

a) are in bondage.
b) have been kept ready.
c) are identified plainly as such.
d) are at the great Euphrates River.

17 What portion of the people on earth will be killed under the sixth trumpet judgment?

....

18 Describe briefly the effect of the sixth trumpet judgment on the behavior of those who are not killed.

....

....

19 Identify what will take place when each of the first six trumpets sounds by matching each trumpet (right) with the description of the judgment associated with it (left).

.... **a**	A third of the waters turn bitter.	1) First trumpet
.... **b**	Locusts from the Abyss torture ungodly people.	2) Second trumpet
.... **c**	Hail, fire, and blood are hurled upon the earth.	3) Third trumpet
.... **d**	Two hundred million troops kill many people.	4) Fourth trumpet
.... **e**	A third of the sun, moon, and stars turn dark.	5) Fifth trumpet
.... **f**	Something like a huge mountain, all ablaze, is thrown into the sea.	6) Sixth trumpet

Self-Test

Multiple choice: Circle the letter preceding the best answer for each of the following questions.

1 According to our study in this lesson, the opening of the first six seals will take place during the
- a) eternal ages that follow the end of time.
- b) millennial reign of Christ.
- c) last half of the Great Tribulation period.
- d) first half of the Great Tribulation period.

2 The purpose of the seal of the living God is to
- a) empower people for service in the Great Tribulation period.
- b) mark those who receive the seal for judgment.
- c) give protection to those who are sealed.
- d) mark those who are sealed for reward.

3 According to the evidence presented in this lesson, the sealed 144,000 people represent
- a) the righteous who are raptured in the midtribulation period.
- b) spiritual Israel of the last days.
- c) the entire multitude in white robes.
- d) the church raptured before the tribulation period.

4 This lesson suggests that the "fallen star" of Revelation 9:1 may be Satan because
- a) this fallen star is referred to as a personal being.
- b) Jesus saw Satan fall as lightning from heaven.
- c) this fallen star is given authority over the Abyss.
- d) all of the above.
- e) both b) and c) above.

5 Locusts from the Abyss will torture ungodly people when the
- a) first trumpet is sounded.
- b) sixth trumpet is sounded.
- c) third trumpet is sounded.
- d) fifth trumpet is sounded.

True-False. Write **T** in the blank space preceding each TRUE statement. Write **F** if the statement is FALSE.

. . . . **6** The act of sealing the 144,000 will permanently end the harming of the earth during the tribulation period.

. . . . **7** The omission of the names of Dan and Ephraim from the list of sealed tribes of Israel appears to symbolize God's hatred of idolatry.

. . . . **8** This lesson supports the theory that the great multitude of people in white robes are all martyrs who are not yet resurrected bodily.

Short Answer. Briefly answer the following questions in the space provided.

9 What will be the function of the winds which the four angels will hold back temporarily?

....

10 What is the significance of the woes that are announced after the fourth trumpet is sounded?

....

Answers to study questions

10 d) all of the above.

1 a 4) 1000 years
b 1) First 3 1/2 years
c 3) Second 3 1/2 years
d 5) Eternity
e 2) Between the two 3 1/2 year periods
f 4) 1000 years

11 Your answer may differ slightly but it should include the basic information we have given. First, the Old Testament shows that it was only the high priest who could use a golden censer to intercede for people before God. Second, the New Testament specifically indicates that Jesus Christ is the only mediator between God and people.

2 b) harm the earth.

12 **a** True
b False
c False
d True
e True

3 d) place a seal on the foreheads of the servants of God.

13 **a** True
b False
c True
d False
e True
f False

4 c) provide protection for them in the midst of judgment.

14 b) hurt people who are not sealed with the seal of God.

5 c) the nation of Israel rather than the church.

15 He is referred to as having previously fallen. Second, the fact that Jesus said He had seen this happen to Satan leads us to connect the two events. Finally, this angel has control over the Abyss, a fact that is symbolized by the key to the Abyss which he holds.

6 Your answer may be slightly different from what we have suggested, but it should contain the same general ideas. They represent the remnant, that is, people from the nation of Israel of the last days who will have become spiritual Israel, the Israel that will accept Jesus Christ as Savior at the middle point of the Great Tribulation period.

16 a) are in bondage.

7 It appears that these two tribes were leaders in apostasy. Symbolically, their omission from the list shows that God hates idolatry.

17 One-third of them will be killed.

8 **a** True
b False
c False
d True
e True
f False

18 They will continue to worship demons and idols and to commit the sins of murder, sexual immorality, and theft, as well as to practice magic arts.

9 The great white-robed multitude is composed of redeemed people who have accepted Jesus Christ as their personal Savior during the first half of the tribulation period. This multitude has been raptured into heaven from all over the earth at the middle point of the tribulation period. These facts indicate that people can be saved during the Tribulation and that they will be caught up into God's presence.

19 **a** 3) Third trumpet
b 5) Fifth trumpet
c 1) First trumpet
d 6) Sixth trumpet
e 4) Fourth trumpet
f 2) Second trumpet

Progress in the Prophetic Panorama

In our last lesson, we considered events that will take place at the middle point of the tribulation period. We focused attention on the trumpet judgments, and we discussed the identity and significance of two companies of people that appear at this point. Moreover, we observed the effect the trumpet judgments will have on the people of the earth. Now we move on to other activities that break into the prophetic stream of action. We will also meet other actors whose roles in the unfolding drama effect the flow of events.

First, we see the mighty angel of chapter 10 and we hear his proclamation. We also see what impact his directions have on the prophet. Then we move to the measuring of the temple and the role of the two witnesses in chapter 11. Finally, we meet a sun-clothed woman and her child in chapter 12, and we obtain clues to their identity, roles, and destiny. Most of the material in this section consists of parenthetical enlargements.

As we address the ongoing progression of this prophetic drama, we must not forget that all believers have one primary goal. After we are saved, we are to share the love of God with those who do not know Him. Since we know the fearful judgments that await unbelievers, we must do our best to make Christ fully known to our generation.

the activities...

◇ Study this lesson and take the self-test on it according to procedures given in Lesson 1.

◇ You may use your Bible to answer study questions and the questions in the self-test.

◇ Review the lessons in this unit in preparation for your unit progress evaluation (UPE). Read the instruction page in your Student Packet, then turn to Unit Progress Evaluation 3. When you have completed the UPE, check your answers with the answer key provided in your Student Packet. Review any items you may have answered incorrectly. (Although UPE scores do not count as part of your final course grade, they indicate how well you learned the material and how well you may perform on the final examination.)

◇ If you have not already done so, make arrangements now with your enrollment office for taking the final examination.

the objectives...

11.1 *State evidence that will help to identify the mighty angel and the significance of his activity.*

11.2 *Describe what John's eating of the little scroll seems to symbolize.*

11.3 *Identify correctly statements that explain what the measuring of the temple implies and how the period of 42 months relates to this action.*

11.4 *Describe the purpose of the two witnesses, their powers, the results of their testimony, and indicate their possible identity.*

11.5 *Explain briefly the emphasis of the seventh trumpet.*

11.6 *Identify the woman of Revelation 12 and describe her flight and preservation.*

the outline...

1 The Mighty Angel and the Little Scroll
- **a** The Mighty Angel
- **b** John's Commission to Prophesy

2 Parenthetical Enlargements before the Seventh Trumpet
- **a** Measuring the Temple
- **b** The Two Witnesses

3 The Sounding of the Seventh Trumpet

4 The Woman and the Dragon
- **a** The Woman Clothed with the Sun
- **b** The Woman's Son: the Ruler
- **c** The Woman's Other Offspring

State evidence that will help to identify the mighty angel and the significance of his activity.

The Mighty Angel and the Little Scroll

We have just seen the results of the fifth and sixth trumpet judgments and the first woe in chapter 9. The next four chapters in Revelation (10–13), however, consist mostly of parenthetical enlargements. We will discuss the first three of these chapters in this lesson. The first parenthetical enlargement concerns the mighty angel and the little scroll.

The Mighty Angel

Revelation 10:1–7

Before further judgment unfolds, John sees another mighty angel coming down from heaven. We have seen the term "another angel" previously in Revelation 7:2 and 8:3. In each case it was used to make a distinction between angels currently in view and one with another function or activity to fulfill. In chapter 7 *another angel* had the seal of the living God. Chapter 8 reveals *another angel* with a golden censer who offered incense with the prayers of the righteous. Now we see *another angel*, a mighty one, glorious in appearance with a special function to perform.

The question is often asked, "Who is this mighty angel?" We will consider this angel's identity first. Then we will discuss the significance of his activity.

The question of the identity of this mighty angel concerns whether he is literally an angel or a symbolical representation of our Lord. Major Bible scholars differ on this issue as we shall see. Some of them view this mighty angel as a symbol of the Lord Jesus Christ. They see points of similarity between the description given here and that of Jesus given in Revelation 1:13–15. Both of these descriptions are seen to resemble that of the heavenly messenger given in Daniel 10:3–5. Some scholars do not believe this messenger with the little book is Jesus because He indicates in verse 6 that He is inferior to God.

Your writer believes that this mighty angel symbolizes the Lord Jesus Christ. In his view, the mighty angel here portrays the act by which our Lord formally claims possession of the earth as our near Kinsman. This is symbolized by his act of placing one foot on earth and the other on the sea (v. 2). In figurative language, God is about to put all things under His authority (Hebrews 2:8). God's plan of salvation is being brought to a close, and this time of completion is moving forward with speed and finality.

proleptic
of or having to do with, an anticipating, especially with the describing of a future event as though it had already happened

At this point (v. 6), the angel in his highly significant stance on earth and sea makes an announcement: "There will be no more delay!" This announcement is called a **proleptic statement*. A proleptic statement is a statement about the future as if what it states had already happened. Isaiah 9:6 is an example of a proleptic statement. It speaks as if Jesus is born about 750 years before His birth. The angel's statement in 10:6 is the announcement of the end. The Greek text states literally "that time no longer shall be." This statement seems to indicate an immediate end to time. However, from the fact that days, months, and years are mentioned in the rest of the book of Revelation, we know that this is not the intended meaning. Here the announcement means that there will be no more delay in the process that leads to triumph over evil. Satan's time to act as the ruler of the kingdom of the air (Ephesians 2:2) and to lead people astray from God's purpose for their lives and eternal destiny is coming to an end. In addition, Satan's man, the Antichrist, whom we shall consider at length in Lesson 9, is facing the end of his *abortive bid for world rule.

abortive
coming to nothing; unsuccessful

We have considered the angel's identity and purpose in this setting. Several further points should be made concerning the little book he holds and reaction to his initial shout (v. 24). John saw that this mighty angel had a little scroll "which lay open in his hand" (v. 2). Some scholars see this "little scroll" as a different book from the seven-sealed scroll because it is said to be small. We believe that the book is said to be small because of its relation to the size of the one taking possession of man's inheritance. It is open and the events recorded in it are about to take place. The central point is that this little scroll has significance in the progression of the prophet's ministry, as we shall see in verses 8–11.

John observed that when the mighty angel took his stance on earth and sea and shouted, seven thunders spoke. What this message was is unknown, for the prophet was forbidden to record it (v. 4). We do know that the end of all things is in view and that the flow of events will move quickly forward to completion.

1 Circle the letter preceding each TRUE statement.

a The term *another mighty angel* used in 10:1 indicates that this being is an archangel.

b The fact that the little scroll which the angel holds is described differently from the seven-sealed scroll may indicate that it is in fact a different scroll.

c The symbolic meaning of the angel's stance on earth and sea indicates a formal claim of possession.

d The announcement that there should be no more delay indicates that the triumph over evil is about to be realized.

e A *prophetic statement* refers to action that has already taken place in the historic past.

2 In your notebook state evidence that tends to indicate that the mighty angel is a symbol of Jesus Christ and evidence that may indicate he was not a divine being.

3 Explain the significance of the angel's announcement that "there will be no more delay."

....

....

Describe what John's eating of the little scroll seems to symbolize.

John's Commission to Prophesy

Revelation 10:8–11

Once again John hears a voice from heaven which instructs him to take the scroll from the hand of the angel. In obedience, he approaches the angel and asks for the little scroll. The angel gives it to the prophet and instructs him to eat it. The angel adds: "Eat it. It will turn your stomach sour, but in your mouth it will be as sweet as honey" (v. 9). John does as he is told and finds that the angel had described quite accurately what would happen. The little scroll tasted as sweet as honey, but it gave John a sour stomach.

In order to understand the meaning of this symbolic activity, we turn to the book of Ezekiel. Ezekiel records an experience similar to that of John in chapters 2 and 3 of his prophecy. There, Ezekiel was handed a scroll on which were written words of lament and warning and woe (2:9–10). He was told to eat the scroll, which he found sweet as honey in his mouth (3:1–3). Immediately afterward, the prophet was told to go to the house of Israel and speak God's words to His people (3:4). It seems obvious that this activity represents in a symbolic way Ezekiel's prophetic commission. This explanation fits the context of Revelation 10 quite well.

The symbol of eating the little scroll suggests that the prophet is to absorb completely the prophetic message. We saw that the seven-sealed scroll concerned terms for the completion of God's purpose of redeeming people. The little scroll here appears to reemphasize the completion of God's divine purpose. John is to absorb the prophetic message completely. In doing so, he will find that it produces mixed feelings in him. The knowledge that God is going to complete His plan for this world by restoring things in it according to His desire produces a sweet experience of joy in all believers. On the other hand, the knowledge that those without Christ—including loved ones—will face eternal damnation is a bitter fact for all believers to digest. Certainly this sobering fact ought to give every believer sufficient motivation to do everything possible to win the lost wherever they may be.

Having received a renewed prophetic commission, the prophet is told, "You must prophesy again about many peoples, nations, languages and kings" (v. 11). While John is at the end of his life, this statement anticipates the impact the prophecy will have as it, together with the rest of the inspired Word of God, is proclaimed in the whole world as a witness to all nations (Matthew 24:14).

4 Circle the letter preceding each TRUE statement.

- **a** The command for John to eat the little scroll is without precedent in sacred Scripture.
- **b** The act of eating a book represents absorbing its contents.
- **c** The message concerning the completion of God's purpose for people on earth produces mixed feelings in those who fully understand it.
- **d** John is told that his influence as a prophet, while exceeding great, would be limited to his own lifetime.

5 In your notebook describe what John's eating of the little scroll seems to symbolize.

Identify correctly statements that explain what the measuring of the temple implies and how the period of 42 months relates to this action.

Parenthetical Enlargements Before the Seventh Trumpet

Revelation 11:1–14

As we focus on the first part of chapter 11, we see more parenthetical enlargements. Some Bible scholars try to spiritualize this passage, saying that no actual events are described. In their minds, the content presents spiritual truth only. However, we do not agree with this notion. We believe that the descriptions given here refer to real events and actions that are vital parts in the completion of God's plan of salvation for people. We move now to the first of these parenthetical enlargements in chapter 11.

Measuring the Temple

Revelation 11:1–2

In verses 1 and 2 John is told to measure the temple and the altar and to count the worshipers. But he is told to exclude the outer court from his measurement because it is given to the Gentiles. Moreover, he is told why the outer court is to be excluded: "It has been given to the Gentiles. They will trample on the holy city for 42 months" (v. 2). What are we to make of these directions?

In these verses one may see a prophecy of the preservation and ultimate salvation of the Jewish people. Shortly before the outbreak of the ruinous Jewish-Roman War (AD 66), Jewish Christians fled from the scene of the conflict. Naturally, this move called into question their loyalty to the state and further strained relations with the orthodox Jewish community. Then as the war reached its climax and drew to its fateful end in AD 70, the city of Jerusalem and the temple were destroyed. At this point Jewish Christians asked the question that Paul had raised earlier concerning the *obstinacy of the Jews to the

obstinacy
stubbornness; act of not giving in; hard to control, treat, or remove

acknowledgment of Jesus Christ as their Messiah: "Did God reject his people?" (Romans 11:1). To this question Paul responded: "By no means!" Then in the course of Romans chapters 9–11 he considered the problem in depth and concluded that the fall of Israel was not permanent. Rather, the nation will yet be reestablished as part of the people of God (Romans 11:26). This is the clear teaching of these three chapters. And Jesus' words in Luke 21:24 agree with this assessment: "Jerusalem will be trampled on by the Gentiles until the times of the Gentiles are fulfilled." Revelation 11, therefore, gives us a prophecy which predicts the preservation and final salvation of the Jewish people.

measuring metaphor refers to the figure of speech employed in which measuring stands for something else: symbolically, something is to be destroyed and something is to be preserved

In Revelation 11:1–2 John becomes a participant in the vision he is receiving (earlier in 10:8–11 he had been a participant). He is told to measure the temple of God and the altar; however, he is to exclude the outer court which has been given to the Gentiles. What are we to make of this *measuring metaphor? Let us first examine the physical aspects of the temple complex and then consider its meaning.

The temple itself (the holy place and the most holy place) was surrounded by three courts. The first or nearest to the temple, the Court of the Priests, contained the altar of burnt offering and the great laver. It was restricted to priests alone. Next to this was the Court of the Israelites, which may have been separated into two parts: one for men and the other for women. The people of Israel who were ceremonially clean could assemble for worship in these latter areas. Outside these inner courts lay the Court of the Gentiles, which was open to all interested people—Jews and Gentiles.

In the present vision all of the inner courts and the sanctuary, together with the worshipers are separated from the outer court—the Court of the Gentiles. As we reflect on the measuring metaphor, we recognize that measuring a city means more than finding out its dimensions. Rather, a comparison of this present symbolism with its use elsewhere in Scripture leads us to the conclusion that measuring symbolizes setting a city apart either to save or destroy it. Your writers also believe that in some scriptural contexts measuring implies God's ownership (See 2 Kings 21:13; Isaiah 34:11; and Lamentations 2:8). In the present case we see a contrast: the sanctuary and its courts are preserved while the outer court and the holy city are not preserved.

Here it is clear that both the outer court and the city of Jerusalem are marked out for destruction by the Gentiles. From Jesus' reference in Luke 21:24 to the trampling of Jerusalem by the Gentiles, we gather that the city, in this case, stood for the Jewish people as a whole. Again, in the present case, Jerusalem stands for the Jewish people. Since the city is contrasted with the temple and its worshipers, which are saved, the meaning seems to be that the nation as a whole is contrasted with a smaller part or remnant who are true worshipers of God.

It seems clear that the temple and its worshipers do not represent all Israel, for they are contrasted with the outer court and the city of Jerusalem as a whole which represent the nation. This suggests a contrast between a faithful remnant of believing Israelites who, in contrast to the city as a whole, are true worshipers of God. The nation of Israel will be trodden down by the nations, and Jewish people will fall under divine judgment because they have become spiritually apostate. This fact is supported by verse 8 in which Jerusalem is figuratively called Sodom and Egypt where the Lord was crucified. Other places in Scripture in which Jerusalem represents the whole nation are: Psalm 137:5–6; Isaiah 40:1–2; and Matthew 23:37.

Verse 2, which says that "they will trample on the holy city for 42 months," takes us back to Daniel 9:27, where it is said that the coming ruler will make a seven-year covenant with the Jews. In the first half of the tribulation period, therefore, Jews will evidently be allowed to worship in their temple, and they will feel that they belong in Jerusalem. However, this parenthetical enlargement in 11:1–2 seems to refer to the middle of the seven year's of tribulation, a point in time when the tolerant policies of the Antichrist begin to come to an end. Then, in the middle of the covenant period, that is after forty-two months or three and one-half years, the Antichrist will break the terms of his covenant with the Jews, annul religious and civil liberties (for the faithful), and set up his image in the temple to be worshiped. This act is the abomination that causes desolation (Matthew 24:15). The end of this last three and one-half years mark the end of the "times of the Gentiles" (Luke 21:20-24). Daniel 7:25 says that "He will speak against the Most High and oppress his saints . . . for a time, times and half a time." Nevertheless, the remnant of faithful ones will be divinely preserved in this time of tribulation.

6 Circle the letter preceding each TRUE statement.

a The reference to the measuring of the temple and the altar and the counting of the worshipers there speaks of the saving of the Jewish people.

b Measuring in chapter 11:1–2 refers to the exercise of finding the size of a thing.

c The trampling of Jerusalem, which stands for the nation of Israel, and the saving of worshipers refers to a remnant who are true worshipers of God.

d The period of forty-two months in which the holy city will be trampled refers to the period of three and one-half years of the Tribulation in which Antichrist will persecute faithful Jews.

e While the first three and one-half years of Antichrist's rule are marked by a tolerant religious policy, this will end at the middle point of his reign.

f While Jews will worship freely in their temple for three and one-half years, they will not feel truly at home in Jerusalem.

g The end of the second three and one-half-year period will bring about the end of the "times of the Gentiles."

Describe the purpose of the two witnesses, their powers, the results of their testimony, and indicate their possible identity.

The Two Witnesses

Revelation 11:3–14

Verses 3–14 give us details of the ministry of two powerful witnesses who will prophesy to an afflicted people during forty-two harrowing months of the tribulation period. While some Bible scholars see these two witnesses as symbolical of the church in its witness, we are led by the detailed description of the two witnesses to see them as two actual end-time individuals who will be sent to the people of Israel to bring about their repentance. In this section we will consider their purpose, identity, time of ministry, detailed description, and death.

We notice first their purpose: they are specially empowered witnesses who will fulfill their specific task of ministry for 1260 days or 42 months (v. 3). One Bible scholar observes that their unique identity as prophets of doom is symbolized by the fact that they are clothed in sackcloth. Sackcloth was a course, loose cloth made of goat's hair which was used to make sacks and the rough garments used by mourners (Genesis 37:34; Revelation 6:12). Rough garments made of sackcloth were also worn in times of great *calamity and in times of repentance to express sorrow for sin (2 Samuel 3:31–32; 1 Kings 20:32; Matthew 11:21).

calamity
a great misfortune, such as a fire, flood, the loss of one's sight

The two witnesses are referred to as "the two olive trees and the two lampstands that stand before the Lord of the earth" (v. 4). You may recall that Joshua the high priest and Zerubbabel were raised up to be witnesses in Zechariah's time. They ministered in the power of the Holy Spirit, which was symbolized by the olive oil used in the lampstands (Zechariah 4:1–6). In those perilous days God reminded His people that it is "Not by might nor by power, but by my Spirit" that His purpose is achieved. Similarly, these two end-time witnesses will execute their prophetic office through the power of the Holy Spirit.

In addition to anointed prophetic ministry, these two have a broad range of power (vv. 5–6). They have divine protection against assaults from enemies, power over natural elements, including the ability to prevent rain, and power to afflict the earth with every kind of plague as often as they wish. One scholar of Bible prophecy notes that these two prophets will have the greatest powers ever given to earthly prophets. This accounts for their ability to survive all attempts to destroy them for forty-two months.

The matter of *when* in the seven-year period the two witnesses carry out their ministry is not clear. Some Bible scholars believe they minister during the first half of the Tribulation. These scholars believe that their ministry will be essential in bringing the 144,000 to salvation. They also insist that since the Gentiles will be oppressing Jerusalem during the second half, there would be no apparent reason for them to witness. Other Bible scholars believe that during the second half of the Tribulation the witnesses' ministry will be especially needed when the Antichrist asserts himself and brings the full force of his power to bear on the Jewish people. These scholars also point out that the second half is a more specific time of judgment and therefore consistent with the purpose of the witnesses' ministry.

In our view the fact that so many people turn to the Lord during the first half of the Tribulation is evidence of the two witnesses' ministry. Whether this great move of God is the result of their ministry, that of the 144,000, or both, or simply a sovereign move of God's Spirit is not clearly stated. We do know that the two witnesses have a dramatic, dynamic, and powerful message which will be accompanied by miraculous signs (vv. 3–6). A comparison of Exodus chapters 7–11 and 1 Kings 17:1–7 with Revelation 11:6 indicates they will have the same power concerning blood, plagues, and rain that Moses and Elijah had.

While the powers listed in verse 6 may suggest the identity of the two witnesses, Scripture does not specifically identify them. Some scholars insist that they are Enoch and Elijah, who must return to earth and experience death, since man is destined to die once (Hebrews 9:27). Obviously, these two men alone of all who have ever lived qualify on this ground. Perhaps these scholars overlook the fact that an entire generation of believers who are raptured will also bypass death.

Other scholars insist that the two are Moses and Elijah since they will have ministries like those of the earlier prophets. This second opinion is also based on the fact that Moses and Elijah appeared with Jesus on the Mount of Transfiguration (Matthew 17:1–7). Moreover, Malachi 4:5 says that Elijah will come "before that great and dreadful day of the Lord comes." Elijah stands as a symbol for prophetic ministry that is exercised in a dynamic and powerful way (Luke 1:17). We believe that Moses and Elijah stood on the mount with Jesus because they fulfilled the Law, represented by Moses, and the Prophets, represented by Elijah. While we do not know for sure their precise identity, we believe they will be two Old Testament-style prophets because they will minister during a time when a segment of Israel will turn to God.

7 In your notebook briefly describe the two witnesses, their powers, and clues about their identity.

As the prophets speak forth God's message, they will undoubtedly face opposition from the ungodly. Nonetheless, potential assassins will be completely powerless to hurt them. In fact, should they try they will be immediately destroyed (v. 5). We must remember that the life of God's people is in His hands. We can serve God without fear, for He will keep us until our task is complete. When the time of death is at hand, each of us, because of His keeping power, can say as Paul did "I have kept the faith" (2 Timothy 4:7). However, when they have finished their task, the beast from the Abyss will attack them and overpower and kill them (v. 7). For the first time in Revelation we have a preview of the coming Antichrist, the beast of Revelation 13.

Verses 8–10 reveal the heartless reaction of ungodly people to the death of the two witnesses. Contrary to the laws of decency and reasonable humanity, the bodies of the two will be unburied and exposed to the greatest indignity for three and one-half days in the streets of Jerusalem. Figuratively, Jerusalem is referred to as *Sodom* and *Egypt*. Sodom speaks of moral degradation and Egypt symbolizes oppression, slavery, and idolatry; however, the true identity of the city is made clear in verse 8.

grisly
frightful; horrible; ghastly

The witnesses' death will prompt a worldwide celebration as people mistakenly believe that the plagues, drought, and judgment come from them rather than from God through them (compare v. 12 with 4:1). However, as modern communications spread the news and show the *grisly remains of the prophets and celebration reaches its peak, the witnesses are resurrected in full view of their enemies. This dramatic change of events strikes terror in the hearts of people as they hear a voice from heaven command: "Come up here" (v. 12). Then as their enemies look on, the prophets are translated to heaven. Before their enemies can return to their ungodly pursuits, however, the city is shaken by the tremors of a mighty earthquake which destroy one-tenth of the city. Survivors are terrified and glorify the God of heaven (v. 13). The second woe has now passed and the third is on its way (v. 14).

8 Based on your knowledge of modern communications, describe in your notebook how it would be possible for people from every people, tribe, language, and nation to view the dead bodies of the two witnesses within a three and a half day period.

9 Combining the evidence that a great multitude will be saved out of the Tribulation with the fact that the two witnesses will have a powerful ministry suggests that their ministry will be
a) limited to Jews in general and Jerusalem in particular.
b) moderately effective in pointing to the judgment to come.
c) highly successful in turning people to God and in pointing to people's accountability to God.
d) successful only in prophesying judgment and preparing people for the coming wrath of God.

10 Match the person (right) with the reason why he is or is not often identified as one of the two witnesses of Revelation 11 (left).

. . . . **a** Identified as the representative of the Law; appeared on the Mount of Transfiguration with Jesus

. . . . **b** Earliest man to be translated to heaven; one of two who qualifies as never having died

. . . . **c** Representative of the prophetic ministry; appeared with Jesus on the Mount of Transfiguration

. . . . **d** Disqualified on the grounds that "man is destined to die once" (Hebrews 9:27)

. . . . **e** Identified by Old Testament prophecy and confirmed by Jesus as one who will come before "that great and dreadful day of the Lord comes" (Malachi 4:5)

1) Moses
2) Elijah
3) Enoch

Explain briefly the emphasis of the seventh trumpet.

The Sounding of the Seventh Trumpet

Revelation 11:15–19

The interlude between the sixth and seventh trumpet has now been concluded. John's prophetic commission has been renewed, the temple has been measured, and the two witnesses have come and gone. Now the seventh trumpet can be sounded, introducing the final period of the end (10:7). It is clear, however, that the statement is *proleptic*, that is, it looks forward to the end of the conflict in chapter 19, speaking as if it were an accomplished fact. But as we shall see, this final period involves an extended length of time.

As the seventh trumpet is sounded, there is no accompanying woe. Rather, an announcement is made that the long-awaited kingdom of our Lord is coming and will be eternal. This means that time is running out for the lawless one, Satan, and those he controls. In response to this announcement the twenty-four elders exult in the anticipated blessing that will flow from the Kingdom. They point out the triumph of our Lord in wresting power from opposing forces as He establishes His reign. Notice the elements associated with His accession to power:

1. The nations were angry (v. 18). Thus, the end does not result in a peaceful *utopia but rather confrontation between a holy God and defiant man.
2. God's wrath is unveiled (v. 18). Up to this point His longsuffering and patience have been emphasized.

utopia
an ideal state or place; a visionary, impractical system of political or social perfection

3. The conclusion brings about the need for judgment (v. 18). In view primarily here is the resurrection of the righteous dead, who will be rewarded. It is also a time for the destroyers to be destroyed.

As this scene concludes, the focus shifts to God's temple in heaven which is opened, revealing the ark of the covenant. In the preceding section we saw that the righteous had to flee from the temple in Jerusalem, but they will not have to flee from God's temple in heaven (v. 19). The temple scene in heaven with the ark of the covenant reminds us that just as God kept His covenant in the Old Testament, so He ever keeps His Word. People, like Israel of the past, may break their part of the contract, but God is faithful to His Word. In the trying times ahead God can be depended on to bring His people safely through to their reward. One scholar observes that the temple being opened in heaven signifies and anticipates our being able to enter directly into God's presence in an unmediated fellowship. That will be a wonderful time as faith gives way to sight and we shall see Him as He is (1 John 3:2). The accompanying lightning, thunder, hailstorm, and earthquake both attend God's presence and signify His wrath as the revelation continues.

11 In your notebook explain briefly the emphasis of the seventh trumpet.

The Woman and the Dragon

Revelation 12:14, 13–17

In the last section of this lesson we examine chapter 12. It is another parenthetical enlargement. While the entire chapter is in focus, we will examine primarily verses 1–6 and 13–17, leaving the subject of the "enormous red dragon" (vv. 7–12) for Lesson 12. We look now at the woman clothed with the sun, her son, and the rest of her offspring.

Identify the woman of Revelation 12 and describe her flight and preservation.

The Woman Clothed with the Sun

Revelation 12:1–6, 13–16

John records the appearance of a great sign in heaven (v. 1). This sign which appears in heaven points to a reality on earth. John sees a mysterious, pregnant woman clothed with the sun, wearing a crown of twelve stars, and having the moon under her feet. She is in the agony of childbirth, nearly ready to deliver, while a great red dragon stands by waiting to devour her child as soon as he is born (vv. 2–4). Nevertheless, the woman safely delivers the child, a male, who is immediately caught up to God. Meanwhile, the woman flees to a place of safety prepared for her by God for 1260 days. This is the substance of the prophet's initial view of the woman, her child, and the great red dragon. We turn now to a discussion of her identity, significance, and future.

Many Bible scholars believe the woman represents Israel. One Bible commentator says that she symbolizes Israel as the matrix from which Christ came. Other women are mentioned in Revelation such as Jezebel (2:20), who represents religion as a false system; the prostitute (17:1–7, 15–18), who stands for the apostate church of the future; and the bride, the Lamb's wife (19:7), who represents the church joined to Christ in glory. Interestingly, the only other place in Scripture where this symbol appears is in connection with Israel (Genesis 37:9).

In the Old Testament Israel is mentioned on occasion as a married woman, the wife of Jehovah (Isaiah 54:1; Jeremiah 3:1–14; Hosea 2:14–23). In fact, Israel is the only group of God's people in Scripture that is referred to as a married woman. The church, by contrast, is referred to as a virgin (2 Corinthians 11:2), never as an expectant mother. Israel is also mentioned in the Old Testament as a woman in travail (Isaiah 26:7 and 66:7; Micah 4:10, 5:3). We conclude, then, that the woman represents Israel. And as the pangs of childbirth point to the approaching birth, so the pains of the woman may represent the signs of which Jesus spoke that lead up to the end of the age (Mark 13:8).

Before we consider the identity of the male child, we must focus on the fate and future of the woman. Verses 6 and 14 state that she will flee from the great dragon (which we will consider in Lesson 12). These two verses indicate something about the place where the woman will flee, how she is able to get there safely, that she will be cared for, and the amount of time she will be shielded from the dragon.

As we have noted previously, at the midpoint of the Tribulation the Antichrist will break his covenant with Israel. His time of accommodation with her will end abruptly, and she will be forced to flee to a "prepared place." Many Bible scholars believe that she will seek refuge in a place located in modern Jordan called *Petra*. In Bible times it was called *Sela* which means "rock" (2 Kings 14:7; Isaiah 16:1). Daniel 11:41 indicates that the Antichrist will invade many Middle Eastern countries, including Israel, but for some reason Edom, Moab, and Ammon will be delivered from his power. It is significant that Petra in modern Jordan is located in part of the area of these three ancient countries. Moreover, God says through the prophet Hosea that He will lead Israel into the desert and deal tenderly with her there (Hosea 2:14).

Petra stands up like a large mountain range in the desert of Jordan. It was originally an Edomite settlement, but about 300 BC Nabateans converted it into the amazing rock-cut city of Petra. To enter Petra one walks or rides on horseback through a narrow passage called the *sik,* which is about a mile long. No large car could pass through this narrow passage, and since Petra is relatively inaccessible, this increases its isolation. Inside there is a twenty-two square mile area which is surrounded by sheer cliffs. Petra has temples, houses, and other living areas carved into the face of the rock. Some scholars estimate that as many as a million and a half people could be housed in Petra. Given the foregoing facts it would not be unfair to call it a *prepared place*.

We do not know precisely how the woman will avoid detection as she makes her escape; however, verse 14 indicates she will receive divine assistance. Perhaps sudden external threats to Antichrist's power will divert his attention long enough for the woman to make her escape in this crisis. Regardless, she will arrive safely at the prepared place where God will sustain her for 1260 days (v. 6) or "a time, times and half a time" (v. 14). (The time frame is the same whether we say 42 months, 1260 days, or 3 1/2 years.) Thus, during the last half of the tribulation period the woman will be preserved in the remote desert.

12 According to our study, the woman clothed with the sun who wears a crown of twelve stars and has the moon beneath her feet represents the
a) bride of Christ.
b) apostate church of the last days.
c) nation of Israel.
d) principle of evil.

13 In your notebook describe the flight of the woman and her preservation.

Discuss the identity and significance of the woman's son.

The Woman's Son: The Ruler

Revelation 12:5–6

Revelation 12 presents a symbolic woman who gives birth to a symbolic child, a male, who is destined to rule the nations with an iron scepter. As with any symbolic figure, there are differing views about the identity of the male child. Some Bible expositors reason that since the woman stands for national Israel, she will produce her own kind, namely a company of Israelites. They believe the male child represents the 144,000 who were sealed in Revelation 7 on earth and who reappear in 14:1–5 in heaven. Other views are also held, but we believe they lack the credibility of the following consideration.

The statement "She gave birth to a son, a male child, who will rule all the nations with an iron scepter" (v. 5) clearly identifies the child: He is God's anointed who is destined to reign over all the earth. This Scripture verse is an obvious reference to Psalm 2 which predicts that the messianic son will receive the nations as an inheritance and rule over them with an iron scepter (Psalm 2:6–9). During the Millennium Christ will indeed rule the nations in this way. Notice that John does not mention any intervening events between the birth of Christ and His ascension. We know that efforts were made to kill Jesus at His birth, but these were unsuccessful. The main point is that by His successful saving work our Lord foiled the evil designs of Satan. Moreover, Jesus' ministry culminated in the ascension and exaltation (Philippians 2:5–11). The result of the dragon's failure to destroy the male child, John noted, was that the dragon turned his attention on the woman and her other offspring. With a view to the future, this means that Antichrist will turn his wrath on Israel and especially those faithful ones who follow the Lord Jesus Christ.

14 It is obvious that the son of the woman is destined for greatness of some kind by virtue of the dragon's efforts to destroy him at birth. In your notebook discuss the identity and significance of the male child.

Objective 11.8

Explain who the woman's other offspring are.

The Woman's Other Offspring

Revelation 12:17

In the last section of this lesson we will focus our attention on verse 17. While the dragon failed in his attempt to destroy the male child and the woman, he will seek to destroy the "rest of her offspring" (v. 17). One notable Bible scholar observes that Israel is hated by the devil not because of any of her own qualities, but because she is chosen by God and vital in His overall purpose for time and eternity. Some Bible scholars believe that as the Palestinian Christian community fled from the approaching ravages of the Jewish War (AD 66–70), so the faithful remnant will flee to the city of Petra for safety. However, apparently part of this remnant described as "those who obey God's commandments and hold to the testimony of Jesus" will not go into hiding. These faithful ones from around the world will be the object of the dragon's wrath.

In summary, it appears that the *woman* will respond to the command that Jesus gave and flee to her "prepared place" (Matthew 24:16). However, there will be those of the remnant of faithful Israel who will not be able to flee to the prepared place. This scattered remnant, then, is referred to as the woman's other offspring. The dragon will attack these faithful ones of Israel wherever they are in an attempt to destroy them completely.

15 Circle the letter preceding each TRUE statement.

- **a** The woman represents Israel, the male child clearly symbolizes the Lord Jesus Christ, and the other offspring are identified as the church.
- **b** The real reason why the dragon is furious is because he has failed to destroy God's program of salvation for people.
- **c** The wrath of the dragon is directed against the other offspring of the woman because of their active ministry in the Tribulation in opposition to his regime.

16 Explain who the woman's other offspring are.

....

....

Self-Test

Multiple choice: There is one best answer for each question. Circle the letter preceding your choice of the best answer.

1 The mighty angel in Revelation 10:6–7 relates a highly significant message to those on earth by indicating that there will be
- a) some delay before the process of victory is achieved.
- b) an indefinite delay before God's program is concluded.
- c) an immediate conclusion to God's redemptive program.
- d) no more delay in the process that leads to divine triumph.

2 The symbolism of measuring the temple complex is that
- a) it enables us to learn about its physical dimensions.
- b) part of it is set apart for preservation and part for destruction.
- c) measuring is a symbolic way of determining who owns it.
- d) the various parts of the temple measured speak of the various elements of which the church is made.

3 The forty-two months when the remnant flees from Jerusalem because it is being trampled on by the Gentiles suggest
- a) a time frame just after the Tribulation.
- b) that the last half of the Tribulation is in view.
- c) that the first half of the Tribulation is in view.
- d) a time just before the Tribulation begins.

4 The sounding of the seventh trumpet, which emphasizes the scene of God's temple in heaven with the ark of the covenant in it, suggests specifically that God
- a) blesses the righteous.
- b) destroys the wicked.
- c) keeps His part of the covenants He makes.
- d) enables us to keep our part of the covenants He makes.

5 The woman in Revelation 12, who represents Israel, will flee to a prepared place and stay there
- a) throughout the tribulation period.
- b) during the first half of the tribulation period.
- c) during the last half of the tribulation period.
- d) just after the tribulation period.

True False. Write **T** in the blank space preceding each TRUE statement. Write **F** if the statement is FALSE.

. . . . **6** The two witnesses of Revelation 11 have a significant purpose: they are to turn the hearts of people to God in a period of great wickedness and spiritual apostasy.

. . . . **7** The sweetness in John's mouth when he ate the little scroll symbolizes the joy the child of God will experience when God punishes the wicked.

. . . . **8** It seems evident that the *rest of the woman's offspring* mentioned in chapter 12 are godly Israelites who will not be in the place prepared for the woman when she flees from the dragon.

Short Answer. Briefly answer the following questions in the space provided.

9 How would the aged John be able to reach out to the many peoples about whom he was told to prophesy again?

....

....

10 We can be clear about the identity of the male child of the woman because of what?

....

....

Unit Progress Evaluation 3

Now that you have finished Unit 3, review the lessons in preparation for Unit Progress Evaluation 3. You will find it in your Student Packet. Answer all of the questions without referring to your course materials, Bible, or notes. When you have completed the UPE, check your answers with the answer key provided in your Student Packet, and review any items you may have answered incorrectly. Then you may proceed with your study of Unit 4. (Although UPE scores do not count as part of your final course grade, they indicate how well you learned the material and how well you may perform on the final examination.)

Answers to study questions

9 c) highly successful in turning people to God and in pointing to people's accountability to God.

1 a False
b True
c True
d True
e False

10 a 1) Moses
b 3) Enoch
c 2) Elijah
d 1) Moses
e 2) Elijah

2 His description is similar to that of Jesus seen in Revelation 1:13–15. Also his action in claiming possession of the earth, his mighty voice, and his announcement suggest an importance beyond that attached to ordinary angels. On the other hand, the fact that Scripture never specifically calls Jesus an angel and that this angel swears by God the Creator assumes that he occupies a lesser position than God.

11 The seventh trumpet emphasizes the coming blessedness of the Kingdom, that judgment is coming, that the end is drawing near, and that God keeps His Word.

3 The announcement indicates that there will be no more delay in the process that leads to triumph over evil.

12 c) nation of Israel.

4 a False
b True
c True
d False

13 Your answer should indicate that the woman, Israel, flees from the rule of Antichrist at the midpoint of the Tribulation. She is helped in her flight to a prepared place, possibly Petra in the present country of Jordan. She will be preserved by God for three and one-half years.

5 Your answer should note that John's act symbolizes absorbing the message contained in the scroll. It is important, for it reemphasizes the completion of God's purpose for people on earth, which will bring eternal reward for believers and judgment for unbelievers. This knowledge brings a mixed response in those who understand the full implications.

14 Your answer should note the fact that Jesus is clearly in view as the male child who is destined to rule the nations. Satan's plan since the beginning has been to frustrate God's plan for man. He seemed to have succeeded in Eden when Adam failed, but the birth, death, and resurrection of Jesus spelled ultimate defeat for him. As we shall see, the Son is destined to universal greatness as He rules and reigns over God's kingdom.

6 **a** True
b False
c True
d True
e True
f False
g True

15 **a** False
b True
c False

7 Your answer. You should have included their attire (sackcloth), their powers (bringing plagues, turning water to blood, and so on), their purpose (to minister powerfully as prophets), their identity (perhaps Moses and Elijah or Enoch and Elijah), and why you believe as you do.

16 Scripture indicates that the other offspring are faithful blood-washed believers of Israel who are scattered throughout the world.

8 Your answer. With present satellite communication systems and various communication networks, news can be filmed as it happens and transmitted throughout the world. Wherever video receivers and satellite dishes are located, these events can be viewed as they occur. As time passes, this capability will become more and more universal, making the phenomenon mentioned here possible.

THE CONSUMMATION OF END-TIME EVENTS

Lessons...

12 The Dragon and His Agents

13 Final Events of the Great Tribulation

14 The Millennial Reign of Christ and Afterward

Procedures...

1 Observe the objectives for key points.
2 Reflect on the headings and subheadings.
3 Study the content identifying key points (highlight, underline, etc.) as you read.
4 Answer the self-study questions.
5 Do the self-test to reinforce key concepts.
6 Review the lessons in this unit in preparation for the Unit Progress Evaluation.

Lesson 12

The Dragon and His Agents

In Lesson 11 we found that events moved progressively along in the prophetic stream of action. Included in these events were: the renewal of the prophetic commission, the measuring of the temple, the ministry of two witnesses, and the description, activity, and destiny of a mysterious woman, her son, and her other offspring. We were able to add these facts to the knowledge we had gained from earlier lessons. Now we turn to an examination of a figure that plays a major role in the events of the Tribulation: the dragon.

We saw the enormous red dragon as a great sign that appeared in heaven when the mysterious woman was introduced (12:3). The dragon is clearly identified in 12:9 as "that ancient serpent called the devil or Satan, who leads the whole world astray." He is God's enemy, the woman's enemy, and our enemy. He appears throughout the whole Bible except in the first two and the last two chapters to try to destroy God's plan and the lives of people. In this lesson you will see that this great red dragon has agents who carry out his will in opposing God. By comparing the facts in this lesson with what we have studied in Daniel, we will see more clearly how Satan's agent will gain power and try to destroy Israel. As you study, we want you to recognize that while Satan is a powerful foe, he is not all-powerful. We also encourage you to withstand Satan and obediently do all you can to help carry out the unfinished task of evangelism while there is time.

the activities...

- ◇ Study the Lesson according to your established procedure. Be sure to read all Scripture references that are not quoted in full in the lesson content.
- ◇ You may use your Bible to answer study questions and the questions in the self-test.
- ◇ Be sure to look in the glossary for the meanings of any key words you do not know.
- ◇ Remember to write your *own* answers to the study questions before looking up the answers at the back of this lesson. This procedure will help you to learn the material more quickly.

the objectives...

12.1 *Identify the dragon and explain the significance of his activity.*

12.2 *Describe the war in heaven and its outcome.*

12.3 *Identify the beast, his origin, source of power, and significance.*

12.4 *Describe the second beast of Revelation 13 and indicate his identity.*

12.5 *Choose statements that give the source of the false prophet's authority and his purpose.*

12.6 *Discuss the mark of the beast and its significance.*

12.7 *Recognize true facts about the great prostitute and her significance in the end time.*

12.8 *Identify facts about the identity, role, and characteristics of the 144,000.*

12.9 *Discuss briefly the proclamations made by the three angels in Revelation 14:6–13.*

12.10 *Choose statements that reflect accurately matters of the harvest and winepress in 14:14–20.*

the outline...

1 An Enormous Red Dragon
- **a** The Dragon
- **b** War in Heaven

2 A Beast Out of the Sea

3 The False Prophet
- **a** His Authority and Miracles
- **b** His Mark, Name, and Number

4 The Great Prostitute

5 Prophecies of the End
- **a** The Lamb and the 144,000
- **b** The Proclamations of Three Angels
- **c** The Harvest and the Winepress

Identify the dragon and explain the significance of his activity.

An Enormous Red Dragon

We now meet the first of several actors in the end-time drama who are introduced in symbolic form. These symbolic figures are usually identified, like the dragon, in the general context so that we know the function and work of each.

The Dragon

Revelation 12:3–4

Sometimes in the course of divine revelation God appears to *draw the curtains* and give us a fleeting glimpse of events in the spirit world. Such was the case in Daniel 10 where God revealed the nature of spiritual warfare. Here in 12:3 Satan is symbolized as an enormous red dragon. Continuing with the symbolism, John notes that the dragon's "tail swept a third of the stars out of the sky and flung them to the earth" (v. 4). You may recall from Revelation 1 that stars represented the angels or messengers of the churches. There may be a reference in verse 4 to a revolt against God in heaven in which one-third of the angels followed Satan and lost their original home (Jude 6).

In 12:9 we are told that Satan leads the whole world astray. The Greek word translated "world" is the one from which we get the word *cosmic* and means "the structured society." Satan exerts a powerful influence over governments, the media, organizations, management, labor, and education. The heads and horns emphasize that Satan is the ruler of a vast spiritual kingdom and stands behind ungodly governments, especially in the last days. The following chart of three names by which the dragon is called in Revelation 12 (Figure 12.1) may help you to know more about the aspects of his character.

NAME AND VERSE	MEANING	REFERENCE
Ancient Serpent (v. 9)	Deceiver	Genesis 3:1–13
Devil (v. 9)	Tempter	Matthew 4:1
	Schemer	Ephesians 6:11
	Opposer	1 Peter 5:8
Satan (v. 9)	Accuser	Zechariah 3:1

Figure 12.1

1 Tell who the dragon is and the significance of his activity.

....

....

Describe the war in heaven and its outcome.

War in Heaven

Revelation 12:7–12, 17:7–18

Revelation 12:7–12 portrays an incredible conflict in heaven. In addition to the facts we gleaned from Daniel 10, Paul tells us that there is a "ruler of the kingdom of the air, the spirit who is now at work in those who are disobedient."(Compare Ephesians 2:2 with 6:10–16.) Comparing Paul's statement with what is said of Satan in Job 1:6–12 and 2:1–7, we learn that Satan has occupied the regions above the earth and had access to the presence of God from the time of his original revolt against God until the present. He will retain this position until he is hurled to the earth in the end time (12:9). Thus, as the tribulation reaches a crucial point, Satan and the evil angels who follow him will lose their place in the heavens as Michael and the other angels of God overpower them.

Such a war in the heavens will have a mighty impact on earth. In fact, those who live on earth are warned about this in no uncertain terms (v. 12). With time running out, Satan will work with diabolical fury in a final attempt to frustrate God's plan. Up to this point Satan has been preeminently the *accuser*. He has used the special method of accusation to attack godly people throughout history. Satan, as we see in the references in Job, accuses believers before God, and he tries to make them feel guilty over sins they have committed which are already forgiven. From this point on, however, he will no longer be "the ruler of the kingdom of the air" (Ephesians 2:2). Evidently, he will no longer have access to the presence of God and the heavenlies; he will be restricted to the physical earth. What an awful time it will be when he is loosed upon the people of the earth without any restraint on his *malevolent power.

malevolent
wishing evil to happen to others; showing ill will; spiteful

This prophecy, which tells of Satan's departure from his place in the heavenlies and the loss of his ability to accuse God's people in His presence, gives us the key to present victory over Satan. The people of God overcome him by "the blood of the Lamb and by the word of their testimony" (v. 11). In spite of Satan's accusations, the believer has victory as long as he surrenders to the control of the indwelling Spirit and allows Him to direct his behavior (Philippians 2:13). We are not perfect, but we are in the process of becoming like Jesus. One day soon we shall be like Him, for we shall see Him as He is (1 John 3:2).

2 From the original revolt until he is hurled from the heavens, Satan's method of attack against the people of God has been

a) primarily physical affliction.
b) mainly psychological attack.
c) insinuation to a person that he has failed.
d) accusation of one to God and to oneself.

3 Describe the war in heaven and its outcome.

....

....

Identify the beast, his origin, source of power, and significance.

A Beast Out of the Sea

Revelation 13:1–10

As this scene opens, John sees the dragon stand on the seashore. The language John uses indicates that the dragon is expecting the next event to occur. John continues, "And I saw a beast coming out of the sea. He had ten horns and seven heads, with ten crowns on his horns, and on each head a blasphemous name" (v. l). Scripture clearly identifies the dragon as Satan within the context of chapter 12. Similarly, the beast is identified within the immediate context. John adds, "The dragon gave the beast his power and his throne and great authority" (v. 2). The *beast* is Satan's man, the tool through which he works in the end time.

We have discussed this one previously as the *little horn* of Daniel 7 and as the *rider of the white horse* under the first seal of Revelation 6. We have considered him in the context of Daniel 9:24–27 as the coming ruler who will make a covenant with Israel, and we have examined his activities in 2 Thessalonians 2:1–

12 that are related to the coming rebellion. Here John describes his appearance and role in the Tribulation in further detail.

It is significant that the beast comes out of the sea. Revelation 17:15 suggests that the sea from which this beast will come represents the peoples of the earth. Scripture thus indicates that the beast is of natural human origin and that he will arise from among the peoples of the earth. The Antichrist will already be a grown man in the world when the Tribulation begins. At the proper time, the dragon will reveal his agent, and Antichrist will move quickly to assume the position of world ruler.

The seven heads and ten horns of the dragon (12:3) and those of the beast (13:1) represent difficult symbolism. You may have noted that in chapter 12 the crowns are on the seven heads of the dragon; whereas, in chapter 13, the crowns are on the ten horns. Most scholars believe that the seven horns stand for seven major kingdoms that have had a major impact on God's people and His plan of redemption. They also feel that the explanation of this mystery in 17:9–14 lends itself to this interpretation. Let us examine this explanation briefly.

Revelation 17:9–10 indicates that the seven heads stand for seven kings or kingdoms. John is told "Five have fallen, one is, the other has not yet come; but when he does come, he must remain for a little while." Egypt, Assyria, Babylon, Medo-Persia, and Greece had come and made their impact on the history of God's people. *One is* certainly seems to refer to Rome which, in John's day, was nearing the height of her power. Rome as an empire died in the west, however, in AD 476. And while nation-states that were once part of Rome's empire have risen and exerted great power, the empire has not been revived in its original form. However, a seventh king is to come to power for a little while. This has prompted these scholars to assert that perhaps the elements that made up the old Roman Empire will be *revived* briefly in a ten-nation coalition as we saw in Daniel 7 before the eighth king, the Antichrist, takes over the entity and subordinates it to his purposes.

This is certainly a plausible explanation. However, as was pointed out earlier, others see some elements of the old Roman Empire and some elements not from the old Roman Empire in the final entity symbolized by the feet of iron and clay in Daniel 2. Keep these explanations in mind as we move on into the description of the Antichrist's significance and activities.

Both Daniel 7:24 and Revelation 17:12 indicate that the ten horns of the beast are ten kings. These Scriptures present Antichrist as an absolute ruler who will exercise authority through ten kings or leaders for *one hour*. This latter note probably indicates the relatively short reign of the Antichrist and those who exercise power under him.

4 Circle the letter preceding each TRUE statement.

- **a** The beast is clearly identified in the general context as Satan's agent.
- **b** The beast is said to arise out of the sea which, according to Revelation 17:15, represents the Mediterranean Sea.
- **c** The beast who rises out of the sea derives his power and authority from the peoples from which he comes.
- **d** Scripture indicates that the sea from which the beast arises represents the peoples of the world and that the Antichrist is a human being.
- **e** Seven heads, according to some Bible scholars, stand for seven kingdoms that have had a major impact on the destinies of God's people.
- **f** The ten horns represent ten leaders of the end time who will exercise power under the Antichrist for a short period.

Verses 3, 12 and 14 of chapter 13, indicate a fatal wounding of the beast out of the sea. The scholars who anticipate the future revival of the Roman Empire point out that only one of the heads of the beast is wounded to death. Thus the old Roman Empire, which is dead, will itself come back to life in a revised form under the Antichrist.

Some, however, interpret this to mean that the Antichrist himself will receive a stroke of death. Thus, verses 3 and 4 show the astonishment of the people of the world at his subsequent resurrection. This feat in turn will inspire the admiration and awe of people everywhere, leading them to ask "Who is like the beast? Who can make war against him?" They will thus be prepared to respond positively when the beast out of the earth makes the "earth and its inhabitants worship the first beast, whose fatal wound had been healed" (v. 12) and orders them "to set up an image in honor of the beast who was wounded by the sword and yet lived" (v. 14). Whether the verse means the actual death and resurrection of the Antichrist or the death and revival of a kingdom, we know that Antichrist will demonstrate remarkable powers that will make him appear to be the perfect leader.

John gives more precise details of this leader's absolute rule in verses 5–8. He says that the beast will exercise power for forty-two months, during which he will utter proud words and blasphemies against God. This description and time frame fit precisely the interpretation God gave Daniel concerning this leader (Daniel 7:24–25). The fact that he will persecute God's people simply underscores what Daniel was told. The prophecies we have studied indicate that the beast will come to power and consolidate his position during the first half of Daniel's seventieth seven; however, he will exercise unlimited power for only forty-two months over the peoples of the earth.

deluded
one who has been deceived, tricked, or led astray

The beast's control is to be so complete that he will receive the worship of all earth's people—all those *deluded by his lies (2 Thessalonians 2:9–12). The people of God, however, will neither worship him nor subscribe to his rule (v. 8). We should notice one significant fact about the beast's power in verses 5–7: the passive expression *was given.* This indicates that the beast derives his power from the dragon, but ultimately he can do only what God permits. More important, his rule is limited to one brief period.

requited
paid back; avenged

Verses 9 and 10 can be interpreted to mean that persecution and death are unavoidable, or they may mean that judgment will be *requited on the enemies of God's people for their hostility to and persecution of God's people. In any case, this time of rule by the dragon's agent calls for the patient endurance of God's people.

5 Explain why people will worship the beast for forty-two months.

....

....

6 What is the significance of the beast's power and activities?

....

....

Describe the second beast of Revelation 13 and indicate his identity.

The False Prophet

Revelation 13:11–18

We have discussed the dragon of chapter 12 and the beast out of the sea of chapter 13. Now we are introduced to *another beast* in 13:11–18. We found that the dragon was identified as Satan (12:9) and the beast out of the sea was identified as Satan's agent, the Antichrist (13:2–4). The second beast of chapter 13 is identified in three places as the *false prophet* (Revelation 16:13, 19:20, and 20:10). Let us review briefly some of the facts about this beast.

1. He comes from the earth.
2. He resembles a lamb, but he speaks like a dragon.
3. He exercises all the power of the Antichrist.
4. He performs great and miraculous signs.

In the book of Revelation, Jesus is symbolized as a lamb (5:6), and Satan is symbolized as a dragon (12:9). Here the beast out of the earth is said to resemble a lamb but to sound like a dragon. The second beast seems to represent Jesus Christ but speaks like Satan. We believe that the second beast represents false Christianity or the apostate church of the last days. This latter beast is a picture of an individual spokesman who brings church and state together in an unbiblical way. He will lead a nonbiblical, *secular church in the end time. In so doing, he will unify the peoples of the world as no one else has ever done. It is no wonder that he is referred to as *the false prophet.*

secular
not religious or sacred; worldly; not belonging to a religious order

With the introduction of the second beast of Revelation 13, we have before us the components of the satanic trinity: Satan, anti-God; the beast, anti-Christ; and the false prophet, anti-Spirit. In terms of activity, we see that the Antichrist represents or manifests Satan, and the false prophet glorifies the Antichrist as he leads multitudes to worship the devil's messiah. This activity represents the greatest imitation ever of the adorable Godhead, but it will not last long. Then, as we shall see, the members of the satanic trinity will be deprived of their power.

7 Describe the beast out of the earth and state his identity.

....

....

Choose statements that give the source of the false prophet's authority and his purpose.

His Authority and Miracles

Revelation 13:12–15

John tells us how the false prophet will exercise authority and he identifies the source of this authority. The false prophet will act in behalf of the Antichrist and make the people of the earth worship the Antichrist whose deadly wound was healed. In addition, John explains how this evil one will deceive the people of the earth. He will use signs and wonders to impress the people of the earth with his seemingly unlimited power (vv. 13–15). However, Paul notes that along with his

counterfeit
false

diabolical power he will use **counterfeit miracles* and engage ruthlessly in every sort of evil, perhaps to shock people with his utter lawlessness (2 Thessalonians 2:9–12). Verse 15 notes specifically that he will make an image of the Antichrist and then, incredibly, cause it to speak and breathe. Then he will force all people either to worship the image of the Antichrist or be killed.

The false prophet will thus channel people's desire to worship in a new direction, that is, toward a new, universal religion: beast worship. Religion without Jesus Christ, however, is a major tool of Satan whether it is named *Christian* or something else. The false prophet will perform great miracles for one reason: to deceive the people of the earth (v. 14). The word *breath* in verse 15 may be properly translated *spirit.* We believe that just as the evil spirit in Luke 8:26–29 is identified as *the demon* and evil spirits in Revelation 16:13–14 are called *spirits of demons,* so the false prophet will command a demon spirit to enter the image of the Antichrist. Then, having entered the image, the demon spirit will cause it to speak, deceiving millions of earth's people.

allegiance
loyalty owed by a citizen to his ruler

Furthermore, the false prophet will exercise means other than deceit to make people give *allegiance to the beast. He will use fear as an instrument of terror: anyone who refuses to worship the beast will be killed. The coming terror on earth will exceed anything man has yet seen. Knowing the savage fury of Antichrist and also the judgment of God on sin, we must face the task of declaring the good news to mankind with an ever-present sense of urgency.

8 Circle the letter preceding each TRUE statement.

a The false prophet, who will exercise great authority on behalf of the beast, derives his authority from the political power of the beast.

b The immediate goal of the false prophet is to do what is necessary in order to deceive earth's people into worshipping the Antichrist.

c The long-term goal of the false prophet and Antichrist is to serve the dragon's interests and defeat God's program.

d While the false prophet may be termed a *trickster* or *wonder-worker,* he is capable only of deception and exercises no real power.

Discuss the mark of the beast and its significance.

His Mark, Name, and Number

Revelation 13:16–18

We have seen that the false prophet will exercise awesome power over the people of the earth. Verses 16–18 indicate the means he will use to unite the people of the world in their support of Satan's agent, the Antichrist. He will require every person to receive the mark, the name, or the number for identification on the right hand or forehead. As we shall see, these indicate support of and loyalty to the policies and aims of the Antichrist. In order to understand the crucial nature of this policy, we must see that all commerce will be affected. *No one can transact business without this identification.* No person, family, state, or nation can conduct its financial or business affairs or receive credit in the world monetary system without being part of the Antichrist's system. This involves people in a decision: will they accept the *mark, the name, or the number of the beast* and avoid the fury of his savage enforcement? Or will they refuse and be killed?

Many people have tried to interpret the meaning of the *number of the beast.* We know only that it is 666, but we do not know precisely what this number means. It appears to us that in Revelation God's number would be 777 to represent the holy Trinity: God the Father, God the Son, and God the Holy Spirit. Moreover, we are led to believe that 666 is man's number and stands for the satanic trinity: Satan, the false god; Antichrist, the false christ, and the false prophet, the false spirit.

Chapter 13 thus introduces us to a solemn view of the future of mankind under a one-world system. Like preceding chapters in Daniel and Revelation, it reveals further detailed elements of the future. Not only will there be a godless dictator, cruel oppression of God's people, fearful signs as the natural world reels under God's judgment but also an oppressive economic system and vile religious control over every aspect of one's life.

Certainly, these facts ought to make every committed believer purpose to live for God and be ready for our Lord's appearing. For the non-Christian the future is hopeless and dark; however, for the Christian the future is bright, for it anticipates eternity with Jesus. May this hope have the effect on us that John speaks of in 1 John 3:2.

9 Discuss briefly the *mark of the beast.*

....

....

10 The significance of the *mark of the beast* is that it
- a) will force all earth's people to decide either to support or oppose the policy and aims of the beast.
- b) speaks only of symbolical support of a policy or person and has no reference to an actual physical mark.
- c) appears to be of utmost importance because one must either support Antichrist's policies or be killed.
- d) all of the above.
- e) both a) and c) above.

Recognize true facts about the great prostitute and her significance in the end time.

The Great Prostitute

Revelation 17:1–18

We have tried to show the progressive nature of Bible prophecy in this study. In general, we have tried to follow the biblical sequence of events. Now, however, since we have the false religious system of the end time in focus and its role in Antichrist's rule, we shall move to chapter 17 and examine the subject in greater detail.

perverted
turned from what is considered true, desirable, good, or morally right; corrupt

Man was made to worship, to respond to God, but throughout history Satan has *perverted this inner urge toward evil ends. From early history man has worshiped everything from nature to the planets. Here false religion is pictured most appropriately as a great prostitute. As modern man becomes more and more inclined to disregard God, reject the rule of law, moral standards, and accountability for his actions, he will become increasingly secular on one hand and inclined

gaudily
what is dressed or decorated too brightly to be in good taste; cheap; showy

liaison
connection between parts of an army or branches of service to secure proper cooperation

flaunted
displayed ostentatiously; paraded boastfully, impudently, and defiantly in the public view

toward the control of evil spirits on the other. His conduct in effect denies the testimony of God in nature and revelation. And since he worships the work of his hands and the evil desires of his heart, he commits *spiritual adultery.* Let us examine the picture John sees as he is carried away by the Spirit into a desert (v. 3).

John sees a *gaudily dressed prostitute on a beast with seven heads and ten horns (v. 4). This is a significant fact. The indication is that early on in the rule of the Antichrist, apostate or false religion symbolized by the prostitute, will play a major role in uniting the world under Antichrist. As the beast comes into prominence, the apostate church or false religion will seek to promote world unity apart from the moral values and principles of the Word of God. The apostate church, which supports eastern mysticism and non-Christian philosophy, will seek to express her aims through political power: a *liaison with Antichrist.

Godless religious systems have historically resisted God and persecuted the church of Jesus Christ; therefore, they have been guilty of the blood of God's people. Moreover, they have *flaunted their corrupt practices before God and His people. The great prostitute will apparently be successful during the beast's rise to power. This is pictured by the prostitute's position on the beast: she appears to be riding the beast and controlling his movements in this symbolical picture.

We notice that the seven heads are interpreted to mean seven *hills,* as well as kings or kingdoms (v. 9). Some Bible scholars believe that the reference to the seven hills identifies the city as Rome, the place from which the false religious system of the last days will be directed. Certain scholars have traced the movement of very ancient Babylonian mystery religions to Rome. These scholars note that certain pagan practices were incorporated into Christian beliefs, creating confusion and blurring biblical requirements for Christian living.

The tradition of men over the centuries has replaced the commandments of the Word of God. In fact, error has been present in the church from its earliest days, but the tendency among many *Christian* churches today is to reject the Bible standard and to substitute a host of other man-made options. This tendency will increase rapidly as the doctrine of devils finds its way into the false religious system of the world. It will reach its zenith near the middle of the seventieth seven as Satan's agent sows his deceitful doctrines and wins the admiration of earth's masses. The degree of success the false system has achieved and will yet achieve is indicated in verse 15: "The waters you saw, where the prostitute sits, are people, multitudes, nations and languages." Then in a very treacherous and dramatic change of mind and policy, the beast and the prostitute part company.

Sometime after the middle, quite possibly near the end of the seventieth seven, the beast will turn against the false system and destroy it completely (v. 16). Then Antichrist will become the supreme symbol of worship and the false prophet will lead multitudes of people to a total commitment to him. In a rigidly controlled world, people will not be able to function without supporting the ungodly policies of Satan's agent. Moreover, with the ten leaders of the end-time coalition supporting him, the Antichrist's system will exercise what appears to be universal control *until* God's words are fulfilled. Significantly, the prostitute is said to be the city that exercises control over the leaders of the earth (v. 18).

11 Circle the letter preceding each TRUE statement.

a Man was created to worship God, but this desire to worship God has been perverted by Satan toward ungodly ends.

b When man worships any other thing than his Creator, he commits spiritual adultery.

c From the evidence given it appears that the prostitute is so-called because she prostitutes her principles in order to achieve unity apart from the values given in God's Word.

d The prostitute can be identified as the apostate church of the end-time or false religion.

e The prostitute will be successful throughout the seventieth seven and rule jointly with the Antichrist.

f False religion is a characteristic of the end time and is thus new in man's historical experience.

g Apparently, the beast will *use* the prostitute to achieve world unity; otherwise, he has no interest in man's religion.

h In the second half of the seventieth seven, the false prophet will lead the world's people into a deep commitment to the beast, which implies support of his policies and aims.

Prophecies of the End

The rest of this lesson is based on Revelation 14. This chapter is another *parenthetical enlargement.* It deals with events that will bring the tribulation period—the period represented by the seventieth seven of Daniel 9:24–27—to an end. Here is a list of six things which, according to Daniel 9:24, are to be accomplished during Daniel's seventy sevens.

1. Transgression will be finished.
2. Sin will be brought to an end.
3. Atonement will be made for wickedness.
4. Everlasting righteousness will be brought in.
5. The vision and prophecy will be sealed up.
6. The Most Holy Place will be anointed.

We believe that item three in the foregoing list was accomplished by Christ on the cross of Calvary. We also believe that the fifth item will be accomplished by the death of the two witnesses of Revelation 11 because they are apparently the final prophetical voices. The rest of the things in the list will be accomplished as a result of our Lord's second coming.

Identify facts about the identity, role, and characteristics of the 144,000.

The Lamb and the 144,000

Revelation 14:1–5

In Revelation 14:1–5 John sees a vision of God's purpose in relation to His chosen people, Israel, and shows that they will be on Mt. Zion when the unfulfilled aspects of Daniel 9:24 are accomplished. In our view the 144,000 who have the Lamb's name and His Father's name written on their foreheads are the same 144,000 who receive a seal on their foreheads in Revelation 7:3–4.

Revelation 14:1 is a parenthetical enlargement of Revelation 7:3–4 because it identifies the seal on their foreheads.

Revelation 14:1–5 does not indicate clearly whether the 144,000 are on earth or in heaven since *Mt. Zion* may refer either to Jerusalem or heaven. Moreover, their identity is uncertain and has inspired various opinions. Some scholars consider them to be identical to the son of the mysterious woman in chapter 12 who was caught up to heaven. They believe that the 144,000 are at this point in heaven. Other scholars, however, believe that these 144,000 are the same as those who were presented in chapter 7. We believe that they represent earthly Israel whose people will inherit the promised land following the Great Tribulation. In fact, one of the purposes of the Millennium, which we will discuss in Revelation 20, will be for Abraham's children to inherit this land, an inheritance that will become eternal (Genesis 17:8). One bit of evidence that supports the view that they are on earth is the indirect reference in 9:4 to judge only "those people who did not have the seal of God on their foreheads." This reference clearly indicates that they are protected on earth—not in heaven. Consistent with what we have noted in our study of Revelation 7 and the ministry of the two witnesses in chapter 12, it appears that the 144,000 who are sealed with God's seal will have a powerful witness during these dark days of the Great Tribulation.

In his description of this select group on Mt. Zion, John indicates the great volume and utter majesty of this glorious symphony as the 144,000 sing a new song of redemption (vv. 2–3). It is a song that only the redeemed can learn and sing. We are told in verse 3 that "the 144,000... had been redeemed from the earth." They are the "firstfruits to God and the Lamb" (v. 4) from the nation of Israel. This group represents the earnest of the larger body from the nation of Israel that will turn to God.

The statement that they "did not defile themselves with women, for they kept themselves pure" has no reference to marriage. Marriage is to be honored by all (Hebrews 13:4). In the general context, their spiritual purity is contrasted with a prevailing spirit of idolatry, which is spiritual adultery.

Concerning the 144,000 as the firstfruits of Israel's people that will turn to God, Isaiah 63:1–6 and Micah 2:12–13 offer some helpful insights. We believe that these passages will help you to understand what will happen to the people of Israel who have fled to the place God has prepared for them in the desert (12:14). The things that will happen to God's people concern the completion of the six things we mentioned in Daniel 9:24.

The picture Isaiah portrays of our Lord in the day of His vengeance is instructive. The One who speaks in righteousness and is mighty to save comes from *Bozrah. Bozrah* means *rock* or *place of protection,* and it describes perfectly the city of Petra we studied about in our last lesson. Micah adds a graphic description of this time of victory after the forces of evil have been defeated and the Lord brings His people back from their place of protection to the center of their national life: Jerusalem. Micah says specifically what is involved in Israel's deliverance in 2:12–13:

1. God will gather the remnant of Israel.
2. His people will be like sheep in a pen or like a flock in its pasture (the Hebrew word for *bozrah* is here translated "pasture").
3. One who breaks open the way will go up before them.
4. They will break through the gate and go out.
5. Their king will pass through before them, the Lord at their head.

The last three statements in the preceding list are especially meaningful in view of our discussion of the city of Petra in Lesson 11. We might say that it will take the awful trauma of the Great Tribulation to get God's people to recognize their need of Him. Sometimes one does not *look up* until he is flat on his back. In the same way, as Israel faces the horrors of life in a world controlled by an absolute dictator who is bent on their destruction, her people will turn to God.

In summary, then, we believe that the Lord Jesus will lead Israel out of Bozrah or Petra to Jerusalem. The Mount of Olives on the east side of Jerusalem will split in two from east to west and form a great valley (Zechariah 14:4). Our Lord will lead His people in through the eastern gate and the glory of God will again fill the temple area in Jerusalem. We believe that the things that remain to be completed to fulfill Daniel 9:24 will be accomplished in the extra days noted in Daniel 12:11–12 following the 1260 days. Thus, God's plan of redemption will be complete and a reign of peace will begin. Transgression will be finished, sin will be ended, a reign of righteousness will begin, and the Most Holy Place will be anointed. At long last the real peace for which man has searched will exist and be maintained under the direction of the Son of David.

12 Match each item about some quality of the 144,000 (right) with its appropriate definition or description (left).

. . . . **a** The 144,000 are spiritually pure, redeemed from the earth, marked on their foreheads, and follow the Lord.

. . . . **b** The 144,000 represent the remnant of Israel who will turn to God and inherit the promised land following the Tribulation.

. . . . **c** The 144,000 protected followers of the Lamb may exert a powerful witness during the Tribulation.

. . . . **d** The 144,000 are protected by the seal of God from His judgment during the Tribulation.

1) Role
2) Location
3) Identity
4) Characteristics

Objective 12.9 *Discuss briefly the proclamations made by the three angels in Revelation 14:6–13.*

The Proclamations of Three Angels

Revelation 14:6–13

In verses 6–11 John hears three angels proclaim important messages to the people of the earth, and in verse 13 he hears a voice from heaven proclaim a beatitude on those who die in the Lord from this point on. All of these verses focus on true worship and false worship: who should be worshiped and who should not be worshiped. They point out clearly the result of falsehood and the result of both true and false worship. Consider the following points that emerge from these verses:

1. The first angel proclaims who should be worshiped (v. 7).
2. The second angel makes a proleptic announcement of the destruction of the apostate church or false religion (v. 8).
3. The third angel makes a proclamation of who should not be worshiped and warns of the curse that will result from false worship (vv. 9–11).

4. Heaven's blessing is declared on those who persist in true worship (v. 13).

The cry of martyrs in Revelation 6:9–11 who had been slain for the Word of God and the testimony they had borne and the knowledge that false religion has so persecuted God's people may explain the advance announcement of the fall of Babylon (v. 8). Those on earth at this time who have turned to God and are suffering at the hands of the beast's system will most certainly welcome word that the end of this corrupt system is at hand.

Revelation 14:9–11 deals with the punishment of those who make a conscious decision to commit themselves to the beast's system. These people will be required to take the mark of the beast and thus identify with him. This decision will purchase a short-lived period of safety; however, it will expose them to the wrath of God and eternal damnation. In effect, those who take the mark of the beast will by this act commit spiritual suicide.

The burning sulfur John refers to in verse 10 is the eternal fire Jesus referred to in Mark 9:42–48. This torment was not prepared for man; it was "prepared for the devil and his angels" (Matthew 25:41). However, those who choose to follow Satan will be forever with him. They will not enjoy the abundant life that our Lord Jesus provides for us. *As we read about their eternal punishment, we must pray that God will give us a new sense of urgency as we present Jesus Christ to a lost world.*

By contrast, faithful worshipers of God who die in Him from this point on will be blessed. Though denounced and killed by the beast and his evil system, they are conquerors in their Lord. These victors in Christ will be blessed with rest from the rigors of life in the end time and they will be rewarded on the basis of their works (v. 13). Indeed, all those who have served the Lord faithfully throughout the ages will be rewarded, and we shall see Him face to face.

13 Based on Revelation 14:6–13, answer the following questions.

a Why did the first angel say God should be feared (vv. 6–7)?

....

b Why is the proleptic statement of Babylon's fall made (v. 8)?

....

....

c What is the penalty for loyalty to the beast and his system (vv. 9–11)?

....

....

d What happens to those who die in the Lord during the Tribulation from this point on (v. 13)?

....

Choose statements that reflect accurately matters of the harvest and winepress in 14:14–20.

The Harvest and the Winepress

Revelation 14:14–20

The latter part of chapter 14 gives us a picture of harvest. The harvest metaphor used in the context of concluding events of the seventieth seven is significant. In this final hour of man's history there will undoubtedly be a great harvest of souls as multitudes turn to God. Jesus used the harvest metaphor to explain how the gospel is to be extended (John 4:35). In addition, we see clear evidence of a judicial harvest in these verses.

We believe that verses 14–16 refer to a great harvest of souls during the last half of the Great Tribulation. Multitudes will doubtless be killed because they will resist the Antichrist's policies. However, it seems likely that as the beast extends his control over the world, he will exert the most control over the areas that are closest to his operations center. To enforce his policies with equal rigor on a worldwide basis might take a longer time than his limited rule will permit. It appears that many will run the risk of losing their lives to save their souls and thus contribute to this great gospel harvest.

In our view, verses 17–20 represent a judicial harvest. The judgment described here will be carried out in the Battle of Armageddon, which is described in verse 19 as "the great winepress of God's wrath." At this time God will call the wicked to account for their opposition to Him and for their evil deeds. The expressions *fury* and *wrath* indicate the reaction of our infinitely holy God against both the source and the various acts of sin throughout human history. While God's patience and mercy have been manifested since the initial fall of man, He has appointed a day in which He will end His appeal to *whoever wishes* to be saved (22:17). Then His wrath will be revealed! The indication is that blood will flow freely in a valley that runs north and south through the land of Israel. This valley can be viewed from the mountain of Megiddo in the northern part of Israel. In fact, this is the source of the name *Armageddon,* which means "mountain of Megiddo."

14 Circle the letter preceding each TRUE statement.

- **a** The harvest metaphor, as used in this section, refers exclusively to judgment.
- **b** Bible prophecy indicates the possibility of a *harvest* of souls during the Great Tribulation.
- **c** Gathering the harvest of grapes into a winepress suggests a judicial harvest.
- **d** Pressing grapes in a winepress is the figure of speech which is used to describe the bloodbath that will occur when God judges the wicked.

Self-Test

Multiple choice: Circle the letter preceding the best answer for each question.

1 The dragon in chapters 12 and 13 is identified
a) clearly as the principle of evil in all times.
b) as Satan, the accuser of man and the opposer of God.
c) indirectly as an evil person on earth in the last days.
d) plainly as a symbol of evil in society.

2 The beast of Revelation 13:1, which John saw emerge from the sea, is identified as the
a) Antichrist who will come to prominence in the seventieth seven.
b) man of lawlessness mentioned by Paul in 2 Thessalonians 2:1–12.
c) second member of the satanic trinity.
d) all of the above.
e) both a) and c) above.

3 The second beast of Revelation 13, which John saw emerge from the earth, is identified in three places as the
a) false prophet and the third member of the satanic trinity.
b) Antichrist who deceives the people of the earth.
c) power behind the Antichrist and his source of authority.
d) personification of evil.

4 Scripture indicates that the people of the earth will view the beast
a) with great wonder and admiration.
b) with distrust and fear.
c) as worthy of their worship and allegiance.
d) all of the above.
e) both a) and c) above.

5 It is possible, according to one point of view of chapter 13, that people will marvel at the beast because of his apparent
a) diplomatic triumphs.
b) military victories.
c) resurrection from death.
d) political achievements.

6 The second beast of Revelation 13 will function primarily to
a) promote the person, policies, and programs of the first beast.
b) gain a personal following for himself.
c) provide an alternative rule to that of the first beast.
d) frustrate social and political development on earth.

7 The first beast derives his power and authority from
a) his political base.
b) the people he controls.
c) his own charisma.
d) the dragon.

8 Revelation 13 indicates that the Antichrist will enforce his policies by means of
a) requiring mandatory allegiance to his rule.
b) a mark which people must have to buy or sell.
c) the threat of imprisonment, torture, and social disgrace.
d) all of the above.
e) both a) and b) above.

9 The penalty for identifying with the Antichrist is the
a) loss of one's life.
b) loss of one's reward.
c) threat of eternal punishment and separation from God's presence.
d) possibility of suffering present shame.

10 Of the great prostitute, the apostate church, we can say most accurately that
a) she *sells* her spiritual principles in return for religious unity.
b) bases her values on tradition rather than God's word.
c) she will be active politically in the attempt to achieve world unity.
d) all of the above.
e) both b) and c) above.

11 Since the great prostitute *rides* the beast, we get the impression that
a) the apostate church will not be supported by the political system.
b) the apostate church will have a major role during the beast's rise to power.
c) she is heady, arrogant, and wants maximum publicity for her *adultery.*
d) here we have an association of evil, deceptive principles.

12 Revelation 17:15–18 indicates that when the beast and the ten supporting kings with him turn in hatred on the prostitute and destroy her, we have evidence that
a) the Antichrist will *use* the apostate church to gain his end.
b) religious toleration will not last long during the tribulation period.
c) the apostate church's spiritual adultery, her fling with the Antichrist, is doomed to fail.
d) all of the above.
e) both b) and c) above.

13 The indication is that those persons who die in the Lord during the Great Tribulation will receive
a) recognition for the brave, courageous lives they have lived.
b) a place in the annals of the faith.
c) rest from their labors and reward for their works.
d) greater rewards than those who do not go through the Great Tribulation.

14 The harvest metaphor used in Revelation 14 speaks of
a) a judicial harvest.
b) a harvest of souls.
c) that fact that man is living in the end of time.
d) both a judicial harvest and a harvest of souls.

15 The figure of grapes being crushed in a winepress speaks quite clearly about the
a) wrath of God that will be revealed in the Great Tribulation.
b) abundance of crops in the world during the seventieth seven.
c) symbolism of fruitfulness and productivity.
d) fruitfulness of the restored land of Israel.

Answers to study questions

8 **a** False
b True
c True
d False

1 He is identified as Satan and the reference to his tail sweeping one-third of the stars from heaven may refer to a past revolt in heaven.

9 It is a mark that represents loyalty to the system of the Antichrist. It will be required for all people to conduct business in any form on earth at this time.

2 d) accusation of one to God and to oneself.

10 e) both a) and c) above.

3 Satan and his evil angels will be defeated by Michael and his angels. As a result, Satan will be hurled to the earth.

11 **a** True
b True
c True
d True
e False
f False
g True
h True

4 **a** True
b False
c False
d True
e True
f True

12 **a** 4) Characteristics
b 3) Identity
c 1) Role
d 2) Location

5 It appears that he will have great power and ability. In what may be a reference to his resurrection from death, he will inspire great admiration and worship. He will arrogate to himself divine prerogatives, and the false prophet will reinforce these claims for the beast.

13 **a** Because the hour of His judgment has come.
b It will most likely encourage those suffering in the Tribulation to recognize that the time remaining for false religion to exercise power is limited.
c Those who give allegiance to the beast will come under God's wrath, suffering eternal punishment and being excluded from God's presence.
d They will rest in the Lord and be rewarded on the basis of their works.

6 He is Satan's agent and will use the power he is given to unite the world in evil against God and His people. (His activities against God's people will doubtless drive them to God.)

14 **a** False
b True
c True
d True

7 He appears as a lamb but is said to sound like a dragon. He is another of Satan's agents. He is identified as the false prophet.

Lesson 13 Final Events of the Great Tribulation

In our last lesson, we were introduced to some of the main characters in the tribulation period. We discussed facts about each member of the satanic trinity, including the work and methods of the Antichrist and his agent, the false prophet. Moreover, we looked once again at the identity and purpose of the 144,000, and we perused the proclamation of three angels in chapter 14 in the light of harvest metaphors. Since the end of the Tribulation is coming rapidly into focus, we shall now consider final events in detail.

As the end approaches, the policies of the Antichrist in attempting to unite the world under the banner of Satan will become unbearable. Meanwhile, the intensity of God's judgments will become more apparent to the people of the earth. The stage will thus be set for the Antichrist's empire to meet its end as the rock "cut out, but not by human hands" (Daniel 2:34) strikes the image on its feet and destroys every trace of human government. This action is a symbolic portrayal of the end of the Antichrist's empire, which will occur at Christ's second coming. Christ's coming is at hand and we must prepare ourselves for that event, doing all we can to make His salvation known to all people. As we engage in the task of evangelism, we may be assured that the time is approaching when we will hear Him say, "Well done! Enter into the joy of the Lord."

the activities...

◇ Study the lesson as usual and read the Scriptures for each section as you come to them in the lesson development._+_

◇ We encourage you to continue to write your own responses to study questions before you turn to those we have provided at the end of the lesson.

◇ You may use your Bible to answer study questions and the questions in the self-test.

◇ Be sure to look in the glossary for the meanings of any key words you do not know.

the objectives...

13.1 *Identify the third great sign and tell why it is so important.*

13.2 *State what the bowl judgments represent and their effect on mankind.*

13.3 *Identify commercial or political Babylon and describe what is symbolized by its fall.*

13.4 *Identify those who give praise in heaven and the subject of their praise.*

13.5 *Describe the wedding supper of the Lamb and identify the significance of the bride's clothing.*

***13.6** Discuss the roles of the warrior-Messiah based on Revelation 19:11–21 and related New Testament teaching.*

the outline...

1 The Preparation for and the Outpouring of the Seven Bowls
 a The Third Great Sign
 b The Outpouring of the Bowls of God's Wrath

2 The Fall of Political or Commercial Babylon
 a The Judgment of Babylon

3 The Second Coming of Christ
 a Thanksgiving for the Judgment of Babylon
 b The Wedding Supper of the Lamb
 c The Revelation of the Warrior-Messiah

Identify the third great sign and tell why it is so important.

The Preparation For and the Outpouring of the Seven Bowls

The interlude, which began following the sounding of the seventh trumpet and continued through chapters 12, 13, and 14, now gives way to the preparation for the bowl judgments. Chapter 15, which is the shortest chapter in the book of Revelation, introduces another great sign: seven angels with the seven last plagues. After they receive the seven bowls of wrath, the seven angels pour out their bowls upon the people of the earth in chapter 16. However, the wrath of God is not poured out indiscriminately; it is visited only upon those who have taken the mark of the beast and worshiped his image.

The Third Great Sign

Revelation 15:1–8

In the flow of revelation, John sees "another great and marvelous sign"(v. l). You may recall that John saw two such signs in 12:1–3: the first was a sun-clothed woman and the second was a great red dragon. Here John observes seven angels who have the seven last plagues of the Tribulation. While the emphasis in this verse is on the word *last* in the original Greek, the number seven is important too. It speaks of *completeness*! In this case it refers to the completeness and certainty of God's wrath against all unrighteousness. The judgments of God thus become more intense as the Tribulation moves toward its climax.

Some Bible scholars believe that the bowl judgments simply repeat the events symbolized in the opening of the seals and the blowing of the trumpets. However, we believe that these scholars tend to ignore the emphasis here on *last plagues*. Since the judgments are called the *last plagues*, the implication is that the seal and trumpet judgments are both different from and earlier than the bowl judgments.

The fact that the bowl judgments are the *last* judgments adds to their wonder and greatness, as does the fact that in them the wrath of God is completed. The advance announcement may indicate that this sign is God's last warning to an *impenitent world. All that remains at this point is final judgment.

impenitent
feeling no sorrow or regret for having done wrong

Verse two shows the victors over the beast standing by the crystal sea holding harps, which were given to them by God. The crystal sea appears to be mixed with fire, which may refer to God's judgment which proceeds from His holiness. The beast believed that he had conquered them by killing them, but their death simply involved a change in location: from earth in the midst of judgment to peace in the presence of God.

As these victors stand beside the crystal sea, they sing a song of praise to God. The theme of their song is deliverance. As the people of Israel praised God for their deliverance from Egypt (Exodus 15), so these ones redeemed out of the Tribulation from the hatred and hostility of the beast will sing a song of deliverance to God. Verses 3 and 4 give us some of the many qualities of God for which they will rejoice.

rhetorical question
question asked only for effect, not information

The *rhetorical question is raised, "Who will not fear you, O Lord, and bring glory to your name?" (v. 4). While the nations do not glorify God nor fear Him in their sin-hardened hearts during the Tribulation, the day will come when they will both fear Him and acknowledge Him as Lord (see also Jeremiah 10:7 and Revelation 14:7). The likelihood of all nations worshiping God is a familiar theme of the prophets, and we see this borne out in the next statement: "For you alone are holy. All nations will come and worship before you." (See also Psalm 2:8–9, 24:1–10, 66:1–4, 72:8–11, 86:9; Isaiah 2:17, 9:6–7, 66:18–23; Daniel 7:14; Zephaniah 2:11; Zechariah 14:9.)

This foregoing statement does not mean that everyone will be saved; it does mean that the kingdom of God will include a fellowship whose members are drawn from all nations. They will worship God and extol His righteous works.

John now sees the tabernacle of Testimony in heaven (vv. 5–6). Since the seven angels of devastation come from the tabernacle of Testimony, the immediate context implies that the final plagues come from the presence of God and are the expression of His unalterable opposition to sin. We believe that these judgments are centered in the very nature of God. Scripture shows that God is righteous when He judges the wicked and when He forgives those who repent of their sins.

One of the four living creatures gives seven bowls filled with the wrath of God to the seven angels (vv. 7–8). The only other context in which the golden bowls are mentioned is in 5:8. There they were full of incense which represented the prayers of the saints. Some thus see a correlation between the prayers of the saints and the visitation of God's wrath on the world. That is, they feel there is a relationship between prayer and divine retribution.

Since God is mentioned in verse 7 as the One "who lives for ever and ever," we are reminded that while evil may seem to rule over the affairs of human history, God is the ever living One whose program cannot be frustrated by either human or satanic resistance.

Now that the bowls of wrath have been given out the temple is filled with the glory of God. It is therefore impossible to enter into the sanctuary until the judgments contained in the seven plagues have been carried out. It appears to us that to enter the sanctuary would interfere with God's wrathful judgment on the world for its rebellion against the love He has expressed in His Son.

1 The third great sign, introduced in Revelation 15:1, is
a) a sun-clothed woman.
b) the great red dragon.
c) seven plague-bearing angels.
d) a potter with a lump of clay.

2 The precise wording of Scripture indicates that the bowl judgments are
a) the same as the trumpet and seal judgments.
b) less intense than earlier judgments.
c) simply a repetition of earlier judgments.
d) to follow earlier judgments in point of time.

3 Explain why the third great sign is so important.

....

....

....

State what the bowl judgments represent and their effect on mankind.

The Outpouring of the Bowls of God's Wrath

Revelation 16:1–21; Exodus 7–12

In chapter 15 John reported on the preparations for the final series of judgments and attendant activity in heaven. However, chapter 16 in its entirety concerns the actual onset of the bowl judgments. There is a striking parallel between the trumpet judgments and the present series of plagues. But while there is some similarity, one should not assume that they are identical. Significantly, the trumpet plagues appear to be partial in their effect while the bowl plagues are universal. And while the trumpet series in a sense calls man to repentance, the bowl series represents the wrath of God. And whereas man was affected indirectly by the first four trumpets, he is affected directly by the bowls at the outset of this latter series of judgments. Moreover, the bowls seem to follow each other in rapid succession.

One who examines the plagues closely will doubtless notice the similarity between them and the Egyptian plagues. We recommend that you read the above reading assignment in Exodus so that you can see this similarity.

At this point it will be helpful to begin this section by reviewing the following chart (Figure 13.1) which compares the seal, trumpet, and bowl judgments. Review it carefully before you continue with the exposition of the remainder of this section.

NUMBER	SEAL	TRUMPET	BOWL
1	White horse rider has bow but no arrows (6:2)	Hail and fire hurled down upon the earth (8:7)	Painful sores upon people with the mark of the beast (16:2)
2	Red horse rider takes peace from the earth (6:4)	Something like a mountain thrown into the sea (8:8)	Death of every living thing in the sea (16:3)
3	Black horse rider brings famine (6:5)	Death of many people from bitter waters (8:10–11)	Rivers and springs of water turned into blood (16:4)
4	Personification of death and Hades (6:8)	Darkening of a third of the sun, moon, and stars(8:12)	People scorched by fire from the sun (16:8)
5	Godly martyrs seen under the altar (6:9)	Locusts of the Abyss torture the ungodly (9:1–5)	Kingdom of the beast plunged into darkness (16:10)
6	The sky recedes and every island and mountain is removed(6:12–14)	One third of mankind killed by infernal cavalry (9:15–19)	Euphrates dried up to prepare way for kings from the East (16:12)
7	Fire from heaven hurled on earth, an earthquake occurs (8:1–5)	Destruction decreed upon the destroyers of the earth through earthquake and hail (11:15–19)	The cry from God "It is done!" is followed by the greatest of all earthquakes (16:17–18)

Figure 13.1

John hears "a loud voice from the temple saying to the seven angels, "Go, pour out the seven bowls of God's wrath on the earth" (v. 1). We must assume that this voice is God's, for all others have been excluded from the temple until the seven angels have completed their mission. In response, John sees the first angel pour out his bowl on the people who had taken the mark of the beast (v. 2). Those who bear the mark of the beast during the Tribulation will now bear the marks of God's wrath. This plague will bring painful ulcers on all who are the beast's. In these times, religion will not be a purely convenient thing. All people will declare their loyalty for either Christ or Antichrist. (Compare this plague with that of the sixth Egyptian plague, in which man and beast suffered with festering boils in Exodus 9:9–11.)

As the second bowl is outpoured, every living thing in the sea dies (v. 3). Like the Egyptian plague (Exodus 7:20-21) and the second trumpet (8:8–9), the waters turn to blood. This plague will have far-reaching implications for all sea life dies. All marine food resources are thus lost, and the sea becomes putrid and unfit for any use. Following in rapid sequence, John observes as the third bowl is outpoured and all fresh waters are turned into blood (v. 4). Water is a critical necessity for life and survival, and even in normal times shortages of water produce crises. But this plague will bring about a universal crisis.

sated
satisfied fully; supplied with more than enough, so as to disgust or weary

Verses 5 and 6 record the words of the angel in charge of water. He notes how fitting this punishment is for the worshipers of the beast. They have become

sated
satisfied fully; supplied with more than enough, so as to disgust or weary

*sated with the blood of martyrs; therefore, they are given blood to drink. God is just in judgment; the penalty matches the crime.

As the fourth bowl is emptied, God appears to overrule the processes of nature, enabling the sun to afflict man. Now the sun is given power to scorch people with fire (vv. 8–9). Though seared by the intense heat, these hardened sinners refuse to repent and instead curse the name of God who has control over these plagues. The indication here is that followers of the universal beast cult recognize the omnipotence of God, but they refuse to repent and arrogantly curse Him instead. Whether the atmosphere is diffused or unusual solar activity occurs, men suffer severely because of this plague.

The fifth bowl plunges the kingdom of the beast into darkness like the Egyptian plague before the Exodus (Exodus 10:21–23). People once again suffer terribly, but instead of turning to God they curse Him for their pains (vv. 10–11). We are not told why people are so anguished and gnaw their tongues in pain. Perhaps the darkness will bring excessive cold for which people are not prepared. Whatever it is, we may be sure that darkness not only intensifies the distress of the previous plagues, but also adds terror all its own.

Verse 12 says, "The sixth angel poured out his bowl on the great river Euphrates, and its water was dried up to prepare the way for the kings from the East." Quite obviously, this is a very complex passage. It is linked to preparations for the Battle of Armageddon. The question is, why would members of the satanic trinity want to gather world rulers to fight against God? They know that Jesus is coming back to reign on earth as King of kings and Lord of lords. They will try to convince world rulers, that under their leadership Jesus Christ can be defeated when He returns. This appears to be the only reason for them to gather the world rulers to Armageddon. Revelation 19:19 indicates that "the kings of the earth" are gathered there for the purpose of making war with Jesus when He returns. Remember that after the death wound experience of the Antichrist, people will ask, "Who can make war against him?" (13:4). Armageddon is about to take place, and all the people of the world will find out there who will defeat the Antichrist in war!

Verses 13–16 are taken by some to be a brief interlude between the sixth and seventh bowls, however, others view these verses as a topical expansion of verse 12. Verse 13 indicates that John saw "three evil spirits that looked like frogs; they came out of the mouth of the dragon, out of the mouth of the beast and out of the mouth of the false prophet." (Here the second beast of Revelation 13 is called for the first time the *false prophet*.) These evil spirits are identified in verse 14 as the spirits of demons working miracles. Their mission is to gather the kings of the whole world for battle. They are *emissaries of the unholy trinity. And, as in Ahab's day, these demons will be highly effective in bringing together the leaders of the nations.

emissaries
persons sent on a mission or errand

Verse 15 breaks into the sequence of events to warn, "Behold, I come like a thief! Blessed is he who stays awake and keeps his clothes with him, so that he may not go naked and be shamefully exposed." What is intended here is that God's people be warned in advance to stay alert. They are not to slumber and say "peace and safety" when destruction is imminent (1 Thessalonians 5:3). Nor are they to assume that security is to be found on the human level instead of in terms of their own relationship to Christ.

When the seventh bowl is poured out, the proleptic statement "It is done" (v. 17) indicates that all is over. That is, the plagues have been poured out and man stands on the threshold of eternity. Notice how the pouring out of the seventh bowl compares with what happens at the opening of the seventh seal (8:5) and at the sounding of the seventh trumpet (11:19). Now comes the reaction: lightnings, rumblings, thunder, and an earthquake (v. 18). John sees the great city here called *Babylon*, which will undoubtedly be the world headquarters of the world government at this time split into three parts and the cities of the nations fall (v. 19). Moreover, the face of the earth changed radically and the mountains disappeared (v. 20). The prophet also saw great hailstones weighing about one hundred pounds each fall from the sky upon people in this fearful plague (v. 21). Finally, notice that people do not repent under the torment of the seventh bowl. Instead, they curse God. There is no indication that people repent under any of the seven bowl judgments!

4 We can say most accurately that the bowl judgments represent
- a) a call for repentance.
- b) the midpoint of the tribulation period.
- c) the wrath of God.
- d) an interlude before the next series of judgments.

5 Which of the following statements represents accurately the emphasis of the IST in this section?
- a) There is a striking parallel between the trumpet plagues and the bowl plagues.
- b) There is some similarity between the Egyptian plagues and the bowl plagues.
- c) John here sets forth a standard of plagues for all time.
- d) All of the above.
- e) Both a) and b) above.

6 Satan, the Antichrist, and the False Prophet will apparently gather the world rulers to Armageddon to
- a) establish which one of them will head the world government.
- b) defeat the Lord Jesus Christ when He returns to the earth.
- c) restore the peace that has been shattered by world war.
- d) make them accept the mark of the beast and accept his rule.

7 Which of the following statements represents the effect the bowl judgments have on mankind?
- a) The bowls lead people to repent and worship God.
- b) The bowls terrify people and make them afraid of God.
- c) People become hardened in their sins and arrogance toward God.
- d) The bowls are simply ignored by the majority of people.

The Fall of Political or Commercial Babylon

As we considered the kingdom of the beast in Lesson 12, we learned that ecclesiastical Babylon stood for false religion and was symbolized by a great prostitute. We saw that after a time of effective cooperation with the beast (the Antichrist), he turned on her and destroyed her completely. Now we turn to the political entity, the survivor of the *illicit relationship after the events of 17:16–18.

John sees that, having divested himself of the prostitute, that is, getting rid of the influence of false religion, the beast will arrogate to himself all praise, honor, and glory. But like the false religious system he destroyed, he himself will be destroyed. In fact, we shall witness the *dissolution and destruction of his empire in chapter 18.

illicit
not permitted by law; forbidden

dissolution
breaking up or ending of any association of any kind

Identify commercial or political Babylon and describe what is symbolized by its fall.

The Judgment of Babylon

Revelation 18:1–24

Whereas *Babylon* in chapter 17 stood for false religion and was symbolized by a prostitute, *Babylon* in chapter 18 stands for rebellious, anti-Christian civilization. It is to be identified as the political and commercial seat of Antichrist's government. Some feel that the city in view here is Rome, which they see as the headquarters of the apostate church. Others believe that whereas Rome will be the religious capital of the world, rebuilt Babylon will be the political and commercial center of world government. However, it is difficult to see how a literal rebuilt city of the future could gain such prominence in view of its rapid rise and very brief tenure. Moreover, Isaiah 13:19–22 indicates that once the city is destroyed, it would never again be inhabited. For these reasons, we prefer to consider Babylon simply as the headquarters of the coming world government, since we have no way of knowing exactly where it will be centered. It could be in London, Zurich, Brussels, or any other great city of the world.

Since verse 1 begins with the words, "after this," we gather that this is a later revelation. Moreover, this revelation is attended by another, that is, a different angel from the one mentioned in 17:1. And while this present angel is described in glorious detail and is said to have great authority, he is not to be thought of as Christ. One scholar has noted that since he has so recently come from the presence of God he casts a band of light across the dark earth. Indeed, Scripture indicates that those who come from God's presence are marked by a lingering radiance (Exodus 34:29–35).

The angel makes an announcement with a mighty voice: "Fallen! Fallen is Babylon the Great!" (v. 2). Coming as it does (immediately following the destruction of ecclesiastical Babylon), one might be tempted to consider the two events as taking place at the same time. However, as we have seen, they are two distinct events.

Chapter 17 makes clear that the false religious system represented by the great prostitute will *ride* the beast. That is, as the system of one world government takes over, it will be helped by the false religious system. The political head, the beast or Antichrist, will *use* the services of the prostitute to further his ends: consolidate his control over the diverse peoples, religions, political persuasions, and economies of the world community. His *woman* will proclaim the glory of collective security through unity. But when he has achieved his ends, the world dictator will quickly cast the prostitute aside.

Chapter 13 makes clear, however, that the beast will blaspheme God, make war on the people of God, and cause all the people of the earth to worship him (vv. 5–8). Obviously, this turn of events requires this arrogant dictator to renounce his temporary liaison with false religion. Thus, in place of the many, many faiths and religions the superchurch has blended together to achieve world unity, the beast will demand to be worshiped. His Minister of Propaganda, the False Prophet, will set up the machinery to enforce beast worship (13:11–17). Only those who take his mark will live; all others will be marked for death. Those who refuse to conform will be prevented from engaging in commercial transactions. The beast will exercise a stranglehold on the world economy. His activities, following the destruction of the prostitute, apparently occupy forty-two months or the last half of the seventieth seven. It is at the end of this period that judgment will fall on his *kingdom*. And it is this anticipated fall that is being announced in chapter 18.

irrevocable
final; impossible to call or bring back

Verse 2 indicates that degree of destruction slated for political or commercial Babylon. It is total, final, and *irrevocable! The sin of arrogant, godless world systems has run its course. The heady intoxication of man's secular political organization throughout history from Nimrod's time until that of the beast has produced a spirit of independence and defiance against God and His law, the objective being to accumulate the wealth of this world. Now the day of recompense has come.

In view of the coming judgment, a warning call is given: "Come out of her my people" (v. 4), and the reasons are set forth. God's people are to get out of the doomed city lest they share in her sins and judgment. A similar call was given by Jeremiah, "Come out of her, my people! Run for your lives!" (Jeremiah 51:45). This warning implies that the beast has not been completely successful in rooting out believers. One has said that the time has come for *spiritual withdrawal from Vanity Fair*, for Babylon's sins have accumulated until they reach heaven. And God cannot forget them (v. 5).

requital
repayment; return

The voice continues to speak from heaven, but now the theme changes. The angels of judgment are now ordered to inflict a just reward on this city (v. 6). This is not revenge but just *requital. Babylon has shed the blood of saints and prophets, and she is about to receive in kind the reward for her own cruelty. Compared to the luxury she has enjoyed in arrogant self-confidence, the coming devastation represents a radical reversal of fortunes (v. 7). And just as she experienced a rapid rise to fame, glory, and power, so she will experience an abrupt fall (v. 8).

Verses 9 and 10 give us the reaction of world leaders to the collapse of the world's capital city. They are unnerved to find that the ultimate form of man's political, social, and economic order has suffered such a sudden and irreversible fate. We note that while they lament at her fate, they do not rush to her rescue. Rather, they keep their distance and mourn her doom.

One has observed that appearances are deceptive. John notes that this center of world government seems to be so great and mighty, beside which the power of the church seems as nothing. In her vanity, she appears to be able to defy God and kill His people at will. Yet, in one hour her doom will come. Then there will be no one to whom those who direct her and depend on her can turn, for they have rejected God in giving their allegiance to the beast.

dirge
a funeral song or tune

Verses 11–19 give a graphic portrayal of the reaction of the merchants of the earth to the death of commercial Babylon. Their grief is caused not because of sympathy for the fate of proud Babylon but because her fate spells economic disaster for them. Government leaders, merchants, and transportation magnates join in this *dirge. And why should they not lament? Their treasure is on earth where moth and rust corrupt and where thieves break through and steal. They have lost everything, and now they face a far worse fate: the loss of their souls!

By contrast, however, the saints, apostles, and prophets in heaven are encouraged to rejoice, for God has vindicated his justice and righteousness (v. 20). In verses 21–24 John sees the portrayal of Babylon's destruction. A mighty angel picks up a large boulder and throws it into the sea, symbolizing the violent overthrow of the city. Babylon's fate will occur at the end of the Great Tribulation in an unprecedented time of destruction. As a result, there will be no further music and joy, building, industry, crafts, light, or marriage celebrations. We gather from this that the city will be dead: silent and dark.

Thus, with the destruction of Babylon the way will be paved for the presentation of the main theme of the book of Revelation: the second coming of Christ. But as we leave the subject of Babylon's destruction, we believe it is appropriate to consider that chapter 18 focuses on the attitude of the world toward material goods. We are living at a time when many people are convinced that material goods somehow bring happiness. Even some Christians are deceived into thinking that many material goods are evidence that they are spiritual. However, this is not the teaching of Scripture. Jesus said, "Be on your guard against all kinds of greed; a man's life does not consist in the abundance of his possessions" (Luke 12:15). Matthew 6:19–34 and 1 Timothy 6:3–11 reinforce this truth and give us insight into true spiritual values. Moreover, the imperative given in Revelation 18:4, "Come out of her, my people," indicates that God's people are not to share the values of the last generation. Remember: it is not wrong to have things, but it is wrong when they have us.

8 Commercial or political Babylon may be identified as
- a) the capital city or governmental headquarters of the beast.
- b) the religious center of the end-time coalition.
- c) a city that Antichrist will build and call his capital.
- d) a spirit or an attitude identified with materialistic people.

9 The destruction of Babylon portrayed in Revelation 18 is intended specifically to represent the fate of
- a) all greedy cities.
- b) merchant and commercial classes from society.
- c) the rebuilt and revitalized historical city of Babylon.
- d) man's secular, political organization throughout history.

10 Commercial Babylon, according to this section, gives us a perfect example of the
- a) highly sophisticated commercial activities of the end time.
- b) ability of man to perfect his situation on earth.
- c) attitude of non-Christian people toward material goods.
- d) low spiritual vitality of end-time believers.

11 In your notebook describe what is symbolized by the fall of Babylon.

The Second Coming of Christ

The initial part of Revelation 19 continues with thanksgiving for the destruction of Babylon. It is a song of thanksgiving to God because He has judged the great prostitute. This thanksgiving contrasts sharply with the wailing of leaders, merchants, and seafarers of Revelation 18 whose fortunes collapsed with the destruction of the beast's economic capital. From this point on the tone in Revelation changes. From the horrors of the Great Tribulation the reader now moves to times of blessing. Chapter 19 ushers in the greatest event ever for man: the second coming of Christ. This event serves as the bridge between the Tribulation and the Millennium.

Identify those who give praise in heaven and the subject of their praise.

Thanksgiving for the Judgment of Babylon

Revelation 19:1–5

With the opposition overthrown and God's righteous judgment vindicated, John hears from heaven. What he hears is the sound of a great multitude shouting "Hallelujah!" In fact, the early part of Revelation 19 tells of a great time of praise in heaven. We note that a great multitude is involved, as well as the twenty-four elders and the four living creatures. In addition, in verse 5 an individual gives praise and exhorts all other God-fearing people to praise God.

We are impressed by the fact that in verse 1 the word *hallelujah* is used for the first time in the New Testament. It is a Hebrew word that means "praise the Lord!" Since the term is used four times in this chapter (vv. 1, 3, 4, and 6), one has been prompted to observe that Revelation 19:1–6 is the New Testament "hallelujah" chorus. God is to be praised for who He is as well as for what He has done. He reigns! Therefore, man for the first time in his existence will be able to live in a perfect environment under conditions of perfect *equity and justice.

equity
being equal or fair; fairness; justice

Praise also refers to the salvation, glory, and power that belong to God. Salvation in this context is more than personal deliverance; it refers to the safeguarding of God's total program of redemption. Not only does God keep His word and fulfill His redemptive promises, but also judges justly and in truth. He has condemned the religious system that corrupted the earth, and He has avenged on her the blood of His servants (v. 2).

Those who unite in worship and praise in these verses are, for the most part, clearly identified. However, it is possible that the one whose voice proceeds from the throne (v. 5), encouraging all God-fearing servants of God to praise Him may be that of the Lord Jesus Christ. Hebrews 2:12, which is based on Psalm 22:22–23, seems to prophesy that Jesus will lead His brothers in singing praise to God. This voice from the throne in Revelation 19:5 may be the fulfillment of this prophecy.

12 Name those who give praise to God in heaven.

....

....

13 The subject of praise for those who praise God in heaven in Revelation 19:1–5 is the

a) overthrow of satanic opposition and God's righteous judgment.
b) character and nature of God, the Author of man's redemption.
c) fact that God's reign has come to begin a time unequaled in human history.
d) all of the above.
e) both a) and c) above.

Describe the wedding supper of the Lamb and identify the significance of the bride's clothing.

The Wedding Supper of the Lamb

Revelation 19:6–10

Verse 6 gives us another glimpse of heavenly praise. The sound that John hears is like the sound of a great multitude of people, like the roar of a mighty waterfall, and like loud peals of thunder. Such an introduction is appropriate for the announcement that God is at last establishing His kingdom on earth. The heavenly multitude responds to the announcement with further hallelujahs and *ascriptions of praise to God.

ascriptions
things attributed to the account of a person or thing

The voice from the throne now announces the wedding of the Lamb, but nowhere is this event described. The proclamation is made simply that the time has come for the wedding to take place. The wedding is a metaphorical way of referring to the final act of redemption when the dwelling of God is with people. He will live with them and they will be His people. Moreover, God Himself will be with them forever.

The word translated "wedding" in verse 7 is the same word translated "wedding supper" in verse 9. This word is used twenty-two times in the New Testament to refer primarily to the wedding banquet or feast. According to Middle Eastern custom in New Testament times, the wedding process consisted of several parts.

First, the marriage contract was arranged by the parents of the couple seeking to be married. We might properly refer to this arrangement as *the engagement.* Should this engagement be broken, it was necessary to obtain a legal divorce (Matthew 1:18–19). Second, when the parents agreed that the couple was ready to be married, the groom was required to go to the home of the bride and take her to his home for the wedding. (This custom agreed with Jesus' indication in Matthew 24:36 that the time of His return is under the Father's control. Thus, when the Father says it is time, the Son will come for His bride and take her to be at home with Him.) Third, there was a supper or banquet to which guests were invited. It was a time of great rejoicing. Examples of the wedding supper are found in Matthew 22:1–14 and 25:1–13. Jesus, you may recall, performed His first miracle at a wedding in Cana in Galilee (John 2:1–11).

Scholars debate whether the wedding supper will take place in heaven or after Jesus and His bride return to earth. If it takes place in heaven, perhaps it will occur while the seven years of the tribulation period are ravaging the earth. It appears to us that the announcement here seems to indicate that it will take place when Jesus returns and the Battle of Armageddon has been fought.

Some scholars do not believe that God's people of the Old Testament will be part of the bride of Christ. They insist that God's people of the Old Testament and earthly Israel will be the guests at the wedding supper. It seems clear to us that both the people of God of the Old Testament and those of the New Testament make up the bride of Christ. It also appears that the guests at the wedding feast will be the angels and the remaining inhabitants of the earth.

In conjunction with the wedding of the Lamb, the bride is said to have made herself ready (v. 7). While the appropriate preparation for heaven is the new birth, which is altogether the work of God in Christ, there must be a human response. First John 3:2–3 gives us a hint about what this response is and 2 Corinthians 7:1 affirms this responsibility.

The bride's attire is given to her to wear. It is a divine gift; nevertheless, those who are privileged to wear these garments have exercised endurance and have persevered in their faith (Revelation 14:12). Verse 8 adds that "fine linen stands for the righteous acts of saints." The plural word *acts* seems to suggest that the bride's attire is made up of those many acts of faithful obedience wrought by those who hold out faithfully to the very end. While we are not saved by our works, after we are saved, our works show that a change has taken place in our lives.

John is told to write of the blessedness of those who are invited to the wedding supper of the Lamb. Based on Revelation 3:20, a shared meal speaks of a special degree of intimacy. Since it is by divine invitation, attendance at the wedding banquet is especially meaningful.

Following these disclosures, John fell at the angel's feet to worship, but he was forbidden. The angel acknowledged that he was a fellow servant with John and that worship should be directed to God alone. Notice in verse 10 how the angel links the testimony of Jesus with prophecy. This verse points out that the Bible is centered on Jesus Christ; all its prophecies focus ultimately on Him.

14 In your notebook describe the wedding supper of the Lamb.

15 According to our discussion, which of the following identifies accurately the significance of the bride's clothing?

a) It is symbolical of the bride's own worthiness for salvation.
b) It represents the good works which are the basis for one's salvation.
c) Her clothing represents the acts of faithful obedience that should characterize the lives of believers.
d) Fine linen represents the elegance of the bride as opposed to the contamination of those who follow the beast.

Discuss the roles of the warrior-Messiah based on Revelation 19:11–21 and related New Testament teaching.

The Revelation of the Warrior-Messiah

Revelation 19:11–21

Having learned of the imminent wedding of the Lamb, which assumes the return of Jesus Christ, John now receives a vision of the event of His return. As you may notice, only one aspect of Christ's coming is emphasized: His victory over the forces of evil. The concept of a warrior-Messiah is seen in the Old Testament prophets (compare Isaiah 13:4,31:4; Ezekiel 38–39; Joel 3; and

Zechariah 14:3) and in apocalyptic literature. The most dramatic portrayal of this concept appears in Isaiah 63:1–6 where an unnamed warrior strides forth in blood-stained garments, wreaking vengeance on His enemies. He treads the winepress of God's wrath, and His garments are spattered with the blood of His enemies. But in the process of judgment His salvation is established for those who receive Him. John thus sees Christ coming as a mighty, victorious warrior in blood-stained garments destroying all the power of the enemy.

This warrior-Messiah concept agrees with New Testament teaching as we shall see. For instance, in 2 Thessalonians 1:7–8 Paul refers to this when he says, "This will happen when the Lord Jesus is revealed from heaven in blazing fire with his powerful angels. He will punish those who do not know God and do not obey the gospel of our Lord Jesus." However, the warrior-Messiah concept does not cancel out the more common Christian idea of the return of Christ which the believer realizes as the blessed hope. Rather, it is a complementary theme which Paul continues in verses 9–10:

> They will be punished with everlasting destruction and shut out from the presence of the Lord and from the majesty of his power *on the day he comes to be glorified in His holy people and to be marveled at among all those who have believed.*

This is Jesus' return as the Lion of the tribe of Judah, the King of kings, and the Lord of lords before whom every knee shall bow. At Jesus' return the battle of all battles, Armageddon, will take place. We trust that as you read this passage you noticed those who are involved in the battle, the order of events in the battle, and the results. Let us review the sequence briefly.

Suddenly John sees heaven standing open. There before him in all His radiant splendor, majesty, and purity is the Lord Jesus Christ. This event is the climax of God's program of redemption. It stands in stark contrast to the fierce judgments that have preceded it. At this *climactic moment the Son of Man shall return, lighting the heavens like a flash of lightning. And all the people of the earth shall mourn because of Him (Revelation 1:7). Israel's grief will be *penitential; whereas, the ungodly shall wail because the terror of divine judgment has overtaken them.

climactic
of or forming a climax

penitential
feelings expressing humble or regretful pain or sorrow for sins or offenses

John saw our Lord return on a white horse (v. 11). This is symbolical and refers to an ancient custom in which conquerors rode white horses as a sign of victory. One of His titles is *Faithful and True*. In this context the title indicates that He can be trusted to keep His covenant. His coming is with justice, and in justice He judges and makes war. The prophet is convinced that the punishment inflicted on the beast and his followers is not arbitrary nor an act of personal vengeance; it is perfectly compatible with truth and justice.

His eyes, which are as a flame of fire, speak of righteous judgment on sin (v. 12). Nothing can escape His penetrating gaze. He is crowned with many diadems (the kingly crown, as we saw earlier), which indicate unlimited sovereignty. The reference to His secret name may mean that the name is veiled from all created beings, or it may express the mystery of His person. Certainly there will always be a mystery about our Lord that our finite minds cannot fully grasp.

The blood-stained garments He wears symbolize His victory in the coming conflict (v. 13). His name, *The Word of God*, emphasizes that Christ in His own person is the Word of God *par excellence*—the embodiment of God's total redemptive plan. He is also the authoritative declaration by which the nations of the world are destroyed.

The armies of heaven are thought to include the redeemed, martyrs, and angels (v. 14). Chapter 17:14 indicates that His followers are *called, chosen,* and *faithful.* Zechariah 14:5 says that "The Lord . . . will come, and all the holy ones with him." The pure garments speak of righteousness. Nothing is said about their armor nor their part in the conflict; this belongs to Messiah alone. However, his followers do share in His victory.

The activity of the warrior-Messiah is given in three figures in verse 15. One, the sharp sword, is a symbolic representation of victory by the power of a word (see Isaiah 11:4). God brought about creation by a word. He simply spoke and it was done (Genesis 1:3 and following, and Hebrews 1:2). Here final judgment is carried out through the word of the Messiah. Second, the figure of ruling with a *rod of iron* refers to destruction rather than firm rule. This is a rod of *retaliation; it is strong and unyielding in its mission of judgment. Third, the figure of the treading of the winepress refers to the wrath of God. And as one prophetic scholar has observed, "There is nothing more inflexible than divine judgment where grace has been spurned."

retaliation
paying back wrong or injury; returning like for like

The designation KING OF KINGS and LORD OF LORDS (v. 16) emphasizes the Messiah's universal sovereignty. He whose right it is to reign has come at last to rule the earth.

Verses 17–19 bring us to the Battle of Armageddon, which was announced in 16:12–16. There we saw that demon spirits were used to entice the kings of the earth to battle. It appears that the peace of Antichrist will be fragile, and perhaps it will be near the breaking point at this time. Scripture gives evidence to support the idea that a struggle is going on within the world empire just before the second coming of Christ. However, our Lord's appearance at the head of the armies of heaven will no doubt cause all the armies of the earthly kingdoms to forget their differences and unify their might against Him.

In contrast to the great wedding supper to which the saints are invited, the *ravenous birds of prey are invited to the great supper of God. Like the feast mentioned in Ezekiel 39, it is provided by God. Verse 18 mentions the flesh of all people. This refers to those who have taken the mark of the beast (14:9–11).

ravenous
very hungry; greedy

Verse 19 describes the great confrontation between Christ and Antichrist. What we have here is not a symbolical struggle in which opposition is gradually overcome but the actual consummation of the conflict between the forces of God and the forces of Satan. Verses 20-21 give the account of the destruction of the beast and the false prophet and the followers of the beast. The beast and the false prophet are taken and cast alive into the fiery lake of burning sulfur. One has noted that the beast is the personification of secular power in opposition to the church, while the false prophet represents the role of false religion in persuading people to worship the anti-Christian power. These two—the beast and the false prophet—have been designated as Satan's masterpieces, and they will precede their master to the place of everlasting punishment.

Verse 21 reveals the destruction of Antichrist's allies. Masses of people will apparently remain unrepentant and hard of heart. They can expect nothing less than judgment and the wrath of God. The chapter thus concludes on a somber note: the multitude of ravenous birds is gorged with the flesh of the wicked.

16 In your notebook discuss the roles of the warrior-Messiah based on Revelation 19:11–21 and related New Testament teaching.

Self-Test

True-False. Write **T** in the blank space preceding each TRUE statement. Write **F** if it is FALSE.

.... **1** The bowl judgments represent God's last call to the ungodly to repent.

.... **2** As a result of the bowl judgments, people will turn to God and accept His Messiah at the Second Coming.

.... **3** The satanic trinity will apparently gather world leaders to Armageddon to defeat Jesus when He returns to earth.

.... **4** Whereas Babylon in Revelation 17 stands for false religion and is symbolized by a prostitute, Babylon in chapter 18 stands for rebellious, anti-Christian society.

.... **5** Commercial Babylon appears to represent the headquarters of the coming world government.

.... **6** Ecclesiastical Babylon will apparently have a major part in bringing about world unity.

.... **7** The wedding supper of the Lamb is fully described in the book of Revelation, as is the accompanying time when believers are rewarded for their works.

.... **8** The bride's clothing indicates both her purity and her productivity in the service of the bridegroom.

.... **9** John describes the second coming of Christ primarily as an event in which Christ's role as *Savior* and *Shepherd* is emphasized.

.... **10** The second coming of Christ is the climax of God's redemptive program.

Answers to study questions

9 d) man's secular, political organization throughout history.

1 c) seven plague-bearing angels.

10 c) attitude of non-Christian people toward material goods.

2 d) to follow earlier judgments in point of time.

11 Your answer should note that the ultimate form of man's political, social, and economic order is doomed to suffer an irreversible collapse. As we saw in Daniel 2 and 7, human government is set to be replaced by the kingdom of our Lord Jesus Christ. Secular man believes that he is evolving upward; however, the truth is that he is still dominated by his sinful nature, and his situation will deteriorate until the end. God has the only solution to this problem as we shall see in the next section of this lesson.

3 It represents the last judgments of God on man during the Tribulation and expresses His wrath.

12 You should have noted that a great multitude, the twenty-four elders, and the four living creatures worshiped God. You may have indicated that our Lord may possibly have been encouraging them in their worship.

4 c) the wrath of God.

13 d) all of the above.

5 e) Both a) and b) above.

14 You should have noted that the wedding supper is announced in the Scriptures, but it is not described. It is a time of reunion in which Christ and His people will be united. It will take place when the Father judges that the time is right. Only those who are invited may come, that is, only those whose lives have been changed by the grace of God. Those who are part of the bride are characterized by purity and zealous activity for the bridegroom.

6 b) defeat the Lord Jesus Christ when He returns to the earth.

15 c) Her clothing represents the acts of faithful obedience that should characterize the lives of believers.

7 c) People become hardened in their sins and arrogance toward God.

16 You should have noted that our Lord is both the agent of God's wrath and the fulfillment of the believer's hope. Christ is seen as meting out dire punishment to the wicked, but He is the source of comfort and glory to His people who witness the perfect justice of His rule.

8 a) the capital city or governmental headquarters of the beast.

Lesson 14 The Millennial Reign of Christ and Afterward

Lesson 13 brought us through the final stages of the tribulation period. We considered the bowl judgments and their impact on mankind at this time. We also examined the downfall of commercial or political Babylon—the seat of the beast's government. Finally, we focused on the praise which will follow when God exercises His righteous judgment, the wedding supper of the Lamb, the second coming of Christ, and the Battle of Armageddon. We now move to a discussion of the content of Revelation 20–22.

Having destroyed the empire of Satan and his allies, Jesus Christ will rule on earth with an iron scepter. The remnant of Israel will occupy all the land God gave to Abraham. And the people of God will rule on earth with Jesus Christ as predicted by the four living creatures and the twenty-four elders (Revelation 5:10). This will be the golden age for which man has longed ever since his expulsion from Eden. The Millennium, however, will end. Then, after a brief and futile satanic revolt, the eternal state will begin, and believers will be forever with their Lord. What an appropriate climax for our study of the books of Daniel and Revelation!

the activities...

◇ Work through the lesson as usual and take the self-test when you have completed the lesson development.

◇ Review the lessons in this unit in preparation for your unit progress evaluation (UPE). Read the instruction page in your Student Packet, then turn to Unit Progress Evaluation 4. When you have completed the UPE, check your answers with the answer key provided in your Student Packet. Review any items you may have answered incorrectly. (Although UPE scores do not count as part of your final course grade, they indicate how well you learned the material and how well you may perform on the final examination.)

◇ If you have not already done so, make arrangements now with your enrollment office for taking the final examination.

the objectives...

14.1 *List one notable spiritual condition that will exist during the Millennium and why it possible.*

14.2 *Identify the participants in the first resurrection and their activity during this time.*

14.3 *Define the word* millennium, *identify what it anticipates, and recognize features of each major view of the Millennium.*

14.4 *Explain why Satan is loosed from his confinement after the 1000 years and what results from this.*

14.5 *Identify facts accurately concerning the final judgment.*

14.6 *Choose explanations that describe accurately what is meant by the terms new heaven and new earth.*

14.7 *Identify details associated with the New Jerusalem.*

14.8 *Explain the importance of various blessings, instructions, and exhortations in 22:6–21.*

the outline...

1 The Millennium
- **a** The Binding of Satan
- **b** The First Resurrection
- **c** Views of the Millennium and Its General Characteristics

2 After the Millennium
- **a** Satan's Final Revolt
- **b** The Final Judgment

3 The New Order
- **a** A New Heaven and a New Earth
- **b** The New Jerusalem

4 A Postscript on Jesus' Coming
- **a** Blessings, Instructions, and Exhortations

List one notable spiritual condition that will exist during the Millennium and why it possible.

The Millennium

As the title of this lesson suggests, we shall consider two major themes with reference to the Millennium. The first main section concerns the Millennium itself, and the second deals with events that follow it. Included in this focus are the matters of judgment and reward, the nature of life following the second coming of Christ, the nature of the eternal state for the blessed and the doomed, the dwelling places respectively of the doomed and of the redeemed. These subjects together with appropriate exhortations and warnings complete the content of the book.

The Binding of Satan

Revelation 20:1–3

At the conclusion of Lesson 13 we saw what happened to the Antichrist and the false prophet. John now sees what will happen to the third member of the satanic trinity: Satan. (You may have noticed that the same four names are used here for this evil leader that were used in Revelation 12:9.) A mighty angel descends from heaven, seizes Satan, and binds him for a thousand years. The vivid description given here obviously employs symbolical language and refers to the radical curbing of satanic power and activity. Or, as one scholar observes, Satan is not merely restricted; he is made totally inactive.

With Satan bound there will no longer be any spiritual warfare. The fact that the Tempter will be bound makes possible the peace and tranquillity foretold by the prophets (as we shall see); consequently, the Millennium can begin. This glorious period, therefore, stands in marked contrast to the Great Tribulation that precedes it, and the final revolt that follows it.

detention
act of detaining; holding back

The effect of Satan's *detention is that he will not be able to deceive the nations during this period. As a result universal peace will be a reality—not a goal. After this he will be released, and true to his nature, he will return to his deceitful ways.

1 List one notable spiritual condition that will exist during the Millennium and why it is possible.

....

....

Identify the participants in the first resurrection and their activity during this time.

The First Resurrection

Revelation 20:4–6

Verse 4, which is a most difficult verse to interpret, includes two groups of people: (1) a group which is identified only as those who had been given authority to judge, and (2) those who have accepted Christ during the Tribulation. Some believe that the first group is composed of the twenty-four elders that we discussed in Revelation 4 and 5 and see evidence for this view in Luke 22:29–30. However, the general emphasis of Scripture is that all overcomers will share in Christ's reign (Revelation 5:9–10; Daniel 7:27; and 1 Corinthians 6:2). Since the evidence is not clear-cut, we will just have to wait and see.

John says of the souls of the martyrs, "They came to life and reigned with Christ a thousand years" (v. 4). The meaning of the word translated "came to life" has caused interpreters some problems. Amillennialists, which we will consider in a moment, see this as "spiritual resurrection" of the souls of the righteous at death. However, the same Greek word is used as *bodily resurrection* in John 11:25, Romans 14:9, Revelation 1:18, 2:8, and 13:14. As a result, many Bible scholars believe that this is the meaning intended in 20:5.

Whether those in this second group come to life at this point, or in what is reported in 7:9–17, or in the harvest of 14:14–16 is a matter of controversy among scholars. In any case, they are now resurrected and reigning with Christ.

There is controversy also over the statement is verse 5, "This is the first resurrection." Those who believe the church will go through the Tribulation point to this statement as proof that up to this point no one has been raised from the dead. However, we saw that the two witnesses were raised from the dead long before this and were then caught up to heaven (11:11–12). Obviously, this one verse shows us plainly that this is not the meaning of the statement in question. Moreover, 20:6 clearly implies through its reference to the second death (which is the lake of fire, v. 14) that the first resurrection concerns the righteous only and that it is a resurrection unto eternal life.

By comparing verses 4 and 5 we see that there are two kinds of resurrection: the first concerns the resurrection of the righteous, and the second involves the wicked. The New Testament does not give clear teaching on a two-fold resurrection, although it implies this (John 5:28–29). Clearly, the first resurrection includes all God's people, including martyrs; therefore, the rest of the dead must include all who have not known Christ. This latter group is not resurrected until after the Millennium, and it is described in verse 12, when the remainder of the dead are resurrected to stand before God's throne of judgment.

Verse 6 declares the blessedness of those who take part in the first resurrection. The first death, according to Hebrews 9:27, is the death that is appointed to all people (except those who are alive at the second coming of Christ). The second death mentioned here is eternal death (see verse 14 and also Matthew 10:28 where the death of the body and soul are contrasted). Those blessed ones who take part in the first resurrection will be *priests* of God and of Christ. One Bible scholar observes that they are priests because they have access to the presence of God and reign with Him in the messianic kingdom.

As we leave this section, we want to make one observation: These blessed ones apparently have resurrected bodies; whereas, the people of the nations (v. 8) will have natural bodies. This should not offend anyone, for our Lord dwelt among His disciples for forty days in His resurrected body. Such are some of the wonders that await us in the glorified state.

2 The participants in the first resurrection are identified accurately in Scripture as the

a) wicked dead who are resurrected to face judgment.
b) people of God of the Old Testament.
c) church, the body of Christ.
d) righteous, including the martyrs of the tribulation period.

3 The activity in which the resurrected dead are said to engage during the Millennium, according to our discussion, is that of

a) sharing in the rule of the messianic kingdom.
b) making peace between warring nations.
c) evangelizing the world in preparation for the eternal state.
d) celebrating the wedding supper of the Lamb for a thousand years.

Define the word millennium, *identify what it anticipates, and recognize features of each major view of the Millennium.*

Views of the Millennium and Its General Characteristics

At this point, we feel it is appropriate to define the term *millennium,* which serves as the major focus of this section. It is a theological term and comes from two Latin words *mille,* "thousand," and *annum,* "year." It is based on the use of the term "thousand years" in Revelation 20:2–7. It is used to refer to the 1000-year period of Christ's future reign on earth in relation to the establishment of the Kingdom over Israel.

The question concerning the "thousand years," which is raised in chapter 20, has aroused endless debate within the church. In fact, various systems of interpretation concerning the events of the end time have tended to be identified according to the way they treat the question of the Millennium. While a number of major views and variations of these views of the Millennium exist, we shall consider three of the most widely held views and the major emphasis of each: Premillennialism, Postmillennialism, and Amillennialism.

Amillennialists do not believe in a literal Millennium. According to them, the 1000 years is a symbolic number and represents the period between the resurrection of Christ and the Second Coming. Adherents of this view do not see in the book of

recapitulates
repeats or recites the main points of; tells briefly; sums up

Revelation a narrative of consecutive events. Rather, they believe that it *recapitulates what has already occurred; for example, in the ministry of the Lord. According to them, the binding and confining of Satan for 1000 years (20:1–3) is to be identified with our Lord's victory over Satan during His earthly ministry.

Postmillennialists believe that the gospel will triumph and that Jesus Christ will return when the church gets the world ready for Him. To these folk, the Millennium is viewed as the final triumph of the gospel in the present age. They believe that the world is getting better and better through the preaching of the gospel. For the postmillennialist interpreter, Revelation 19 does not portray the second coming of Christ. Rather, in a symbolic way it describes the triumph of Christian principles in human affairs and the victory of Christ through the church. However, Scripture nowhere depicts the bringing in of a golden age by the preaching of the gospel. The gospel will be proclaimed (Matthew 24:14), but as the end comes, it is presented in the midst of apostasy—not universal revival (2 Timothy 3:1–5).

Premillennialists believe that the events noted in Revelation 20 refer completely to the end of the age. They believe that the second coming of Christ will be followed by the binding and confining of Satan and the resurrection of the righteous, who will join their Lord as He reigns on earth over a temporal kingdom. This kingdom age will end with Satan's final revolt and the final judgment.

A variation of this view is that of *dispensationalism.* The dispensationalist sees the millennial kingdom as an aspect of God's theocratic program. He perceives the kingdom age as a fulfillment of the promise given to David that his kingdom would continue forever. He views the 1000 years as a literal period of time. Moreover, he sees it as a period in which Christ will literally rule on earth as supreme ruler. Israel will thus occupy a prominent place in this kingdom, and the Gentiles will also be blessed. Prominent in this system, also, is the idea of a restored priesthood, sacrifices, and rituals as indicated in Ezekiel 40–48. Moreover, the dispensationalist fails to see any present spiritual aspects of the kingdom fulfilled in the church.

theocracy
literally, the rule of a nation or of the world by God; government by God

While verses 4–6 give us some information about the Millennium, other Scriptures give us characteristics of the *kingdom age.* The form of government will be **theocracy* for Christ shall rule, and the capital of His kingdom will be Jerusalem. Christ will thus have an earthly center in the holy city in the holy land. Other characteristics are as follows: There will be

1. universal peace (Psalm 46:9; Isaiah 2:4, 9:6–7; Micah 4:3–4).
2. universal prosperity (Isaiah 65:21–24; Amos 9:13–15; Micah 4:4–5).
3. universal justice (Isaiah 11:3–5; Jeremiah 23:5).
4. universal knowledge of the Lord (Isaiah 11:9; Habakkuk 2:14; Zechariah 8:22–23).
5. a restoration of the earth to its first state of fruitfulness (Isaiah 35:1–2; Amos 9:13–15; Ezekiel 36:8–12).
6. no ferocious nature in animals (Isaiah 11:6–9, 65:25).
7. a change in the way earth receives the light of the sun and the moon (Isaiah 30:26).
8. a greatly increased life span (Isaiah 65:20-22).

More details on some of the characteristics of the Millennium are found in Zechariah 8:4, 12–13, and 16–21. Chapters 40–48 of Ezekiel give a detailed description of Israel after the nation's people have returned to the land promised to Abraham. The Millennium will make possible the fulfillment of this promise, and after the Millennium, Abraham's descendants will dwell in this land forever. *God keeps His promises.*

4 The word *Millennium* comes from Latin words which mean

....

5 Match each major view of the Millennium (right) to the description of that view (left).

. . . . **a** Jesus will return when the world is ready for Him.

. . . . **b** The world will experience a literal 1000-year messianic reign following the Second Coming.

. . . . **c** The world will not experience a literal 1000-year reign of Christ on earth. Revelation recapitulates events that have already occurred.

. . . . **d** Revelation 20 looks to a future fulfillment. Thus, the second coming of Christ is followed by the binding and confining of Satan and the resurrection of the righteous who will reign with Christ for 1000 years.

1) Premillennialism
2) Postmillennialism
3) Amillennialism

6 Circle the letter preceding each TRUE statement.

a Christ will rule the world during the Millennium, and the form of government He will head is called a *theocracy.*

b According to Scripture, Babylon will be the seat of Christ's government during the Millennium.

c Based on what we have studied about the Millennium, we can assume there will be no unemployment, no war, no injustice, and no poverty.

d The earth will be restored to its first state of fruitfulness and human life expectancy will be greatly increased.

e The people of Israel will occupy the land given to Abraham from this time forth and forever.

After the Millennium

In the second part of chapter 20, we consider two important matters that follow the Millennium: Satan's final revolt and the final judgment. These subjects allow us to focus our attention on Satan's end and that of those who have been deluded by him.

Explain why Satan is loosed from his confinement after the 1000 years and what results from this.

Satan's Final Revolt

Revelation 20:7–10

John notes that once he has been freed from his confinement, Satan wastes no time in raising the flag of revolt. He sets out to deceive the nations of the entire earth. The people he attempts to seduce are apparently the saints who survive the Great Tribulation and the children of those who enter the Millennium. Outwardly, these people will conform to Christ's rule and will profess obedience. However, inwardly there will be no reality to their confession; consequently, when Satan is released many of them will follow him in a rebellion against God.

From the record given here, it appears that a vast multitude of people will follow him in this rebellion (v. 8). However, no battle will actually take place, for as they surround the city He loves, God will intervene and destroy the entire rebel force (v. 9). Thus, Satan's last stand will become history, and he, together with the beast and the false prophet, will be confined in the lake of burning sulfur forever (v. 10).

In view of the widespread support for this satanic revolt, we must ask ourselves this question: Why would God allow Satan to be loosed? The indication is that it may be that God will allow Satan to be loosed because those born during the Millennium will not have had the opportunity to choose to live either for or against Jesus Christ. You may recall from 19:15 and other Scriptures that our Lord will rule these nations with an iron scepter. Nevertheless, God gives every person the right of free choice.

A robot cannot love; love is a matter of choice. We are made in the image of God, and this includes the ability to choose. Throughout Scripture, God has allowed man to choose whom he will serve. Adam and Eve made their choice, and every one of their descendants has made his choice either for or against God. Satan's presence among those born during the Millennium will give them an opportunity to choose. And, in a sense, the outcome is a foregone conclusion. Man will still like to have his own way, to run his own life. As a result, multitudes of these folk will yield to temptation and *converge on the holy city in defiance of earth's rightful Sovereign. But before they can unleash their attack, they will be destroyed by fire from heaven and their attempted revolt will be brought to an abrupt end (v. 9).

converge
to come together; turn toward each other

7 In your notebook explain why it appears that Satan will be loosed from his confinement and what will result from this.

Identify facts accurately concerning the final judgment.

The Final Judgment

Revelation 20:11–15

We now come to the final judgment, the second resurrection, and the judgment and sentence of the wicked dead. In this phase of the vision, John sees heaven and earth flee before the *grandeur of God on His judgment throne. One Bible scholar has noted that as it flees from the presence of God, there is no place for a terrified universe. Like the Psalmist, all realize that there is no place where one may flee from God's presence (Psalm 139:7).

grandeur
magnificence or splendor of appearance

All the dead from all walks of life and degrees of importance appear before the throne. Since they are standing, we assume they know the verdict and are awaiting the sentence. There are no mistakes. Each person is judged on the basis of his works. All has been recorded; the record does not lie. But beyond one's works there is another fundamental basis for judgment: The Book of Life. All whose names are not recorded in this book are sentenced to eternal damnation and *consigned to the lake of fire.

consigned
handed over, delivered; set apart; assigned

The issue of judgment here should not confuse us. What is in focus at this point is not salvation by works but works as evidence of salvation. We are saved by grace through faith, but faith is always revealed by the works it produces.

In verses 13 and 14 death and Hades are personified, just as they are under the fourth seal in Revelation 6:7–8. As you read about Hades, did you think about who will be there to be resurrected? It is a very sobering thought; however, only those who have died in an unsaved condition will be there.

Death and Hades are now thrown into the lake of fire. The lake of fire indicates not only the stern punishment awaiting the enemies of the righteous, but also their full and final defeat. It is the second death, that is, the destiny of those whose temporary resurrection results only in return to death and its punishment.

8 Circle the letter preceding each TRUE statement.

a The final judgment is a general judgment for all people who have died whether righteous or wicked.

b Revelation 20:11–15 indicates that one is saved or lost on the basis of good works.

c Whether one suffers eternal damnation or not depends on whether his name is recorded in the book of life.

d The final destiny of those who reject God's offer of salvation is the lake of fire.

The New Order

In the last chapters of his book, Isaiah foretells the creation of new heavens and a new earth (65:17) that will endure forever (66:22). The fulfillment of this prediction that begins to take place before John's eyes is recorded in the last two chapters of Revelation. Here the holy city, the New Jerusalem, descends from heaven to take its place on a completely *renovated earth. The description of the new heaven and earth form the last major event of the book (21:1–22:5).

renovated
made like new; made new again

Choose explanations that describe accurately what is meant by the terms new heaven and new earth.

A New Heaven and a New Earth

Revelation 21:1

In Revelation 20:11, John described the dissolution of the old heaven and earth. In very graphic language he described their flight from the presence of God. Now John sees a new heaven and a new earth. While some see in this statement a new act of creation, many other prominent Bible scholars feel that the statement implies the renovation of what already exists. One may see clearly that throughout the Bible the destiny of God's people is an earthly destiny. In their usual dualistic fashion, the Greeks believed that the universe was divided into two realms: the earthly or temporary and the eternal or spiritual world. To them, salvation involved the flight of the soul from the *transitory sphere to the realm of eternal reality. By contrast, biblical teaching has man on a redeemed earth, not in a heavenly realm removed from earthly existence.

transitory
passing soon or quickly; lasting only a short time

In this regard, it may be helpful to point out that the meaning of the expressions "a new earth" and "the first earth had passed away" (v. 1). In the Bible, three Greek words are translated "world": *aion,* which is more accurately translated "age," *kosmos,* which refers to "the structured society," and *ge,* which usually means "earth." The terms *aion* and *kosmos* are sometimes spoken of as having ceased to exist, but the term *ge* is never referred to as having ceased to exist. With this in mind, let us see what the expression "the first earth had passed away" really means.

When Paul uses the expression "the old has gone" (2 Corinthians 5:17), "has gone" means basically the same thing as "passed away" does in Revelation 21:1. Paul's term refers to one's acceptance of Christ. The question is, does one cease to exist in order to make way for the new person he is to become when he accepts Christ? Of course not! Nonetheless, when one is made new, he is changed. Likewise, "the first earth had passed away" in Revelation 21:1 simply indicates that the first earth will be changed—not that it ceases to exist.

Romans 8:18–22 gives us some indication of the coming change that will take place in the created order. Then Peter paints a graphic picture of the process by which the change will occur (2 Peter 3:10–13). In this context, the word translated "destroyed" can also be translated "loosed," a translation that harmonizes more completely with our concept of a changed earth. Peter strongly emphasizes the final expression in this passage, "a new heaven and a new earth, the home of righteousness." We believe that earth's greatest change will be from a place of much wickedness to "the home of righteousness."

9 According to our study here, the expression "a new heaven and a new earth," is taken to mean that the

a) present universe will be totally dissolved and a new creation will be required.
b) present heaven and earth will undergo a renovation.
c) future order of creation is not described here or elsewhere in Scripture.
d) chosen people move to a parallel universe and abandon this one.

Identify details associated with the New Jerusalem.

The New Jerusalem

Revelation 21:2–22:5

Since this section of the lesson focuses on the New Jerusalem, we have provided a brief three-point outline of this rather lengthy passage on the New Jerusalem. We will use it to direct our comments and questions in the outline.

I. Summary Description of the New Jerusalem (21:2)

II. Dwelling Place of God With His People (21:3–8)

III. Detailed Description of the New Jerusalem and Life Within It (21:9–22:5)

I. *Summary description of the New Jerusalem* (21:2). While we often think of the heavenly Jerusalem as the permanent dwelling place of God and His departed people (Galatians 4:26; Philippians 3:20; Hebrews 12:22), it is only the temporary home of God's people between their death and the resurrection (2 Corinthians 5:8; Philippians 1:23; Revelation 6:9–11). In the new order, however, the heavenly Jerusalem will be relocated on earth.

The fact that the New Jerusalem is said to come down out of heaven from God seems to imply that it is already in existence. In our view, it is necessary to comment on the subject of the bride of Christ. We feel that a comparison of verse 2 with verses 9 and 10 might cause some to confuse the bride of Christ with the city prepared for her. Some believers, for example, have claimed that the city, not the believers, is the bride of Christ. It is obvious from previous descriptions of this bride, however, that the bride is not the city. That would be totally *erroneous. Let us illustrate this point.

erroneous
containing error; wrong; mistaken

In Luke 13:34 when Jesus said, "Oh Jerusalem, Jerusalem, you who kill the prophets and stone those sent to you," He was not indicating that the walls, buildings, gates, and streets of the city were responsible for killing the prophets. It was the people who lived there about whom He was speaking. In a similar way, Jesus may appear to be rebuking cities in Matthew 11:20-24; however, He is actually rebuking people who are living in them. Thus, the New Jerusalem will not be the bride of Christ, but it will be the home of believers who will make up that bride.

II. *Dwelling place of God with His people* (21:3–8). In the new eternal order of things, the New Jerusalem will be God's dwelling place with people. In the

Old Testament economy, His presence was manifested in the tabernacle and later in the temple in the *shekinah*, or glory. Then in the person of Christ, He dwelt for a while among us (John 1:14). Presently He indwells the church by His Spirit, and we know His presence by faith. But in the future eternal order we will see His face (22:4).

At this future time, God will wipe away every tear from His people's eyes (v. 4, 7:17, and Isaiah 25:8). There will be no more tears, for all the evils and ills that have oppressed mankind will be forever banished as the curse is lifted (22:3). The emphasis here is not on people's *remorse but on the comfort that God gives. God will even wipe away the tears of believers that will result from the sorrow for those that are dear to them who have been cast into the lake of fire at the final judgment. Not only will tears be no more but also death, mourning, crying, or pain. All these tragic emotional experiences will have passed, for they are associated with the old order of things (v. 4).

remorse
painful regret for having done wrong

He who is seated on the throne told John that He was making everything new (v. 5). *Everything new* indicates things new in character and new in the sense of being recently made. Drastic change is indicated. Thus, the physical world will be liberated from the bondage of the curse (Romans 8:21). John is therefore instructed to record what he has seen and heard, for that which has been revealed is trustworthy. Moreover, the phrase "It is done" signifies that God is bringing to a conclusion His work concerning the whole history of man until the eternal state. Not only has God's program of redemption been completed, but also the future has been made secure by the One who is the First and Last, the Author of creation and redemption (v. 6).

The one who thirsts is promised a satisfying drink of the water of life. Thirst here depicts the desire of the soul for God. David reflected this in Psalm 42:1: "As the deer pants for streams of water, so my soul pants for you, O God." (See also Psalm 36:9, 63:1, and Isaiah 55:1). God is "the spring of living water" (Jeremiah 2:13) that satisfies thirst and wells up to eternal life (John 4:14). In application of the promise in verse 6 to our everyday lives, Jesus promised that those who truly believed in and committed their lives to Him would have streams of living water flowing from within them (John 7:37–39). Jesus used the term *living water* to refer to the Holy Spirit. We earnestly pray that God will give you such a thirst for this *living water* that you will be filled with it and that the overflow will then surge out and create a similar desire in others.

The one who overcomes is promised all things. However, he is required to be faithful and loyal to Christ in the face of opposition (v. 7). By contrast, those who do not accept God's grace can expect nothing but eternal damnation in the fiery lake of burning sulfur (v. 8). Notice especially the eight classes of ungodly people who will be placed in the lake of fire. The cowardly, who head the list, are those who are afraid to accept Christ, live for Him, and let it be known. The second class, the unbelieving, remind us that more is required in *believing* than mental assent. (Compare John 3:16 with James 2:19 and John 1:12.) Believing demands that one make Christ the Lord of his life and live consciously and actively for Him.

III. *Detailed description of the New Jerusalem and life within it* (21:9–22:5). We now examine the New Jerusalem, the *prepared city* (compare verse 3 with John 14:1–3), where the people of God will reside forever. John is carried away in the Spirit to see the matchless beauty of the heavenly city. It is no accident that the scene is identical with that in 17:1, where the prophet was caught away to view Babylon. John undoubtedly intends a deliberate contrast between the harlot city and the heavenly city where God dwells.

Most striking is the fact that the city bears the glory of God. Scintillating in the reflected light of God, the city sparkles like a many-faceted diamond.

Some have wondered why the city has a wall. We must remember that this may simply be part of the description of an ideal city as conceived by ancient people who were accustomed to the security of strong outer walls. The city also has gates of pearl, in fact, twelve of them (v. 12), each consisting of one pearl. And on the gates are written the names of the twelve tribes of Israel. This stresses the continuity of the church of the New Testament with the people of God under the old covenant. And the names of the twelve apostles on the twelve foundations emphasizes once again the unity of ancient Israel with the church. It seems very clear from the description of these gates and foundations that both the Old Testament and New Testament people of God are in the bride of Christ.

We pointed out in our chart near the end of Lesson 4 that the number *twelve* means *final completion*. Notice in 21:12, 14, 16, 21 and 22:2 the significance of the number twelve and its multiples in regard to the New Jerusalem.

Verses 15–17 record the measuring of the city. Unlike the measuring recorded in chapter 11, this is done to indicate its impressive size and perfect symmetry. The city measures some 1500 miles long by 1500 miles wide by 1500 miles in height. It is a perfect cube. These dimensions reflect perfect symmetry, vastness, and completeness.

Verses 18–21 describe the 216–foot wall of jasper that rests upon twelve foundations each of which is a precious gem stone. The twelve gates are made of twelve immense pearls and the streets are of transparent gold. One may only contemplate the effect of the light in the city as it filters through the various colors of the foundations and the crystal-clear jasper wall itself and then diffuses in lustrous softness on the golden pavement.

John observes that there is no temple, for the temple is replaced by the Lord God Almighty and the Lamb (v. 22). The temple was supremely the place of God's presence in the old economy. But now symbol has given way to reality. Nor is there any need of stellar light, for the glory of God enlightens the city (v. 23). This city is unique by the very things that are missing: there is no temple, no sun, no moon, no darkness, no abomination, no tears, no parting, no pain, no thirst, no hunger, and no death.

Verse 24 indicates that the nations will walk by the light of the city. John may mean that since in the eternal state the redeemed will consist of people from every nation, tribe, and tongue, they will not lose their national identity. Or it may be simply an affirmation of the universality of the knowledge of God.

Access to the city is limited to those whose names are written in the Lamb's Book of Life. The gates of the city are open because with the destruction of evil no security measures will be necessary. In addition, there will be no night there. One has noted that in God's Word darkness is the usual metaphor for life apart from the presence of God (Matthew 6:23, 8:12, 22:13); however, all darkness will be abolished in the presence of God and the Lamb.

The vision John saw that began in chapter 21 is continued and completed in chapter 22. Verses 1–5 give us further information concerning the heavenly Jerusalem. First, we learn that a river of life as clear as crystal flows from the throne of God down the middle of the great street of the city. The river is thus central in the city. Man's earthly story began initially beside a river (Genesis 2:10) and now continues eternally beside the essence of life. This has prompted one eminent Bible scholar to note that the existence of the river of life

picturesque
quaint; vivid

is a *picturesque way of showing that death with all its sinister attendants has been abolished and life reigns supreme.

The tree of life from which Adam and Eve were driven now reappears, producing a different fruit each month (v. 2). It will not have to go through the cycle of budding, blossoming, fruitbearing, and harvest, giving but one or two crops per year. Rather, it will be weighted down with fruit every month, prompting one scholar to note that this represents the complete triumph of life over death. This fruit will promote the enjoyment of life to the full. Moreover, the curse will be lifted! This fact has prompted J. B. Smith to write:

> And there shall be no more curse—perfect restoration. But the throne of God and of the Lamb shall be in it—perfect administration. His servants shall serve him—perfect subordination. And they shall see his face—perfect transformation. And his name shall be in their foreheads—perfect identification. And there shall be no night there; and they need no candle, neither light of the sun; for the Lord giveth them light—perfect illumination. And they shall reign forever and ever—perfect exultation *(A Revelation of Jesus Christ,* 295–296).

While Moses could not see God's face and live, the redeemed will see God's face. His name will be on their foreheads. In their glorified state the redeemed will be fully transformed; they will be like Him and they will reflect His likeness. The seal on their foreheads indicates ownership and likeness.

It is difficult to imagine the New Jerusalem and life within it. Naturally, John used earthly language to describe what was too sublime for description in such language. What a great city the New Jerusalem will be! It is beyond our ability to describe or even imagine adequately.

10 Circle the letter preceding each TRUE statement.

a Heavenly Jerusalem is the permanent dwelling place of God.
b According to our study, the New Jerusalem is identified as the bride of Christ.
c When the text speaks of spiritual thirst, it is referring to the desire of the soul for God.
d *All* things are promised to the one who overcomes.
e The gates of the New Jerusalem, which bear the names of the twelve tribes of Israel, and the wall on which are the names of the twelve apostles of the Lamb emphasize the unity of the church with the Old Testament people of God.
f There is no temple in the New Jerusalem because the time and need for worship has ended.
g In their glorified state the redeemed will actually see God's face.

A Postscript on Jesus' Coming

Revelation 22:6–21 is primarily a postscript on the all-important subject of the soon coming of the Lord Jesus (vv. 7, 12, 20). At this time we will have arrived at the point in eternity's beginning where we see the statements of Revelation 22:3–5 about life in the New Jerusalem fulfilled. Then we will know through experience that what we suffered on earth is not worth comparing with the glory we will be enjoying (Romans 8:18).

Explain the importance of various blessings, instructions, and exhortations in 22:6–21.

Blessings, Instructions, and Exhortations

Revelation 22:6–21

In verse 6 the message-bearing angel describes the nature of the message he is declaring: "These words are trustworthy and true." Moreover, the angel's statement that the Lord is "the God of the spirits of the prophets" indicates the relationship between prophets and prophecy: all true prophets are voices or channels of the Spirit of God because they yield their spirits to His direction and control. Finally, the angel indicates that he has been sent "to show his servants the things that must soon take place." *Must soon take place* is the same expression that we saw in Revelation 1:1 and discussed in an earlier lesson. The word *soon* is emphasized again in verse 7 in Jesus' statement "Behold I am coming soon." *Soon* means certainly and suddenly in both verses 6 and 7. The church of all times has been encouraged to live in a state of expectancy (Matthew 24:42–44).

In Lesson 5 we saw that there are seven beatitudes in Revelation. The last two are in verses 7 and 14 of chapter 22. In verse 7 a blessing is pronounced on those who *keep* the words of this prophecy, and in verse 14 the blessing is pronounced on those who "wash their robes," that is, *do* God's commandments. Since "keeps the words" (v. 7) actually means to do what the words say, both of these beatitudes clearly indicate that people who receive the blessings must do what the Word says and not merely listen to it (James 1:22). Those who receive the blessing in verse 14 have the right to the tree of life and to go through the gates into the city. We should remember that God's primary purpose in giving us the prophecies in Revelation is to show us how to live and not simply to fill us with information.

In verse 8 John identifies himself as one who is well-known to the churches of Asia Minor. Thus, he adds no other identifying names. He does, however, verify the visions and experiences recorded here. Responding as he had on an earlier occasion, John fell at the angel's feet, but he was forbidden and told to worship God (v. 9).

You may recall from our discussion of Daniel 12 that Daniel was told to "close up and seal the words of the scroll until the time of the end" (vv. 4, 9). However, with reference to the same prophetic message John is told: "Do not seal up the words of the prophecy of this book" (Revelation 22:10). Why was Daniel told to seal up the message while John was told to make it known? Quite obviously, Daniel's prophecy was very obscure until John wrote Revelation. Until then it was beyond human understanding. John's message is a *revelation* that was to be heard throughout the Church Age. Its warnings are important to every church of every age. The book of Revelation shows what God expects of His people, and it warns His people to obey His Word. In our view the clear implication in verses 10 and 11 is that even if the proclamation of the prophetic message in Revelation does not cause people to repent, it will encourage the true believer to continue to do right and to be holy.

The exhortation in verse 11 applies both to the believer and the unbeliever. Those who are living holy lives are exhorted to persist while the ungodly are challenged to persist in their ungodliness. One Bible scholar has noted that as concerns this verse, no neutrality is possible. One must be either for or against the claims of the gospel. There is a sense in which one's choices now shape his character; nevertheless, there will come a time when change will be impossible. Current choices tend to become permanent in character.

Again the Lord stresses that His coming will be without warning and that He will bring His reward with Him to repay everyone according to what he has done. We have seen the reward of the ungodly at the final judgment in 20:11–15 and that of the godly in 21:1–22:5. It is obvious that there are certain rewards for serving God. Moreover, it is equally clear that judgment on the basis of works is emphasized throughout the New Testament (Romans 2:26; 1 Corinthians 3:10–15; 2 Corinthians 5:10; Revelation 2:23).

Verses 13–16 reveal the majesty of the Eternal One who verifies prophecy. These verses, like 21:8, list those who will be outside God's eternal city whose place will be in the fiery lake of burning sulfur. Verse 15 specifically warns people that if they are to enter the New Jerusalem, they cannot continue to sin. They must repent, accept Jesus Christ as Lord of their lives, change their minds and their behavior, and live for Him. Verse 15 lists dogs among those on the *outside.* In Isaiah 56:9–12 *dogs* is a word that refers to ignorant, false shepherds, or prophets. Romans 1:24–27 and 1 Corinthians 6:9–10 explain what the term *sexually immoral* includes.

In verse 16 our Lord mentions two of His titles. (1) As the *Root and Offspring of David,* Jesus fulfills the prophecy in 2 Samuel 7:16 in which David was promised an eternal heir for his throne. The term *Root* speaks of Jesus as *God* who gives the family tree of David unending life. The term *Offspring* speaks of Jesus as *Man* who is the rightful, legal heir to David's throne. (2) The *bright Morning Star* speaks of Jesus who will bring about first the Millennium and then the new, eternal order of things. This Star anticipates the coming dawn of a glorious day. In order to experience that day, however, we must know Jesus, the bright Morning Star.

In verse 17, the Bible's last invitation is given to people to live freely and eternally with God, to come to the source of spiritual life. Notice especially the fourfold nature of this invitation. The word translated "wishes" means not only wanting or desiring, but also the exercising of one's will to get what he wants. Those who are to give this last invitation to people are the Holy Spirit, the bride of Christ, and anyone who hears the invitation. (Here the word *hears* refers not only to physical hearing, but also to mental and spiritual acceptance of Christ.) Thus, anyone who accepts Jesus should immediately invite others to accept Him.

distortions
things that have been distorted or twisted out of shape

authenticated
made valid or authoritative

Verses 18 and 19 give us the last warning in the Bible. It is a warning against tampering with the divinely inspired prophetic record. In the Old Testament Israel was admonished along these same lines (Deuteronomy 4:2). What John is speaking to here is deliberate *distortions and perversions of the divinely *authenticated Word.

Verse 20 opens with the testimony that Jesus is coming without delay and closes with John's *amen*, which echoes the church's longing for that great occasion. This longing stands at the heart of the Christian faith; apart from Christ's return, His redemptive work remains forever incomplete. His return is the only sure hope for the future of the world.

John concludes with an appropriate benediction (v. 21). He pronounces it on all those who read this prophecy or hear it read. As we await our Lord's coming, may we, with John say "Amen. Come, Lord Jesus" (v. 20). And may we like our Lord during His days on earth, purpose to be about our Father's business (Luke 2:49, KJV).

At the conclusion of this study, we trust that you have been both enlightened and challenged by the unveiling of the future. We trust that what you have learned will motivate you to apply the talents and the time God has given you to the great task of preaching the gospel to every creature. And may this knowledge lend a sense of urgency to your work. This is our prayer.

11 Circle the letter preceding each TRUE statement.

a The term "the Lord God of the spirits of the prophets" suggests that prophets are channels of the Spirit and are under His direction and control.

b The blessings pronounced in 22:7 and 14 concern those who *do*, that is, fulfill God's commandments.

c Daniel's prophecy was to remain *sealed* because it was relevant only for the Old Testament period.

d The command for one who is holy to continue to be holy suggests that present choices shape one's character.

e Judgment both in Revelation and throughout the Bible is said to be based upon one's works.

f Among the ungodly who cannot enter the New Jerusalem are *dogs* who will instead be eternally damned.

g The last invitation in the Bible is given to people to attend the wedding supper of the Lamb.

h The last exhortation in the Bible indicates that people should neither add to nor take away from the divinely inspired Word of God.

Self-Test

Multiple choice: Circle the letter preceding the best answer for each of the following questions.

1 Which of the following conditions will exist during the Millennium?
a) There will be no spiritual warfare.
b) Wars will be limited to purely local struggles.
c) People will not be subject to spiritual tests or temptations.
d) All of the above.
e) Both a) and c) above.

2 Which of the following will occur at the beginning of the Millennium?
a) The final judgment
b) The second coming of Christ
c) The resurrection of the righteous dead
d) Satan's final revolt

3 Which of the following statements identify correctly the status of our Lord, His people, and Satan during the Millennium?
a) Our Lord will reign during the entire millennial period.
b) The people of God will share in Christ's millennial rule.
c) Satan will he bound throughout the 1000-year period.
d) All of the above.
e) Both a) and b) above.

4 According to our study, the Millennium will be characterized by
a) universal peace, prosperity, justice, knowledge, an increased life span, the absence of the ferocious nature in animals, and theocratic rule.
b) the spiritual awakening of multitudes of people who will then serve Christ willingly out of their love and commitment for Him.
c) the greatest time of evangelism ever as the Spirit is poured out on all flesh.
d) the emergence of an undercurrent of revolt against the benevolent rule of the Lord Jesus Christ.

5 Amillennialists believe that
a) the world will not experience a literal 1000-year reign of Christ on earth.
b) the world's people will be saved by the preaching of the gospel.
c) revelation recapitulates events that have already occurred.
d) all of the above.
e) both a) and c) above.

6 Premillennialism is a view which holds that
a) Revelation recapitulates events that have already occurred.
b) the 1000 years is a symbolic number and represents the period between the first coming of Christ and the Second Coming.
c) the world will experience a literal 1000-year messianic rule following the second coming of Christ.
d) the Millennium represents their final triumph of the gospel in the present age.

7 Postmillennialists believe that the
a) Second Coming is followed by the binding of Satan, the resurrection of the righteous, and Christ's 1000-year rule.
b) gospel will triumph and that Jesus will return when the world is ready for Him.
c) world will not experience a literal 1000-year messianic reign.
d) 1000-year terminology is purely symbolic.

8 Following the Millennium, Satan will lead a revolt against God. The ones who will follow him are

a) the resurrected wicked.
b) the people from the nations which were subdued by our Lord at Armageddon.
c) those who survived the Tribulation and the children of those who enter the Millennium.
d) those angels who originally sinned.

9 The final judgment which follows the Millennium, may be described best as

a) a general judgment for all people who have died whether righteous or wicked.
b) the judgment in which the righteous are judged according to their works.
c) a preliminary judgment of the wicked which indicates where they are heading if they fail to repent.
d) the final judgment at which those present are judged on the basis of whether or not their names are in the Book of Life.

10 Which of the following are included as instructions, invitations, or exhortations in the final part of Revelation?

a) Readers are warned against tampering with the divinely inspired prophetic record.
b) Readers are invited to come to the source of spiritual life.
c) Believers are urged to persist in holy living.
d) All of the above.
e) Both a) and c) above.

Unit Progress Evaluation 4 and Final Examination

You have now concluded all of the work in this Independent-Study Textbook. Review the lessons in this unit carefully, and then answer the questions in the last unit progress evaluation (UPE). When you have completed the UPE, check your answers with the answer key provided in your Student Packet, and review any items you may have answered incorrectly. Make sure you have sent to your enrollment office the materials indicated on the cover of your Student Packet in the section *Checklist of Materials to Be Submitted to the Enrollment Office*. If you have not already done so, make arrangements as soon as possible with your enrollment office to take the final examination. Review for the final examination by studying the course objectives, lesson objectives, self-tests, and UPEs. Review any lesson content necessary to refresh your memory. If you review carefully and are able to fulfill the objectives, you should have no difficulty passing the final examination.

Answers to study questions

6 a True
b False
c True
d True
e True

1 There will be no spiritual deception on earth because Satan will be bound for a 1000-year period.

7 You should have noted that apparently Satan will be loosed from his confinement to give the people born during the Millennium an opportunity to choose either for or against God's rule. As a result of his release, multitudes will join his revolt and converge on the city of Jerusalem. Before they can attack, however, fire from heaven will destroy them and Satan will be confined forever in the lake of burning sulfur.

2 d) righteous, including the martyrs of the Tribulation period.

8 a False
b False
c True
d True

3 a) sharing in the rule of the messianic kingdom.

9 b) present heaven and earth will undergo a renovation.

4 1000 years.

10 a False
b False
c True
d True
e True
f False
g True

5 a 2) Postmillennialism
b 1) Premillennialism
c 3) Amillennialism
d 1) Premillennialism

11 a True
b True
c False
d True
e True
f True
g False
h True

Glossary

The right-hand column lists the lesson in the Independent-Study Textbook in which the word is first used.

			Lesson
abortive	—	coming to nothing; unsuccessful	11
abstinence	—	the act of keeping oneself from doing or entering into something	1
adversity	—	condition of being in unfavorable circumstances; misfortune; distress	7
affirmation	—	a positive statement, assertion	5
allegiance	—	loyalty owed by a citizen to his ruler	12
allegory	—	a long and complicated story with an underlying meaning different from the surface meaning of the story itself	4
apocalyptic	—	like a revelation; portending a violent upheaval; Apocalyptic also describes a class of Jewish and Christian visionary literature written between 200 BC and A.D 200.	4
apostasy	—	the losing of one's religious faith or moral principles	1
archangel	—	ruling angel; chief angel	5
Armageddon	—	in the Bible, the great and final conflict between forces of good and evil at the end of this age	8
arrogate	—	claim or take without right	12
Artemis	—	a goddess in Greek mythology, identified by the Romans with Diana, apparently regarded in earliest times as a nature goddess, and especially worshiped by women as presiding over childbirth	6
ascriptions	—	things attributed to the account of a person or thing	13
astrology	—	study of the stars to tell what will happen; study or science which assumes that stars and planets exert a direct influence on people	1
atrocities	—	monstrous wickedness or cruelty; very cruel or brutal acts	2
authenticated	—	made valid or authoritative	14
avenge	—	inflict, execute, or carry out deserved or just punishment (upon someone)	3
awesomeness	—	having the power to inspire emotion in which dread, wonder, and veneration are variously mingled	3
beatitude	—	all of the declarations made in the Sermon on the Mount (Matthew 5:3–11) that begin with "Blessed are" or "Blessed is"	5
calamity	—	a great misfortune, such as a fire, flood, the loss of one's sight	11
censer	—	an ornamented container in which incense is burned, especially during religious services	10

			Lesson
charisma	—	a mysterious power to fascinate and attract; great personal magnetism or glamour	8
climatic	—	of or forming a climax	13
coalition	—	alliance of political parties or groups for some special purpose	2
coexist	—	to exist together or at the same time; to live in peace with each other	10
consigned	—	handed over, delivered; set apart; assigned	14
consummation	—	bring to completion; fulfillment	8
contemplates	—	thinks carefully about	11
contemptible	—	deserving contempt or scorn; mean; low; worthless	3
converge	—	to come together; turn toward each other	14
convulsed	—	what has been shaken violently	10
counterfeit	—	false	12
deception	—	a deceiving; a being deceived; a thing that deceives; trick meant to deceive; fraud; sham; hoax	3
deluded	—	one who has been deceived, tricked, or led astray	12
demoralized	—	having been weakened, or disheartened	1
desecrated	—	having been used or treated without respect	3
detention	—	act of detaining; holding back	14
diabolical	—	very cruel, wicked, or fiendish	2
diadems	—	kingly power or authority; the victor's crown or crowns	9
dire	—	causing great fear or suffering; dreadful	10
dirge	—	a funeral song or tune	13
dissolution	—	breaking up or ending of any association of any kind	13
distortions	—	things that have been distorted or twisted out of shape	14
divination	—	act of seeing the future or discovering what is obscure by supernatural or magical means	1
emissaries	—	persons sent on a mission or errand	13
end time	—	as an adjective it relates to the end of the present world system or the events associated with it in religious expectation	8
entity	—	something that has real and separate existence	1
epiphaneia	—	Greek word which in relation to Christ's coming means ''brightness" or "splendor"	8
equity	—	being equal or fair; fairness; justice	13
erroneous	—	containing error; wrong; mistaken	14
extra biblical	—	non-biblical material; that which goes beyond scriptural authority	7

flaunted	—	displayed ostentatiously; paraded boastfully, impudently, and defiantly in the public view	12
gaudily	—	what is dressed or decorated too brightly to be in good taste; cheap; showy	12
grafted into	—	a shoot or bud from one kind of tree or plant inserted into a slit in another closely related kind of tree or plant, so that it will grow there permanently	10
grandeur	—	magnificence or splendor of appearance	14
grisly	—	frightful; horrible; ghastly	11
harpadzo	—	Greek word which, in relation to our Lord's coming, means "to snatch away by force"	8
holocaust	—	great or wholesale destruction; complete destruction by fire, especially of animals or human beings	3
icons	—	pictures or images of Christ, an angel, or a saint, usually painted on wood or ivory, and venerated as sacred	7
illicit	—	not permitted by law; forbidden	13
imminent	—	likely to happen soon, about to occur	5
impending	—	about to happen or take place	6
impenitent	—	feeling no sorrow or regret for having done wrong	13
impiety	—	lack of respect or reverence for God	1
incense	—	any substance producing a pleasant odor when burned	10
indemnity	—	payment for damage, loss, or hardship; money demanded by a victorious nation at the end of a war as a condition for peace	3
indenture	—	a written agreement, such as a contract or deed; contract by which a servant or apprentice is bound to work for someone else	9
insurrection	—	a rising against established authority; revolt; rebellion	3
irrevocable	—	final; impossible to call or bring back	13
intrigue	—	underhanded planning to accomplish some purpose	2
liaison	—	connection between parts of an army or branches of service to secure proper cooperation	12
malevolent	—	wishing evil to happen to others; showing ill will; spiteful	12
manipulation	—	clever use or influence; change made for one's own purpose or advantage	2
martyrs	—	persons killed because of their beliefs	10
measuring metaphor	—	refers to the figure of speech employed in which measuring stands for something else: symbolically, something is to be destroyed and something is to be preserved	11
medieval	—	of, having to do with, or belonging to the Middle Ages (the years from about AD 500 to about AD 1450)	7

		Lesson
Messiah	— Jesus, the expected King and Deliverer of the Jews and Savior for all mankind	6
messianic	— of or relating to Jesus	4
meteorites	— masses of rock or metal that enter the earth's atmosphere from outer space with great speed and reach the earth without burning up	9
millennial	— of or having to do with the period of one thousand years during which Christ is expected to reign on earth	10
Millennium	— the period of a thousand years during which Christ is expected to reign on earth	4
Nicolaitans	— may have been those who supported the idea of elevating the clergy above the laity; may have been people in the first century AD who claimed one could be a Christian and practice all kinds of immorality	6
obstinacy	— stubbornness; act of not giving in; hard to control, treat, or remove	11
occultism	— use of the mysterious or magical; belief in and use of evil spirits and their power	1
omniscience	— universal or complete knowledge	5
orthodox	— having generally accepted views or opinions, especially in religion	6
overcomer	— one who surmounts or prevails over obstacles or enemies	6
paradox	— statement that may be true but seems to say two opposite things; for example: "More haste, less speed"	3
parenthetical-enlargement	— a close-up view, a fuller description, of one part of a subject that has already been mentioned	4
parousia	— Greek word which means "a personal arrival or coming"	8
penitential	— feelings expressing humble or regretful pain or sorrow for sins or offenses	13
personified	— represented or regarded as being a person	9
perverted	— turned from what is considered true, desirable, good, or morally right; corrupt	12
physique	— bodily makeup	5
picturesque	— quaint; vivid	14
ponder	— consider carefully; think over	11
preincarnate	— describes activities of our Lord before He was embodied in flesh and became *God with us*	3
prerogative	— right or privilege that no one else has	12
pristine	— as it was in its earliest form or state; original; primitive	6
professing	— laying claim to; pretending; claiming to be; often used to contrast those who "claim to be Christians" with those who are actually Christians in life and behavior	7
proleptic	— of or having to do with, an anticipating, especially with the describing of a future event as though it had already happened	11
prototype	— the first or primary type of anything	7

ransomed	—	delivered, especially from sin or ignorance	9
rapture	—	a carrying away or being carried away in body or spirit; as used in Bible prophecy, refers to the "catching away of the church, the bride of Christ, at the Second Coming"	8
ravenous	—	very hungry; greedy	13
recapitulates	—	repeats or recites the main points of; tells briefly; sums up	14
remorse	—	painful regret for having done wrong	14
renegade	—	deserter from a religious faith; traitor	3
renovated	—	made like new; made new again	14
reputable	—	well thought of	11
requited	—	paid back; avenged	12
requital	—	repayment; return	13
resplendent	—	very bright; shining; splendid	9
restrainer	—	one who limits, restricts, or keeps under control	8
retaliation	—	paying back wrong or injury; returning like for like	13
retribution	—	a deserved punishment; return for evil done	7
rhetorical question	—	question asked only for effect, not information	13

sacrilege	—	an intentional injury to anything sacred	3
sated	—	satisfied fully; supplied with more than enough, so as to disgust or weary	13
secular	—	not religious or sacred; worldly; not belonging to a religious order	12
sealing	—	of or having to do with the act of making someone or something secure from harm	10
selectively protected	—	refers to the way God protects His own in the midst of judgment on the wicked. For example, while the plagues affected Egyptians, they did not affect Israelites, leading us to say they were selectively protected	8
self-indulgence	—	act of gratifying ones own desires, appetites, and passions with too little regard for the welfare of others	1
Septuagint	—	the Greek translation of the Old Testament that was made, according to ancient tradition, in about the third century before Christ	4
skeptics	—	those who question the truth of theories or apparent facts	3
sorcerers	—	those who practice sorcery, wizardry, or magic	1
stringent	—	strict; severe; rigorous; convincing; forcible	11

temporal	—	not religious or sacred; worldly; secular; lasting for a time only	1
theocracy	—	literally, the rule of a nation or of the world by God; government by God	14
thievery	—	the act of stealing; theft	8
transitory	—	passing soon or quickly; lasting only a short time	14

			Lesson
trauma	—	an emotional shock which has a lasting effect on the mind	3
turbulent	—	causing disorder; unruly; violent	9
uniqueness	—	the state of being different from all others and having no like or equal	8
usurper	—	one who seizes and holds (power, position, authority) by force	3
utopia	—	an ideal state or place; a visionary, impractical system of political or social perfection	11
validated	—	made valid; given legal force; confirmed	3
vultures	—	any of certain large birds of prey related to eagles, falcons, and hawks that eat the flesh of dead animals	8
watchword	—	a motto that embodies a principle or guide to action of an individual or group	5